ROUTLEDGE LIBRARY EDITIONS: POLICE AND POLICING

Volume 19

POLICE AND PUBLIC ORDER IN EUROPE

POLICE AND PUBLIC ORDER IN EUROPE

Edited by
JOHN ROACH
and
JÜRGEN THOMANECK

R Routledge
Taylor & Francis Group

LONDON AND NEW YORK

First published in 1985 by Croom Helm Ltd

This edition first published in 2023
by Routledge
4 Park Square, Milton Park, Abingdon, Oxon OX14 4RN

and by Routledge
605 Third Avenue, New York, NY 10158

Routledge is an imprint of the Taylor & Francis Group, an informa business

British Library Cataloguing in Publication Data
A catalogue record for this book is available from the British Library

ISBN: 978-1-032-41114-9 (Set)
ISBN: 978-1-032-42661-7 (Volume 19) (hbk)
ISBN: 978-1-032-42709-6 (Volume 19) (pbk)
ISBN: 978-1-003-36390-3 (Volume 19) (ebk)

DOI: 10.4324/9781003363903

Publisher's Note
The publisher has gone to great lengths to ensure the quality of this reprint but points out that some imperfections in the original copies may be apparent.

Disclaimer
The publisher has made every effort to trace copyright holders and would welcome correspondence from those they have been unable to trace.

POLICE
AND PUBLIC ORDER IN EUROPE

EDITED BY JOHN ROACH AND JÜRGEN THOMANECK

CROOM HELM
London   Sydney   Dover, New Hampshire

©1985 John Roach and Jurgen Thomaneck
Croom Helm Ltd, Provident House, Burrell Row,
Beckenham, Kent BR3 1AT

Croom Helm Australia Pty Ltd, Suite 4, 6th Floor,
64-76 Kippax Street, Surry Hills, NSW 2010, Australia

British Library Cataloguing in Publication Data

Police and public order in europe.
   1. Public policy (Law) – Europe   2. Police
   – Europe
   I. Roach, John   II. Thomaneck, Jurgen
   363.3'094   HV8049

   ISBN 0-7099-2242-6

Croom Helm, 51 Washington Street, Dover,
New Hampshire 03820, USA

Library of Congress Cataloging in Publication Data
Main entry under title:

Police and public order in Europe.

   Includes index.
   1. Police – Europe – Cross-cultural studies.
2. Public policy (law) – Europe – Cross-cultural studies.
3. Offenses against public safety – Europe – Cross-
cultural studies. I. Roach, John, 1938-
II. Thomaneck, Jurgen.
HV8194.A3P65   1985   363.2'3'094   85-16831
ISBN 0-7099-2242-6

Printed and bound in Great Britain
by Billing & Sons Limited, Worcester.

CONTENTS

CONTRIBUTORS

ACKNOWLEDGEMENTS

INTRODUCTION   1

1. BRIXTON AND AFTER   7
   The Rt. Hon. The Lord Scarman, O.B.E.

2. POLICE AND THE SOCIAL ORDER   15
   John C. Alderson, C.B.E.

3. THE BRITISH POLICE SYSTEM: 33
   with Special Reference to Public Order Problems
   Frank E.C. Gregory

4. THE CIVIL POWER AND AIDING THE CIVIL POWER: 73
   The Case of Ireland
   Trevor C. Salmon

5. THE FRENCH POLICE   107
   John Roach

6. POLICE AND PUBLIC ORDER IN THE FEDERAL
   REPUBLIC OF GERMANY   143
   Jurgen Thomaneck

7. THE BLUNT INSTRUMENTS: ITALY AND
   THE POLICE   185
   Richard O. Collin

8. THE POLICE SYSTEM OF SPAIN   215
   Iain R. Macdonald

9. THE POLICE IN SWEDEN   255
   Clive Archer

10. EUROPEAN POLICE COOPERATION   273
    Paul Wilkinson

INDEX   287

Contributors

The Right Honourable the Lord Scarman, O.B.E., has become a leading authority on public order issues following the publication of his report on: <u>The Brixton Disorders, April 10-12, 1981</u>, London, Her Majesty's Stationery Office. Cmnd. 8427 (November 1981).

John C. Alderson, C.B.E., Q.P.M., LL.D., D.Litt. Formerly Chief Constable of Devon and Cornwall, he has written several books on the relationship between the police and the state including: <u>Policing Freedom,</u> Plymouth, Macdonald and Evans, 1979, and his latest work, <u>Law and Disorder</u>, London, Hamish Hamilton, 1984.

Frank E.C. Gregory, B.A., M.Sc., is Lecturer in Politics at Southhampton University. He has written widely on issues of government and the police, and he is preparing a book on the subject to be published by Harvester. His latest book is, <u>Dilemmas of Government: Britain and the European Community,</u> Oxford, Martin Robertson - Blackwell, 1983.

Trevor C. Salmon, M.A., M. Litt., is Lecturer in Politics at the University of St. Andrews. He is a specialist on Irish affairs and has published several studies on Irish Foreign and Domestic policies.

John Roach, B.A., Ph.D., is Lecturer in French at the University of Aberdeen. He specialises in all aspects of Contemporary France and is preparing a study on <u>The Politics of Education in France</u>.

Jurgen Thomaneck, M.Ed., Dr.Phil., is Head of the German Department, at the University of Aberdeen. He has a special interest in German history and society and has published widely on various aspects of these subjects.

Richard O. Collin, B.A., M.A., D.Phil., is Associate professor at Coastal Carolina College, University of South Carolina. At the time of writing his contribution to this volume he was a Research Fellow at the University of Oxford. He has written several works on Italian history and society including <u>De Lorenzo Gambit,</u> London, Sage, 1976, and a novel, <u>Imbroglio</u>, London, Gollancz, 1981. He is presently completing a book on the role of the Italian security forces during the Transition from Liberalism to Fascism.

Iain R. Macdonald, M.A., Ph.D., is Senior Lecturer in Spanish at Aberdeen University. He is a specialist on Spanish culture and society and among his publications is a study of Gabriel Miro, London, Tarmesist.

T. Clive Archer, B.Sc.Econ., Ph.D., is Deputy Director in the Centre for Defence Studies, University of Aberdeen. He was previously a Lecturer in International Relations and is a specialist on the politics of Scandinavian Countries. His latest book is International Organisations, London, Allen and Unwin, 1983.

Paul Wilkinson, M.A., is Professor of International Relations at the University of Aberdeen. He has an international reputation as an expert on terrorism, on which he has published several important studies, including Terrorism and the Liberal State, a new edition of which is soon to be published by Macmillan. His book, The New Fascists, was published by Pan Books, 1983, in a revised and enlarged edition.

Acknowledgments

This volume could not have been completed without the help of a large number of people in the various countries, many of whom cannot be named individually. To all of them we wish to express our thanks. The Editors would like to thank in particular, Lord Scarman for finding time to be a contributor: Mr. John C. Alderson and Mr. Derek J. Snoxhall of the Encyclopaedia Britannica for giving us permission to print the text of Mr. Alderson's Encyclopaedia Britannica Public Lecture on 'Police and the Social Order', given in Edinburgh on Wednesday, 8th February 1984: Herr Holger Johannsen, Leck, German Federal Republic: Ms. Wendy Adam and Mrs. Lorna Cardno for their help in preparing the final copy.

INTRODUCTION

Over the last twenty-five years there has been a sharp increase in public order conflict throughout Europe, not only in the number of incidents but more importantly in the nature of the incidents and in the response to them by governments. The street has become the locus for protest and protest has come from an ever growing diversity of quarters and with a mounting readiness to resort to violence on the part of protestors and the police. To the many traditional forms of grievances have been added serious conflicts arising from social tensions caused by a deteriorating economic situation after years of affluence and rising expectations, resulting, for example, in overt class antagonism and racial animosity. Hardly a day goes by without public order and police issues finding their way into the homes of the European public, either through newspaper headlines, radio bulletins, or television pictures. The media cover industrial conflict, demonstrations, marches, crowd troubles, road blocks, riots and many other instances of confrontation between citizens and those other citizens, the police, whose task it is to impose the constraints determined by the state.

The role of the police in public order contexts gives rise to powerful polemics and to widely differing perceptions. This is sharply evident in Britain at the time of writing, but it is also true of all other European states. Public order has clearly moved into the foreground of political debate and policy. The importance attached to police matters is evidenced by the way in which policing is placed high on the agenda of any political discourse and the extent to which it is given a high priority by all political parties in every country. At party conferences and in party manifestoes, the issues are often placed under the title of 'law and order' and wielded in the general propaganda war which parties wage between themselves and within their own ranks, discussion usually focusing on the rising crime rate, the problem of drugs, hooliganism, the death penalty and so on. But at the centre of all such political considerations, certainly after May 1968 and following the escalation of international terrorism after the Munich massacre in 1972, there has been the issue of public order. Governments' policies on police matters have, more and more, made public order their priority concern, even though their public declarations do not disclose this. The amendments to existing laws, the introduction of new laws reinforcing police powers of surveillance, search and arrest, the increasing restrictions and controls placed on protest, the great increase in the allocation of resources to the police especially in equipment and training which have a direct bearing on public order policing, all suggests that the measures introduced and the political reasons for them, have a public order purpose. The rise in police numbers in all the European forces is only partially a conventional response to the rise in crime (it certainly has not resulted in a higher detection rate, still less the prevention of crime), fundamentally the increases have been motivated by governments' need to provide themselves with the means by which to meet the growth of mass protests and the rapidly changing nature of those protests. Similarly, while great advances have been made which contribute to more effective general policing of crime, such advances have an equally if not more potent application to public order policing, thus, for example, the resources and equipment available for electronic equipment and the facilities which result from computerised data banks have an immediate significance for the covert police services in their public order functions. Some innovations in strategies and in equipment have exclusive public order objectives: the formation and training of special squads, the introduction of specialised riot equipment, personal protection and special weapons, strategic planning such as saturation policing, right up to the development of vehicles specifically designed for public order operations. Similarly organisational procedures and structures have been evolved in response to and in anticipation of, public order disturbances. In Britain, for example, there has been a significant move towards centralisation by the centralised operational direction of the police during the miners' strike. Throughout Europe public order has taken on a high priority in police activities, in strategic thinking, in resource allocation, in organisational changes. Public order priorities and the kind of policing which we have witnessed in Europe over the last twenty-five years have brought about fundamental changes in policing and in the public's perception of the police. In an increasing number of occasions the police of today are quite unrecognisable, often in a literal sense, from the traditional image of the police, especially when the police are clad in all their sophisticated public order apparel which makes them appear more like a para-military force than a civil force. Furthermore the kind of confrontation policing associated with public order influences the normal pattern of policing, with damaging consequences for police-public relations. Thus the study by the Policy Studies Institute into "Police and People" in London showed that police procedures which are aggressive lead to alienation and destroy co-operation between the public and the police thereby reducing police efficiency in the fight against crime. For example, the use of stop and search powers was shown to be counter-productive in that such procedures solve few crimes, moreover they damage public support for the police and thus reduce the police's ability to solve crime let alone prevent crime. Furthermore, powers which are claimed as necessary for effective policing, that is, the reduction of crime and social conflict, in fact generate conditions for public order violence. "Without controls on stop and search powers, the unpublicised individual conflicts which are a feature of everyday life in parts of Inner London will turn into tragic occurences involving the community as a whole." (Dr. M. McConville, The Guardian, 18.7.83) The same is true for most of the major cities of Europe.

The increasing number of public order incidents and the nature of the reporting of public order troubles, means that the subject has an immediate impact on the public, whose response is often emotive and frequently ill-informed. This is because though the police are, for most of us, our most evident and closest encounter with the powers of the state (after the taxmen!) most people simply acknowledge the existence of the police as some sort of universal and immutable institution, very rarely are the police recognised as an essential branch of government. The police are usually considered as some sort of abstraction 'The Police' and few people concern themselves with acquiring an understanding of police organisation, operational procedures and powers. The police themselves are frequently very secretive, perhaps believing that secrecy generates the kind of distance and awe from which comes respect. More usually, however, such secrecy only breeds misunderstanding, fear and hostility. Secrecy produces suspicion and prejudice all round and through a lack of proper communications and information, preconceptions are built up and sustained which create conspiracy theories about the police and within the police. But information is not easy to come by. Most of the studies about the police (they are numerous and increasing in number) tend to be of a very specialised nature requiring either expert knowledge or considerable familiarity with the subject. For the most part such studies are not concerned with police organisation and operations, but with more narrowly technical aspects of policing. However, as P.J. Stead writes, "This very important aspect of civil government (should be treated)

3

on the classic lines of history, analysis and comparison. The subject is too important to be left on the shelf of mere technical instruction and to be regarded as something which is on the one hand dismally regulation-bound and on the other so intimidatingly empirical that it defies humane and academic enquiry." (The Medico-Legal Journal, vol.33, 1965, p.3.) Yet very few books on government deal with the police. We feel that this is a serious omission since in all countries the police constitutes a major institution and one which profoundly conditions the relationship between the citizen and the state. Through its history, its organisation, its operations, a nation's police force reflects many of the essential political and social values of that nation.

We have adopted a broad, threefold approach: History, Organisation, Procedures. Within these guidelines the relationship between the components clearly could not be the same for each country. Contributors have structured their essay so as to place emphasis on those features which they feel are the most pertinent to the police of their country. In this way we have sought to achieve continuity and to allow cross references to be made, while giving proper importance to those aspects which make each country's police something unique to it. We hope that the approach and the range will encourage readers to (1) gain information and insight into a nation's police organisation, and its response to public order, (2) to recognise the police as an institution and to relate the police to other institutions of government within that country,(3) to make comparisons between the various countries dealt with in the book.

We begin with Lord Scarman's reflections on the Brixton riots, in which he raises issues which go beyond the specific context, issues which are central to the whole concept of police and public order. There is no doubt that Lord Scarman's Report is a seminal study which brings out questions which are fundamental to healthy police-public relations and to the well being of any society. The collapse of public order such as that which occurred in Brixton and Toxteth reminds us of the fragile structure of social order. Lord Scarman's report highlighted the complexities of the issues involved. The police have a key role to play in protecting social order by maintaining public order, but if their function is reduced to that of reactive and repressive policing sustained by increases in numbers and equipment, then they will not be able to contain let alone help to resolve the problems. Suppression and repression are not conducive to good public order policing. This is something which John

Alderson brings out in his essay, advancing an argument which he develops more fully in his latest book, Law and Disorder (Hamish Hamilton, 1984). Indeed, it is a measure of the public concern with police matters and the importance of public order issues that such professionals as John Alderson, Sir Robert Mark, Sir Kenneth Newman, James Anderton, have emerged as prominent public figures and that each of them has expressed himself forcefully on the subject of the role of the police in society with special reference to the police's public order function. Lord Scarman and John Alderson's overviews are followed by essays on separate countries and in the closing chapter, Paul Wilkinson examines the ways in which European police co-operation has evolved towards greater concern with political crimes and thus to increased surveillance and to the pooling of information so as to meet possible public order troubles. We are all too aware that each of the sections could have been a book, but exhaustive study of each police force was not our aim. We have sought to provide essential information on the tradition, the organisation and the public order functions of a nation's police so as to encourage readers to recognise the police as an institution of the state, a branch of government and thus to generate informed debate on the subject of the role and the importance of the police in a nation's system of government. We have focused on public order because it represents the clearest instance of government and police power coming together, when the police are most overtly the instrument of government authority and thus when the police may be seen most clearly as a branch of government.

All governments in the countries represented here (1) are confounded by considerable public order problems in trying to maintain order in a democratic context which tries to balance rights and constraints(2). The police are representative of a government's democratic principles and of the social health of a nation. A government's policy on public order is executed by the police, and the procedures and strategies adopted reveal the thin line between the desire for results and legality, the protection of authority and the defence of justice which makes the difference between a democratic police force and a police state. Between what John Alderson calls the 'police as preservers of liberty', the police as law enforcers, to the police as government policy enforcers.(3)

FOOTNOTES

1. We had intended to include chapters on Holland and Switzerland, both of which reveal very interesting aspects of police organisation and the maintenance of public order. Personal circumstances meant that our contributors were unable to complete their studies. However, we would like to thank Professor Dr. Alfred Heijder, now Prosecutor-General at the Court of Appeal in The Hague, and Dr. Kurt Truninger, now a producer for Swiss television in Zurich, for their help and their suggestions.

2. The situation in Northern Ireland is sadly abnormal, for this reason we felt that it could not be covered within the framework we adopted, for one thing the restrictions on length imposed on our contributors would run an ever greater risk of simplifying complex issues. However, Paddy Hilliard gives an excellent insight into the problem in his chapter on 'Law and Order' in: <u>Northern Ireland, The Background to the Conflict,</u> ed. J. Darby, Syracuse, Syracuse U.P., 1983, pp. 32-60.

3. In his foreword to T.A. Critchley's, <u>A History of Police in England and Wales,</u> London, Constable, 1978, Sir Kenneth Mark commends the change in the role of the police from "mere law enforcement to participants in the role of social welfare and even more importantly to that of contributors in the moulding of public opinion and legislation". The odd use of 'mere' suggests the desirability of a more overt political role for the police. Such a development would have profound implications. See: Malcolm Dean, 'The Finger on the Policeman's Collar', <u>The Political Quarterly,</u> April-June 1982, pp. 153-164. Recent events and figures show the extent to which public order is a police priority in Britain. Of the 120,000 police officers in Britain, 20,000 have had riot training; forces are to make 10% of their effectives available to the National Reporting Centre; 13 mainland forces stock plastic bullets (20,000 of which half are in London.) In 1985 NATO countries will conduct Wintex-Cimex 85 an exercise designed to test responses to the breakdown of public order in the event of war.

Chapter 1

BRIXTON AND AFTER

The Rt. Hon. The Lord Scarman, O.B.E.

I constantly ask myself two questions. Has any good resulted from the Brixton Inquiry? And, what now remains to
be done?

The Brixton Inquiry was set up by the Home Secretary
under powers vested in him by section 32 of the Police Act
1964. It was an inquiry into the policing of a specific
area, Brixton. The task was "to inquire urgently into
the serious disorders in Brixton on 10th to 12th April
1981, and to report, with the power to make recommendations". The report was submitted six months later, on
the 30th October 1981 and presented to Parliament in the
following November.

It is not possible to make effective inquiry into
policing whether generally or in a specific area without
going way beyond policing. The success of policing operations depends in the last resort not upon questions of
technique or professional expertise but upon the degree of
confidence felt by society in its police. In the Introduction to the Report it was said to be an obvious truth
that policing policy and methods reflect to some extent a
reaction by established authority to the society which is
being policed. [B.R., Cmnd. 8427, 1.5] If the reaction
is socially acceptable, all's well. But ours is an ethnically diverse society. What if policing policy and
methods, though acceptable to some groups in our society,
are unacceptable to others? Inevitably, the policing
problem becomes complex. It is the complexity of the problem (concealing, as it does, many policing dilemmas)
which makes it necessary that the policy (and the rest of
us) should analyse and understand the art of winning confidence in plural society.

The disorders of 1981 fully justify the underlying
premise of the Inquiry, that good policing is built upon
social confidence. The young blacks (most of them of
Caribbean origin) who confronted the police in Brixton and

7

developed their confrontation into a violent and devastating conflict had no confidence in the police. They saw themselves as the victims specifically of police harassment on the streets and, more generally, of social and economic deprivation and frustration. The police, as a force, were, of course, in no way responsible for their social and economic disadvantage. Yet the police, by their refusal or inability to adjust their methods to the social situation with which they were confronted, angered and alienated them. The police failed in their fundamental duty, which is, and always has been, the maintenance of public tranquillity. Unwillingly they contributed to the spirit of disquiet which was one of the reasons for the disorders.

How did this failure come about? What can be done to reduce the chances of such a failure again? The Brixton report made answer to these two questions. The history of policing in Lambeth in the years immediately preceding the disorders was a sequence of missed opportunities and misunderstanding, culminating in an unwise operation against street crime which was given the extremely unfortunate code-name within the Force of "Swamp". My conclusion, so far as the police were concerned, was that the senior command had not sufficiently adjusted itself to the problems of policing a multi-racial community, [B.R. 4.79]. And I detected a failure in the Metropolitan Police as a whole to appreciate the true importance of good community relations to the success of policing a multi-racial society. Basing myself on this conclusion, I made a number of recommendations for the reform of police policy, methods, and operations. They are to be found in Part V of the Report. To what extent have they been implemented?

Recruitment

"Them", the enemy, and "Us", the victims, represented the attitude in 1981 of the young blacks in Brixton towards the police. The police were seen as the arm of oppression, a force hostile towards them and set apart. Black faces in police uniforms were few and far between. There was no chance of bridging the gap unless young black people could be encouraged to enter the police force. My recommendation was:

> I therefore recommend that the Home Office, with Chief Officers of Police, and in consultation with Police Authorities and representatives of the ethnic minority communities, conduct an

urgent study of ways of improving ethnic minority recruitment into the regular police and of involving the ethnic minorities more in police-related activities such as the Special Constabulary. The object of policy must be that the composition of the police fully reflects that of the society the police serve. Nothing less will suffice.

The recommendation has been accepted. But the results are so far disappointing. Numbers of "ethnic minority" policemen are increasing: but far too slowly. There are now a few hundred black constables: and one or two senior officers are black. This is not enough. The difficulty is not in lack of will on the part of the Home Office or Chief Officers of Police but in deepseated attitudes both in the ethnic minorities and within the police force. A young black man faces the hostility and contempt of his friends, even social ostracism if he elects to join the police. But there are, also, problems of racial prejudice between white and "black or brown" officers in the Force, as the Study by the Policy Studies Institute into "Police and People in London" has revealed. (P.S.I., III, p.163). The Study concludes that black or brown officers do face particular problems in their relationships both with the public and their colleagues, but that these problems are not overwhelming, (emphasis supplied).

A start has been made, but progress is painfully slow. Nothing is more important than that the drive for greater recruitment from the ethnic minorities should continue.

Training

I was particularly concerned that the recruit should have the benefit of an adequate initial training both in duration and in syllabus and should then proceed to a probationary period during which he would be undertaking police duties under the supervision of an experienced officer. Sir David McNee had begun a comprehensive reform of training methods a year or so before I reported. Excellent progress has been made. The young police officer now entering the Force is a better trained, better understood, more closely monitored officer than his predecessors: and he has more help in his early days. He will understand the complexities of the community he helps to police. The initiative has been taken by the police themselves: and they deserve the credit.

Discipline

My specific recommendation was that racially prejudiced behaviour should be included in the Discipline Code as a specific offence, [B.R. 5.41]. This has not been done. The P.S.I. Study has confirmed the existence of racially prejudicial attitudes amongst policemen. But it finds that racially prejudicial _conduct_ is not common, though (as I also found) it certainly occurs. Until racial prejudice is specifically outlawed by the Discipline Code (or its equivalent), the ethnic minorities (and others) will find it hard to accept on the "say-so" of senior officers that racial prejudice is not tolerated by the Force in attitudes, actions, or social intercourse. No single formal change is more necessary than an effective declaration that racially prejudicial conduct is an offence against police discipline. I understand that a code of ethical conduct is being prepared for the guidance of the Metropolitan Police. If it has teeth, by which I mean that failure to observe it will attract disciplinary penalties (including dismissal in a serious case), my recommendation will be met. But, if not, the situation will continue to create trouble and loss of public confidence.

Complaints against the Police

My conclusion was:

> "that there is a widespread and dangerous lack of public confidence in the existing system for handling complaints against the police".
> [B.R.5.43]

I commented that people do not trust the police to investigate the police. I advocated a strengthening of the independent element in the system.

I devoted a substantial part of the Report to the problem.[B.R.7.11/7.29] The conclusion has, I think, been largely accepted: but not my recommendations. The solution advocated in the Report was a system of "independent investigation". The Government has, it would appear, ruled out a system in which police have no investigative role as being impracticable. But they have adopted my alternative suggestion of "a package of more limited measures" which would incorporate a genuinely independent supervision of the investigation. It is too early to reach a judgment on the Government's proposals, which will (I am glad to note) be given the authority of statute. But the decision to increase the independent element is

10

welcome: and I would give the proposals a chance to prove themselves.

One aspect of complaints investigation, considered in the Report, is, I believe, of great importance. It is that of increasing the element of conciliation in the handling of minor complaints. Discourtesy, abusive words, plain rudeness of behaviour by a policeman either in a public place or a police station, do untold harm to the repute and local estimation of the police. Yet they are features more often of a policeman's uncertainty and apprehension than of his unfitness to develop into an efficient and understanding officer. A conciliation process, if operated with the consent of the complainant and the policeman, might be very valuable to both and to the good name of the Force: more especially, if one of the conciliators could be an independent layman drawn from the local community. Other police forces (notably the Toronto Metropolitan Police) operate such a system: and I believe it is a success. If the process could be linked with the arrangements for local accountability and consultation, so much the better: by doing so, one would strengthen both the conciliation process itself and the consultative machinery upon which success or failure of healthy police/community relations may come to depend. There are indications that a concilation process may be developed. There are difficulties (including the safeguarding of the rights of the policeman against whom complaint has been made): but I believe it is now accepted that they can be satisfactorily met.

Policing Methods

Here there have been substantial improvements since 1981 – all of them designed to foster good community relations without impairing efficiency in the enforcement of the criminal law. Four recommendations made in the Report have been implemented [B.R. 5.54], namely:

1. more foot patrols;
2. the integration of the Home Beat officer into the mainstream of operational policing.
3. opportunities for officers of all ranks to get to know the community they are policing;
4. "a balanced spread" of officers of different ages in inner city areas.

One of the defects in the structure of the Metropolitan Police in 1981 was the great preponderance in numbers of young, comparatively inexperienced, policemen. This resulted from the influx of recruits following upon the acceptance of the Edmund-Davies police pay proposals. As time goes by, this defect is diminishing.

Consultation and Accountability

The importance I attached to these aspects of policing is now well known [B.R. 4.72-74, 5.55-70]. My recommendations will be largely met if the Police and Criminal Evidence Bill, now before Parliament, becomes law. I will, therefore, content myself with repeating my emphasis upon the need for local communities as well as the police to work positively to establish a good relationship. This is, indeed, happening in Lambeth, the district of South London of which Brixton is the centre.

The P.S.I. Study

The study was commissioned by Sir David McNee before the 1981 disorders. It is a study of police and community behaviour in London. It exposes as the area of major public concern the safety of people on the streets. Police exercise of the power to stop and search on the streets is seen to be a major aggravating factor so far as young people of Caribbean origin are concerned. This, of course, was a major factor contributing to unrest in Brixton. The Study stresses the many factors that make policing a diverse society so difficult. Age is one: the generation gap between the young people on the street and their community leaders is far from closed. But also the ethnic minorities differ in the way they see the police: and young whites differ from both. These complexities have contributed to what the Study concludes is a dangerous lack of confidence in the police amongst young people generally. The Study goes so far as to describe the lack of confidence amongst young blacks as "disastrous".

It is too early to be certain that the study's diagnosis is correct. But such experience as I gained in the course of the Brixton Inquiry leads me to treat their warning as one to be treated very seriously indeed. The authors of the Study see the way forward in a radical changing of police attitudes, but argue that this must be achieved not merely by improvements in training but by reforms in the management, structure, and consultative arrangements of the Force. I find myself in agreement with their appraisal and with most of their proposals, though I cannot agree with the suggestion that the period of initial training of a recruit should be shortened so that he spends a longer period as a probationer attached to a police station under supervision. Both periods are vital: the one should not be sacrificed to the other.

Conclusion

I have confined this essay to a discussion of progress in the policing of Brixton since publication of the Report. But what is true of Brixton is largely true of policing elsewhere in the country. The disorders of 1981 have woken us up to the fragility of public order in a plural society, if that society is blind to its plurality. At least Britain is now aware of its ethnic diversity and is beginning to accept the necessary implications. But the policing problem is only one aspect of deeper social problems. Until racial disadvantage is rooted out and the equality of opportunity becomes the unspoken and fundamental premise on which our society is built, we cannot expect to eliminate the sense of deprivation, disadvantage and alienation which led young black people into the disorders of 1981. Their violence is not to be excused: but society can hardly be surprised by violence on the streets, if it sleeps while grievances fester. I would, again, recall the words of President Johnson with which I ended the Report [B.R. 9.5]:

"We should attack these conditions [discrimination, slums, poverty, unemployment] not because we are frightened by conflict but because we are fired by conscience."

Further Reading

Policy Studies Institute, vol. III, "Police and People in London", PSI, London 1983.
Scarman, Lord, Report on an Inquiry by the Rt. Hon. Lord Scarman: The Brixton Disorders 10-12 April 1981, Cmnd 8427, London, HMSO 1981.

Chapter 2

POLICE AND THE SOCIAL ORDER

John C. Alderson, C.B.E.

Introduction

It can hardly be denied that there are few benefits more
important to a civilised society than a degree of public
tranquillity conducive to the enjoyment of both freedom
and security. Assessing the degree of success in achieving such a social condition early regard will often be had
to the role of the police system and its place in the social order. In wishing to steer the subject away from too
hasty a recourse to such a pursuit I wish to emphasise
that a police system is but the product and a reflection
of a society's values at a particular time and in a particular place, rather than the converse. In this sense a
society really does get the police it deserves. There are
both historic and contemporary examples to support this
axiom.

But room must be left in a polemic of the kind I am
to embark upon for the notion that a society may seek to
diminish as well as to extend the role of its official
police. Room must be left for the idea that it is not inevitable that public tranquillity should continue to demand a constant extension of police power and its con-
comitant diminution of liberty and the erosion of personal
civic obligation and participation and duty. However I
should seek to explain and to clarify how the term police
may be properly employed.

We owe the origin of the term 'police' to the Greeks,
stemming as it does from their polis, the city, and
politeia, a comprehensive term describing the safety and
the welfare of the inhabitants. The politeia in the Greek
city state was within the concern and influence of all
citizens as a collective and democratic responsibility.
The Romans having adopted and latinized the term into
politia placed the power which it represented with the

15

Emperor under the fiction of imperial sovereignty. Police power was regarded as lying at the heart of state authority.

Now without wishing to put too fine a point on it, some aspects of the contemporary debate on policing in the world mirror the competing ideas of Greek and Roman in this regard. Superficially, it can be observed that the existing French police system leans to Rome, whilst the British leans, albeit perhaps less than it should, towards ancient Athens. That the British system so leans had been enabled by early tribal custom, by the tradition of local government and later by democratic local government (to which I will return in due course) and by nine-hundred years of evolution free from conquest and alien rule. I believe it is an endangered species. The Romans are gaining ground.

When I say that the British system leans a little towards the ancient City State of Athens I mean only to emphasise that in Britain police power has not been regarded as lying at the heart of state authority. And further to stress that the wider meaning of police in the Greek sense of the general safety and welfare of the inhabitants is an idea which brings the maintenance of a tolerable social order within the influence of many and varied democratic institutions. Room has to be left in the vocabulary of the policing debate for both meanings. More of one, the wider, may mean less of another, the narrower.

Meanwhile I intend to illustrate my earlier assertion that a police system reflects the social and political values, at a given point in time and space. In doing so I wish to acknowledge indebtedness to a former acquaintance, the late Professor Brian Chapman of the University of Manchester, for his work on the evolution of European Police States.(1)

The Police State

According to Chapman jurists in the universities of continental Europe around the 16th Century rediscovered and refined the fictional lex regia of Roman law into the constitutional doctrine of absolute monarchy and the divine right of kings. But it was in 18th Century Prussia that Europe was to witness the first creation of a police state. Following the devastation of the Thirty Years' War, the reforms of Frederick William of Prussia no doubt came to the people as a blessing. The yearning for order and security transcended notions of liberty and freedom. Dedicated to the protection of the populace, the welfare of the State and its citizens, and the improvement of society, the benevolent despot established a police bureaucracy, using the term in its widest sense, at every level of administration. Very much a Hobbesian scenario. Police authorities were endowed with wide powers to enact rules and ordinances regulating all manner of social conduct. Nor were police officials amenable to judicial sanctions, but only to the control of their own bureaucracies. Well intentioned measures no doubt in their time but measures which contained the seeds for future corruption of the system.

Totalitarianism

In the final analysis and given the stark choice a people will opt for safety before freedom. When order is being wrought out of chaos police can acquire a constitutional ascendancy which can remain long after the need for it exists. Some two-hundred years later in a bestial and never to be forgotten caricature and distortion, the totalitarian police state of Nazi Germany was to be created out of the Polizeistaat of an idealistic king, and the chaos of the ill-fated Weimar Republic. When the positive interventionist police philosophy is harnessed to an authoritarian regime the police in effect become the state. The overthrow of liberal democracy is a prospect which all too often may become a reality.

'Low' and 'High' Police

In France meanwhile we can see an example of a modern liberal democratic state with a highly centralised police bureaucracy quite distinct from our own. Its present form emanates largely from the post-revolutionary period, though the Gendarmerie, the soldier police, (of which we have yet no equivalent), claims its origins in earlier times. It was Fouché, Duc d'Otranto, who as Minister of Police to Napoleon developed to a high degree the ideology of police suitable to time and circumstance. Perhaps the nearest example to Fouché in English policing might be Thomas Cromwell the exponent of espionage whilst councillor and secretary to Henry the Eighth who, in 16th Century England, was likewise concerned with bringing order out of chaos. Fouché divided the police function into two levels, 'low police', whose function was to maintain order in the streets and market places, (the equivalent of the English watchmen and parish constables), and the 'high police'. Of the latter's function he commented that they were, "the regulating power which is felt everywhere, without ever being seen, and which at the centre of the State, holds the place which the power which sustains the harmony of celestial bodies holds in the universe, a power whose regularity strikes us although we are unable to divine the cause ... Every branch of the administration has a part which subordinates it to the police."(2)

Meanwhile in Westminister the 1822 Parliamentary Committee on the Police convened to consider how to control the London equivalent of the Paris mob, fearful of the threat of crime and disorder to life and government in the capital, reported: "It is difficult to reconcile an effective system of police with that perfect freedom of action and exemption from interference which are the great privileges and blessings of life in this country."(3)   The police ideology of post-revolutionary France, unlike its wine, did not travel well to Britain at the time.   The position of police in the social order differed in place, if not in time.   But let us remain with this notion of the 'high police' a little longer.   A French writer described this idea in the following terms:

> Even without written instructions the police knew instinctively how to recognise crimes and offences. The police knew, too, that they alone could judge correctly the action to be taken against delinquents because they had a general moral sense – a sense which all mankind had been naturally endowed – and nature spoke so strongly in them that they admitted only with difficulty that a man who disagreed with them on some point or another could be honest and sincere. And they were alone in allying this moral certitude with a profound knowledge of the needs of public order.(4)

Similar sentiments have been expressed by contemporary police officials in liberal democracies too.

Put like this the police begin to see themselves not only as legal actors and keepers of the peace but also as the moral custodians and political censors of society. Of course the rise and independence of the French magistracy has since brought the system much nearer perfection. But, nevertheless, some seeds lie deeply imbedded. President Mitterrand of France was until recently the subject of a fat police dossier; he was regarded as a subject worthy of secret police attention and potentially subversive. Shortly after his election he ordered the destruction of the police records of himself and other politicians of the Left, whilst curtailing such Fouché-inspired activities.

It is rather as if Mrs. Thatcher were to use MI5 to compile dossiers on Mr. Kinnock, Mr. Steel, or Dr. Owen ...
Had Napoleon's Minister of Police been witness to the
events he may have quietly murmured, "Plus ça change".

Police in the U.S.A.

When one turns to consider the police system in the United
States of America it undoubtedly features as the most
democratic to be found in policing systems of great nations, if such systems are to be judged by the criterion
of control by elected representatives. It is of course
too much the subject of political caprice and manipulation
for British tastes but it is undoubtedly more democratic.
After all, in the cities, the elected Mayor appoints the
Police Chief and holds him accountable, in the counties
the Sheriff is elected by the people, whilst in the States
the elected governor is the Police Authority. That is of
course concerning what Fouché called 'low police'.
    The 'high police' of the F.B.I. and the C.I.A. are
federal bodies located in Washington. It was here that
the late J. Edgar Hoover presided over high police activities. He would no doubt have agreed that his 'moral certitude' and 'profound knowledge' were indispensable to the
welfare of the State. The obsessive watch for communist
sympathisers and other anti-bodies not only fuelled the
outrageous McCarthy witch-hunt in the 1950's and later the
harassment of Martin Luther King and others during the
civil rights movement, but his amassing of gossip, tittle-
tattle, and information about the private lives of politicians made him too powerful to be replaced. No President
or Attorney General was the match for his Fouché-like interpretation of his role in the social order of the United
States. Those of his officers who failed to live up to
his own moral standards were dismissed or despatched to
remote assignments so that he became surrounded by what
might be described as his own likeness. It is not to be
wondered at that given the ideology, the police, high or
low, will seek to extend their role accordingly.

Power

Policing like politics is to a great extent concerned with
the use of power. In this context power takes diverse
forms. In addition to the formal legal powers there is
the power represented by information and knowledge as well
as of the physical and technical resources at the disposal
of the directors of operations. Police such as Fouché and
Hoover might possess no more legal power than other police

but their possession of informational power and control over its collectors makes them relatively omnipotent.

In Britain, at least in modern times, the nature of the system of policing and of parliamentary democracy has made it difficult, if not impossible, for a Fouché or a Hoover to establish such personal ascendancy.

British Police

I should acknowledge my awareness of the different paths along which police in Scotland and police in England and Wales have evolved. In particular one acknowledges the influence of the French legal and policing tradition on the Scottish institutions. Suffice it to say for present purposes the two systems have tended and tend to converge. We can speak now of a British police idea.

The main thrust of the idea has been that policing whilst under the supremacy of parliament and subject to the rule of law should be based upon the responsibility of local government except in the Metropolitan area of London. Whilst there were plans to establish a national police system in the mid-19th Century, the present system did not evolve under such a grand plan much less under police ideological stimulus. Its strength as well as its weakness has been as an adjunct of the great principle of local government. Speaking in 1963, after the Royal Commission on the Police of 1962 had rejected the idea of a national police, the Home Secretary, R.A. Butler, (later Lord Butler) said, "I am convinced that it would be wrong for one man or one government to be directly in charge of the whole police of this country. Our institutions are based on checks and balances. This has kept our liberty throughout the generations."(5) Checks and balances therefore are deemed to be fundamental to control of police in the social order. But even though the principle may be immutable the form may and does change. In the thousand years since Alfred the Great (in what was then Saxon England), established the idea of collective responsibility for keeping law and order in the settlements of his subjects, four major historical shifts in policing have taken place, each a reflection of the social order of its time.

Firstly, the Anglo-Norman system of policing through the Shire Reeve (later the Sheriff) and the oath of 'Frank Pledge' required that all males over 14 years should help keep the peace and join the 'hue and cry' for malefactors. Each person bound by his oath together with others of his group of ten families was obliged to produce for trial those who committed crime. And, particularly under the harshness of early Norman rule, to be punished in default. A system which in some degree is similar to the policing in the Chinese People's Republic at the present time. Secondly, the provisions of the Statute of Winchester of 1285 led to the appointment of city Watchmen, the first paid police. The growing wealth of the medieval trading cities required more effective policing to deal with growing crime. Not for the last time were affluence and juxtaposed poverty to fuel criminality of an acquisitive nature.

But within less than a hundred years the degree of disorder and crime was such that Edward the Third passed the Justice of the Peace Act in 1361. An Act which set up a policing system throughout England and Wales based on the local responsibility of sheriffs, justices and constables. A system which save for a break of two years during which Cromwell's military police took charge, lasted well into the nineteenth century. The Cromwellian system following the Civil Wars had a continental ring about it. Established in August 1655, ten – later eleven – Major Generals were given new powers within their respective districts not only to hold down Royalist insurrections but to improve the moral climate of the nation. But in the words of Cromwell's most recent and respected biographer,Antonia Fraser:

> Oliver might have done better to have rested his case purely on the requirements of security. His fatherly concern for the moral tone of his people met with no answering response where the hated Major Generals were concerned.(6)

Within two years policing reverted to Edward the Third's fourteenth century creation until the growing pains of the Industrial Revolution caused the then Home Secretary, Sir Robert Peel, to address Parliament in the following terms:

> The time has come when from the increase in its population the enlargement of its resources, the multiplying development of its energies, we may fairly pronounce that the country has outgrown her police institutions.(7)

It was 1828 and the occasion was the introduction of a Police Bill for London. The Home Secretary was to be, and still is, the police authority for the Metropolitan area.

The ancient City of London retained, as it still does, its own responsibility for police affairs. Local city forces were established under their committees, and county forces under the justices of the peace, later under committees including councillors. Britain by the end of the nineteenth century had created a web of modern local police forces democratically accountable to local government. At the same time Britain did not develop any equivalent of Fouché's 'high police'. Unlike its counterpart in the USA the police were the beneficiary of central as well as local funding and the subject of annual inspection by Her Majesty's Government. So far as security of the realm was concerned it was to be the military who created and administered intelligence systems known as MI5 and MI6, particularly during the First World War. The police in London, in response to the Irish Fenian terrorism of the 1880's formed a special branch of the CID to counteract it. Later other forces created similar branches so that today each force under its chief constable is responsible for that part of security whilst the functions of what were MI5 and MI6, counter-espionage and espionage respectively are constitutionally separate. The security services and the special branches now work very closely together so that in effect the nation is both covered and served without the creation of an FBI, a CIA, or Deuxième Bureau. Though clearly there lies within the system the potential for the establishment of such an organisation.

My purpose has been to offer a context of police and the social order within which I might comment upon police in contemporary and near future Britain, to which I now turn.

In believing that in some ways our policing is at a watershed I do so out of a conviction that the social order is itself at a watershed. And in arriving at this view I am bound by my earlier assertion that a policing system reflects the values which a society places upon itself.

Ten years ago the distinguished historian, the late Arnold Toynbee, wrote: "The economic deterioration in developed countries indicates the onset of a new way of life, a severely regimented way of life which would have to be imposed by a ruthless authoritarian government."(8) Our economic deterioration is admitted, only the extent and the continuance of the deterioration is a matter of controversy.

No consideration of police and the social order can evade the connection with economics, be it a matter only of degree. Though eighty per cent of the work-force may be enjoying comparative affluence at the present sufficient for the large majority to be reasonably content, some twenty per cent or one in five are not. The declining asset of North Sea oil further cushions the effect of economic ravages. However, I do not perceive the ranks of

the economists forecasting a certain continuance of Western prosperity. The strains on Western societies are
showing. Doubts are cast upon the ability of the economy
to sustain both increases in untaxed income and the maintenance of the health and social security benefits and
services. The rising costs of State pensions index-linked
and extrapolated, cause treasury officials to wince. One
does not need to be an economist to consider the social
consequences of economic deterioration; they are evident
in all that one sees, hears and reads.

I agree with Toynbee to the extent that a nation be-
set by the trauma of dramatic economic deterioration and
change faces the prospect, though not necessarily the reality, of both disorder and ruthless authoritarian government. Economics and policing are related in more ways
than one. Neither do I believe it fanciful to pose the
question that should economic deterioration gather speed,
what would be the prospects for policing by consent?
After all the urban poor of London in 1829 were not policed by consent, and to suggest otherwise would be to court
ridicule. Can the social order be adaptable enough to
avoid Toynbee's prediction?

His ruthless authoritarian government would require
an executive arm capable of exacting its purpose, namely
the police, and of course as in Northern Ireland though
for different reasons, the Army, though I do not propose
to develop that line of argument. Such a role for the
police in Britain is against our recent traditions though
we have, over the last twenty-five years, been acquiring a
police organisation which could quite easily be converted
into an offensive arm for such a government. It is a
highly mobile force with excellent national communications
and data banks and an intelligence system. It is well
armed, possesses the appropriate riot equipment including
the dreaded and lethal plastic bullet. It has developed
highly trained companies of riot police with the best protective equipment. In the technological sense the British
police is as advanced as any of the national forces on the
continent and elsewhere. Neither is there a shortage of
legal powers, soon to be strengthened, though administrative checks on its abuse are proposed. All of this is
quite capable of justification, but it raises the question
of control to a more critical level. Emergency regulations could be passed to give further essential powers
without the prospect of obstruction in Parliament.

On the police side there would be little likelihood
of widespread disaffection for the task. The British
police is a well disciplined organisation, comparatively
highly paid and tightly knit. Though able to serve an

authoritarian regime, however, the police ideologically lean more to the authoritarian right than to the authoritarian left. This is partly due to innate conservatism and partly to the fact that the ideology of the far left has a long tradition for criticising the police as part of an established order which they despise and wish to change. Equally the far right tends not to criticise the police even for admitted shortcomings or excesses believing that regrettable though they may be, it would tend to weaken the police as part of the establishment which they wish to see strengthened.

If Toynbee's ruthless authoritarian government came from the Right there would be few problems in converting the existing system. A fact which may give comfort to many and discomfort to others. If on the other hand such a government came from the Left there could be problems, though they would arise not from the technical and legal resources but from the ideological and political preferences of some police officials. Some chief officers and police spokesmen in England, (I am not aware of any in Scotland) have made no secret of their dislike for the politics and policies of the Left or for local control. But the Police Federation in England and Wales and the Police Superintendents' Association have retained Conservative Members of Parliament as their advisors and for many years have abandoned the convention of retaining a member of Her Majesty's Opposition. Their political campaigns between and during general elections have coincided closely with those of the Conservative manifesto. Increased penal severity, capital punishment, tighter measures for dealing with juvenile offenders, increases in police powers, and severance of the police from local government, have all been the subject of campaigns or public speeches. It is equally fair to say that the police generally steer clear of political intrigue. In this sense Britain is very fortunate.

It may be of course that Toynbee's scenario may not come to pass even if economic deterioration caused by social convulsions does happen. After all, we may be blessed with leaders and a political system and philosophy to match the time. When all is said and done the British are amongst the most governable of people, though I would wish to argue that even they have their limits.

Contemporary society is not of such a form to take severe economic strain without considerable prospects for crime and disorder. Those parts and characteristics of the social order which used to represent homogeneity and consensus have gradually changed as the impulses which fuel social dynamism have found their outlets in social

24

mobility. The demography is new, and materialism has become pronounced. People do not give up hard won privileges any more easily than assertive ones accept with docility what they perceive to be injustice or unfairness. Nor even are they immune to envy, that running mate of greed. When a society develops in this way, as many western societies have in recent times, people begin to rely more on the law for discipline and stability rather than those traditions of social cohesion and fraternity. The Land of Hope and Glory is still sung, though more with nostalgia then reality, and never in certain of our deprived areas and the schools located within them. Society is more bitchy and dissension is abroad whilst the political parties' struggle for ascendancy divides the nation. Although it cannot be said that iron has entered the soul to a dangerous extent, there is iron in enough souls and it seems to warrant the preparation of the police to meet it. In a passive submissive society where consensus prevails, as in Frederick William's eighteenth century Prussia, policing is a comparatively straightforward task, but when a society begins to mount a challenge to authoritarianism, policing becomes more burdensome particularly at the point where the challenge mounts and authoritarianism has not begun to recede. This represents a turning point, since if those possessed of political power decline to use it for demanded changes, the police will be called upon to play a major role in producing social stagnation. It is likely that in such a condition two societies will emerge, the privileged and the deprived, the protected and the suppressed, and prospects for the eruption of communal violence will increase. The police will operate at this interface since they are on the side of the status quo and will both suffer violence from, and apply it to, the dissenters.

The 1981 riots in London and other English cities whilst fuelled in adverse social conditions were ignited by police practice, which is the essential lesson to be learned from the Scarman Inquiry. People will put up with a lot in the way of social deprivation without resorting to violence, for they often have a propensity to blame themselves for their predicament, but when the predicament is compounded by seeming undue repressive policing the breaking point will be reached much earlier than it otherwise would.(9)

Sensitive use of police is much more important in this sense where social conditions are bad. Where social conditions are good, insensitive use of the police will result in complaints through formal channels provided for such contingencies; where they are bad they will result in riot. It gives me no satisfaction to say that two years before the riots in England I wrote and published a work drawing attention to this social phenomenon in the following terms;

> The decaying inner-city areas are breeding grounds for crime and disaffection. To leave them to the vagaries of law enforcement would be unwise. There are now sufficient examples of how neglected social problems which have been allowed to fester to a dangerous state, but which have been covered over and policed by force, can break out in public disorder. In such cases the police are trapped into a dilemma. On the one hand they perceive (or should perceive I may add) the problem, but not having the solution they gradually become a solution of expediency, though sooner or later social repair and reconstruction has to begin. From a police point of view the sooner the better.(10)

In this sense policing becomes part of the problem. But the police system is no longer as well placed as it was to respond to social diversity, to feel the impulses of small communities in their varied circumstances, needs and desires. Where there is no dialogue there can be no understanding, where there is no accountability there is no compulsion to serve. Both these assertions apply pari-passu to many other government services. To examine the issues critically is not to blame the police any more than to seek to cast blame on any well intentioned efforts to cope with change.

The more complex a social order becomes the more the services which tend to its needs require the flexibility to adapt to local as well as regional and national circumstances. However, there is in fact a divergence of interest and perception. Thus whilst British society has become infinitely more diversified and pluralistic the services upon which it depends, including the police, have become more remote and bureaucratic.

Policies which are fashioned and laid down by large bureaucracies remote from local diversity and sentiment do not always fit the kaleidoscopic nature of the receivers of those services. An example of this divergence is to be found in the evidence of the Commissioner of Police of the Metropolis to Lord Scarman's Inquiry on the Brixton riots in London.(11) The policies of the Force, it was reported, had been reviewed in the wake of the riots and it was felt that there was no need to change them. The inquiry, and subsequent police reflection, however, found that in the particular locality the policing policies were a major factor in producing violent communal reaction on a serious scale.

Police and Local Government

Any examination of the divergence between community needs and bureaucratic distance, so far as the policing system is concerned, has to begin with changes in the structure and the health of local government since it is claimed that our policing is based upon it.

The creation of larger units of local government in Great Britain following upon the Local Government Acts of 1972 (in England and Wales) and 1973 (Scotland) greatly enlarged police bureaucracies. The police of Strathclyde and of Greater Manchester could by no stretch of imagination be called local police forces. In going for the benefits of scale, and there are some, including better use of resources, coordination of effort and so on, local roots and accountability were needlessly sacrificed. Although the creation of District Councils, and in Scotland, (though not in England and Wales), Community Councils, provided a role in some aspects of local government, they were to have no role so far as policing was concerned. Great and ancient cities and towns were to be policed by regionally administered forces. At the same time as these changes were taking effect another phenomenon calculated to compound the situation was the growth of police professionalism.

Police Professionalism

By police professionalism I mean the idea that the role of the police in the social order becomes defined by the police. When the weakening of local influence is combined with professional certitude the way is opened up for police to become an institution in itself. Police and the police system is so complicated and enlarged, that only the police can understand and define its purpose. The development of police technology adds a further seductive dimension in the same direction. Sophisticated computer directed responses, the impressive mobility and systems of communication can create a feeling within the organisation that it possesses power enough to be efficient without seemingly old fashioned notions of 'politeia' or public participation and influence. This condition is more marked in some systems than in Britain, but there are ominous signs of a drift in this direction here too.

27

Recent research has, for example, confirmed that so far as the detection of crime is concerned as much as 85 per cent of reported cases are detected wholly or in part by the public. The police compile the reports and collect the evidence. This suggests that in clearing up crime police technology is less important than public contact and support.(12)

Research carried out jointly in Devon and Cornwall and Greater Manchester highlighted a further significant trend in perceptions of the role of the police in the social order.(13) Whereas the public tended to judge delivery of police services in terms of the human qualities, skills, understanding and problem solving, the police officers believed they were being judged on their technological modernity and reactive efficiency in, for example, responding quickly and activating the police machine. The result was that the police over-estimated the public regard for the way in which they functioned. An ominous trend if it were to continue without in some way being corrected.

The combination of scale, remoteness of local government administration of the police, and the growth of police professionalism has contributed to misunderstanding, conflict, and uncertainty about the place of the police in the social order which is not as good for the police nor as reassuring for the public as it might be. Police authorities have found difficulty in knowing how to discharge their function in obtaining the accountability which the system provides for. The dilemma, and one police authority's response, was expressed by Margaret Simey, chairperson of the Merseyside Authority in the following terms:

> The message which emerged from the mini-Scarman inquiry conducted by the Merseyside Police Authority after the disturbances of 1981, was that it was democracy which had failed the people of Toxteth and not the police. Put bluntly it was the failure of the police authority to fulfil its political duty to ensure that the people were policed by their own consent and according to their own wishes, so far as was possible, which had brought the situation to flashpoint.(14)

These views are close to my own, since I believe that we are better served by increased democratic influence and greater accountability. Margaret Simey's comment that 'it was democracy which failed the people' is an arresting one; an informed and sagacious insight. It draws our attention to the social phenomenon that weakness in democratic activity opens the door to injustice and misuse of power. In its extreme form, as in the German Weimar Republic, it exposes liberty and justice to a crushing defeat.

The state of democracy in Britain today is germane to the subject before us. Democracy in Britain today is too stunted to warrant optimism or to justify complacency. From apex to base there are weaknesses. The House of Lords makes no pretension to being a democratic institution whatever its other virtues may be, and it has many. But the assembly of the House of Commons, our bulwark, at the present time fails to reflect the growing diversity of political opinion among the electorate. Anxiety in this regard is reflected in broad agreement among some members of all political parties. Whilst strengthening the government of the day it alienates loyalties. It serves power at the expense of democracy.

The picture is no rosier at local government level. Not only is it not 'local' any more but it is being weakened and demoralized by the radicalism of central government. A conflict which is likely to intensify. There is a huge vacuum at community or neighbourhood level and it is here that the lack of means for democratic participation creates prospects of direct action.

The trade unions are also at bay - partly due to abuses of their power which disturbed too many in the recent past, and partly due to the same radicalism of the present government, combined with the threat of unemployment. When democracy is weak or abused greater recourse to repression by those charged with government is foreshadowed.

An additional weakness which becomes more pressing as bureaucratic power increases is the absence of a Bill of Rights to protect individuals and groups. Although Britain was a founder member of the Council of Europe and one of the architects of the Convention of Human Rights, we have been singularly lacking in training our police and other officials in its spirit and purpose.

The combination of defective democracy, the absence of a Bill of Rights enshrined in our domestic laws, the continuing economic deterioration and laissez-faire policies are all leading to a divided nation. All of these factors are likely to increase reliance on the criminal sanction and to lead to increases in repression and surveillance, thereby fundamentally shifting the place of the police in the social order.

Having now opened up a much wider perspective than I had intended I am obliged to narrow it again. For the last part of my essay I intend to concentrate on the problem of anchoring the police to communities. I believe that if they are so anchored they themselves will gain much. They will feel more secure as an institution, they will receive more public help and guidance in the delivery of their services. A way will be opened for democratic impulses in society to balance the growth of bureaucratic power.

I believe that for all kinds of reasons, apart from policing, the creation of community forums is a pressing need. In a confident, expanding society people will gradually disengage from mutuality. In a contracting and apprehensive society, mutuality assumes greater importance. If this movement is facilitated it offers a counter to excessive reliance on the strong leader. The former, that is communitarianism, will strengthen the social order whilst preserving freedom and developing democratic participation, whereas the latter, the strong leader, will call for the sacrifice of these things.

Community forum areas would be drawn up on a definitive map by local authorities. Residents would appoint delegates, not representatives, street by street. Delegates rather than representatives, to avoid undue politicisation. To make them manageable, at least in the cities and towns, they would serve between ten and twenty thousand inhabitants. Participation in community affairs would be an individual right. A programme of education, both for the young and the adult, would be designed to stimulate understanding and participation. The police and other agencies providing a community service would be locked into these primary cells of democracy . The welfare and safety of the inhabitants would provide the terms of reference.

In due course such forums would number tens of thousands, some more active and well conducted than others no doubt. The well-springs of democratic activity would in this way be primed. This would not be another tier of government but a forum or platform to generate local initiative, action and concern. A Minister for Community Affairs and local government Community Affairs Committees would share the responsibility for setting up and nurturing them.

As for the police, the intermediate level of their informal accountability would be at district level, where consultative groups set up for the purpose would provide this link. Following upon Lord Scarman's recommendations a statutory duty to create these groups in England and

Wales is included in the Police and Criminal Evidence Bill at present before Parliament. The third level of police accountability would rest as it does now, formally with the police authorities, at what I call regional level.

It should be emphasised that the police role in the social order is primarily that of keepers of the peace, and preventors of crime. This function can only be activated where the primary level of activity is rooted in neighbourhoods. It is here that police officers have to toil in the foothills of the social order. The enforcement of laws is adjunct to this primary function and should not be its usurper. The success of our _politeia_ should not only be judged by the efficiency with which we can build larger prisons, increase penal severity, and enlarge the population of detention centres and prisons. It should be judged also by our success in relying less on the criminal sanction to protect the social order (to which at present I see no diminution) and more on innovation and ideas of preventive activity in those primary cells of the body politic to which I have referred.

All the signs are that Britain's police traditions will be seriously tested in the years to come. They would be better served by an increase in democracy and in openness and accountability and a decrease in the prospects of violent conflict. Whilst much of this may have bemused an Imperial Roman it may have been well understood by an Ancient Athenian.

FOOTNOTES

1. B. Chapman, The Police State (Macmillan, London, 1971), p. 11.
2. Ibid., p. 30.
3. T.A. Critchley, History of Police in England and Wales (Constable, London, 1976), p. 47.
4. Chapman, op.cit., p. 41.
5. Critchley, op.cit., p. 292.
6. A. Fraser, Cromwell: Our Chief of Men (Weidenfeld and Nicolson, London, 1973), p. 557.
7. Critchley, op.cit., p. 29.
8. In an article in The Observer in 1974.
9. It may be that the absence of anti-police riots in Scottish cities in 1981 reflects less repressive police policies, a more community orientated social order, fewer cultural differences, or homogeneity. If this be the case it goes some way towards proving much of my thesis.
10. J.C. Alderson, Policing Freedom (Macdonald and Evans, Plymouth, 1979), p. 177.

11. The Scarman Report on the Brixton Disorders (HMSO, London, 1982), para. 4.79.

12. Home Office Research Study No. 67 (HMSO, London, 1982), p. 29.

13. University of Cardiff, Department of Social Administration, Unpublished, 1982, p. 174ff.

14. The Guardian, 23.11.83.

Further Reading

1. J.C. Alderson, Policing Freedom (Macdonald and Evans, Plymouth, 1979).

2. J.C. Alderson, Law and Disorder (Hamish Hamilton, London, 1984).

3. B. Chapman, The Police State (Macmillan, London, 1971).

4. T.A. Critchley, History of Police in England and Wales (Constable, London, 1976).

Chapter 3

THE BRITISH POLICE SYSTEM - WITH SPECIAL REFERENCE TO PUBLIC ORDER PROBLEMS

Frank Gregory

Introduction

After the riots in Britain during the summer of 1981 some
commentators attempted, quite rightly, to put the events
into a historical perspective. Gaskell and Smith survey-
ed the literature on the 'crowd in history' and pointed
out that, 'It is perhaps somewhat comforting that these
studies show such disturbances to be a fairly regular
occurrence in many countries, including Britain. They
sometimes hasten change in the political system, but they
are not the beginning of the end of civilisation.'(1)
        The study of the British police system and public
order problems should be prefaced by some general observations on the development of police systems. Whitaker
points out that only '... in comparatively recent times
has policing been linked mainly to law and order ... The
Greek politeia, like the Roman politia, meant the art of
governing the city-state for its comprehensive good,
...'(2) The linking of those who are paid to exercise
supervising powers, over others, with the system of
government has become identified with the continental
civil or Roman law system of policing. In this system
the policeman is very definitely the servant of the
government, as is the case in France. By contrast,
Britain's common law tradition makes the individual
citizen responsible for helping to preserve order and
uphold the law. Consequently the British policeman has
an individual responsibility, as the holder of an office
from the Crown, to act as a servant of the law.
        However, while in theory the Roman law and common law
based police systems are distinct in practice, there is an
inevitable blurring of the differences. The reality -
and the origin of many of the problems of the police - is
that laws simultaneously provide both the necessary
framework of order to protect people's rights, and also
are an expression of class rule. In other words as

political parties, when forming a government, pass laws, and the police have to enforce the laws, if there is a lack of popular consensus on a particular law, the police are inevitably identified with the governing party's "side", as can be the case with laws relating to trade union activities.

In Britain today it can be argued that the police system is something of a hybrid model. It is neither the 'pure' Anglo-Saxon decentralised common law police system nor is it, yet, a nationally organised government controlled system. A former HM Inspector of Constabulary and Chief Constable, Colonel Sir Eric St Johnston, argued in the Guardian of 10th August 1981:

> The police service has already gone a long way towards nationalisation. There are standard conditions of service and discipline: the training of recruits and senior officers is standardised under the control of national committees: wireless equipment owned by the Home Office and rented to police forces: while forensic science laboratories under the control of the Home Office are on a national scale. There are also national and regional crime squads to deal with the problems of criminals who commit crimes in more than one police area.

Increased national level "supervision" for particular police methods was encouraged in 1983 when the current Chief Inspector of Constabulary, Sir Lawrence Byford, required Chief Constables to report on their emulation of the Metropolitan Police Commissioner's (Sir Kenneth Newman) new strategy of "policing by objective", that is "proactive" rather than simply "reactive" policing.

However, to balance these apparent moves towards a national de facto if not de jure police system it must be noted that there has, recently, been considerable discussion about making the police more accountable, in a supervisory sense, to local political authorities. The position of the Home Secretary, as the police authority for London has also been attacked as unfair to the elected representatives of the Greater London Council area.

Therefore the police are under a variety of external pressures concerning their future lines of development. Also, internally, the police are experiencing pressures for change. It has always been argued that, in Britain, there exists a system of policing with popular consent, contrasted with the expectation of opposition in a Roman law or authoritarian political police system. Although

34

it remains a valid contention that the policeman needs the cooperation of the general public, the increasing complexities of criminal activities and the availability of new technology or technical aids has, at times, seemed to create a more remote police system. An early symbol of these developments came when the policeman on the beat was often replaced by the "Panda" car patrol. These developments have been examined in depth by Manwaring-White who has coined the rather sensational term "technopolice" to describe developments in police tactics, equipment and technology some of which are related to the duty of the police 'to cause the peace to be kept and preserved' when terrorist campaigns, large scale demonstrations and riots threaten the rights and safety of the law-abiding citizen. These incidents are usually described, in general terms, as 'public order' problems.(3)

In this chapter the study of the British police response to public order problems will be analysed from a number of perspectives. The historical evolution of the British police system will be outlined. Next consideration will be given to Britain's legal regime on public order and the related political considerations regarding the maintenance of public order. These sections are followed by a discussion of the organisational forms by which police forces can respond to public order problems. The presentation of the material is then related to a review of the major public order problems in Britain since 1945, especially the riots of 1981. In the final, forward looking section, the emphasis is placed upon identifying the most realistic and likely trends in the official response (political, legal and police) to possible public order issues. The long running emergency in Northern Ireland is not considered because the legal regime and police system in Northern Ireland (and Ireland under British rule before partition) have always been distinct from those in England, Scotland and Wales.(4)

The Evolution of the British Police

In the British Isles, whilst many generalisations are perfectly correct in descriptions of the police system a number of exceptions need to be clearly understood. Firstly, both currently and historically there exist three distinct legal regimes, England and Wales with a legal system based on common law, Scotland with a partly Roman law based system and Northern Ireland (and previously all of Ireland) being subject to those types of legislation, involving losses of normal civil liberties, common when states of emergency are deemed to exist.

The differences between the Scottish legal system and the legal system in England and Wales are not very great but in some respects they do affect the powers and duties of the police. In particular, whereas in England and Wales the police, with reference in certain cases to the Director of Public Prosecutions, are both investigators and through police lawyers, the prosecutors, in Scotland part of the direction of police investigations and the decision to prosecute plus the actual prosecution are the responsibility of civilian officers of the Lord Advocate's department known as Procurator Fiscal. There has always been some concern in England and Wales, about the police having both investigating and prosecuting duties, and in the debate about the proposed new Police and Criminal Evidence Bill suggestions have been made that England and Wales should have a separate prosecution service like the Procurator Fiscal.

Northern Ireland not only has a much more authoritarian legal system during emergencies it also has a very distinct police system. One of the first proper police forces to be established in the British Isles was in Ireland in 1814. This police force, later to be known after the 1835 Irish Police Act as the Royal Irish Constabulary, was formed as an armed para-military barracked police force whose primary task was the maintenance of public order. With these characteristics the RIC served as the model for many of the police forces Britain established in her colonies. The political situations were similar, namely the need to impose the rule of an external polity on unwilling native inhabitants. Thus the British police forces in Ireland, including today's permanently armed Royal Ulster Constabulary, have always been identified as government police forces in contrast to the situation in England, Scotland and Wales where the policeman has been presented as merely a citizen in uniform serving the law.

The Development of the police system in England, Scotland and Wales

In the nineteenth century the traditional British dislike of standing armies was linked to a disdain for the authoritarian political systems in Europe. Therefore any reforms of the old haphazard system of local parish constables needed to be carefully structured to avoid a continental style of military policing system. Sir Robert Peel, the Home Secretary in 1822-27 and 1828-1830, who had been instrumental in reforming the police system in Ireland, could not, in his desire to bring law and order to an increasingly urbanised society, use his Irish model, unchanged. Moreover popular opinion would not accept a version of the French Gendarmerie, an army unit, given the additional task of providing a civil police force.

What Peel did, as a first step, by the Metropolitan Police Act of 1829, was to provide London, but under the Home Secretary's authority, with an unarmed, civilian police system based on the common law traditions of the ancient office of constable. Each constable, whilst a member of a force organised along some military lines (because the military model was the only one available to give the necessary command and control structures), had and has, unlike the soldier an individual duty to uphold the law which transcends his duty to obey his superiors in the police service.

The 1835 Municipal Corporation Act required urban authorities to establish police forces and in 1839 counties were similarly empowered, though not required, to raise police forces. Scotland was slightly ahead of England and Wales as the Local Improvement Act had enabled Glasgow to raise a police force in 1800, and Edinburgh to raise one in 1805. By 1848 there were 182 police forces in Britain and by 1859 there were 239. This decentralised system of a large number of separate autonomous police forces was to exist in Britain until 1966. The only significant developments during the period from 1829-66 were the slow formation of special Criminal Investigation Departments (CIDs), consisting of non-uniformed officers better known as detectives, during the later half of the nineteenth century. There was also the formation, in 1883, (and until 1961 in the Metropolitan Police only) of the Special Branch, plain clothes detectives with particular responsibility for gathering intelligence on individuals and groups threatening the security of the state, ie, concerned with political crimes.

After World War II the British police system had, by an evolutionary process, developed a number of anomalies. Some national standardisation was taking place because 'The Home Office-backed Police College and Training Centres increasingly helped to establish common links between the force, holding more opportunities for the exchange of methods and information and the spread of ... ideas'. However, it was difficult for Parliament, whilst obviously concerned about crime or traffic as national issues, to question the working of the police system as a whole. The Home Secretary was only directly responsible for the police in London and Home Secretaries '... frequently rebuffed enquiries (from MPs about other police forces) by replying that the forces were autonomous ...'(5)

In 1960 that very British procedural device for difficult political issues, a Royal Commission, was set up to review police pay and 'the constitutional position of the police throughout Great Britain, the arrangements for their control and administration'. This Commission was unanimous in concluding in 1962 that the creation of a national police force would not be either constitutionally objectionable or politically dangerous and they argued that a police state arises from the nature of a government not its police. In a minority report one Commission member, Dr Goodhart, went further and argued that, 'The danger in a democracy does not lie in a central police that is too strong, but in local police forces that are too weak'.(6) However, no political party has, as yet, put forward a policy for the creation of a national police.

Instead, a typically British compromise was adopted in the 1964 Police Act. The Home Secretary was given the de jure powers that he had already exercised de facto to oversee the local forces, remove inefficient Chief Officers and promote cooperation between or even the amalgamation of police forces. A degree of central control and over-sight that was reinforced by the fact that half of each force's funds came from central government. In parallel the local police authorities, partly (2/3) elected local councillors, partly (1/3) magistrates, lost powers. In practice their powers were limited to receiving an annual report from the Chief Constable and agreeing on funding for equipment and capital items like buildings, there was no provision for the discussion of police methods and policy. In the aftermath of the riots in parts of Britain in the summer of 1981 some local police authorities did try to effect police policy through budgetary control. For example, the police authority for Gwent voted against the Chief Constable's request for £33,000 for three armoured Transit vans and allowed only an expenditure of £8,250 on 150 protective helmets and overalls.

Since 1966, partly as a result of changes in local government boundaries and structures, the number of separate police forces has declined rapidly. In 1966 the number of separate forces was 117; it is now 42. Some writers have argued that this concentration of police power into the hands of a smaller group of Chief Constables has allowed some of the more vocal of these officers, like Sir Robert Mark, James Anderton and John Alderson to become very public advocates of certain types of law and order policies.

The latest available police statistics for England and Wales (31 Dec 1982) show the strength of the police in the following terms: the total police strength in England and Wales (population. 1981 - 49.5m) was 120,951 with 801 authorised vacancies. In Scotland the police strength was 13,214. The largest force is the Metropolitan Police with a strength of 26,615, eight forces are more than 3,000 strong (all in areas of large urban population concentration). Only four police forces are less than 1,000 strong. The overall population to police ratio is 413:1. Apart from the special circumstances of the force area of the City of London Police, the lowest population to police ratio of 275:1 is to be found in the Metropolitan Police district (London). The part-time Special Constabulary has a strength of 15,160 but the Specials are not normally considered as reserves for public order duties but as a reserve which could release full-time officers for public order duties if and when necessary.

In a brief but interesting article a police officer, P.M. Cook, suggests that in terms of structure and policing philosophy there are pressures for both centralisation and decentralisation within the British police. Cook cites the 'national' centralising influences of the Home Office, the Police Staff College and the national police staff associations. Moreover a reactive form of policing requires centralisation and strong organisational control. By contrast a proactive form of policing (a very comprehensive form of preventive policing involving community and quasi-social work) requires decentralisation and a loosening of organisational control. However, on balance it seems most likely that Britain will continue with a decentralised police system although the numbers of separate forces could decline and the emphasis is certainly on the standardisation of training and equipment.(7)

"Public order" - a legal and political concept

Under common law and by statute there has developed what has now been generally accepted as an unsatisfactory legal regime and the 1936 Public Order Act and related legislation has recently been extensively debated following the Conservative government's publication of the 'Review of the Public Order Act 1936' (Cmnd 7891, 1978) and the subsequent report of the Commons Home Affairs Committee on 'The Law Relating to Public Order' (House of Commons Papers Nos 756-I and II, 1980). Before examining these reports it is useful to refer to Ingraham who has carried out a general comparative study under the title Political

Crime in Europe.
It can be argued that we understand some of the extreme forms of the activities of protesting citizens as constituting a public order problem as distinct from activities labelled simply as criminal partly as a consequence of the reactions of the authorities within a state. As Ingraham defines the crime, '... the "political" nature of the crime depends on the kind of local response the act evokes from those in authority ...'. A particular feature of the response is the stress on preventive measures rather than punishment because '... the political crime, or at least that act which aims at the seizure of the reins of power is one form of crime that is either prevented or it may never be punished'.(8)

As a contrast to the legal position in Britain in a civil (Roman) law system, such as the French, there exists the more widespread concept of ordre public, '... used widely throughout French law to provide an exception to a general rule for the sake of "exigences supérieures"... ...'.(9) Ordre public is sometimes translated into English as 'public policy' or 'law and order'. The concept can perhaps be best understood in English referring to the discretionary powers of the executive to grant or withhold permission for something.

Under the British legal system 'The fundamental assumption in our law is that a citizen is free to do something unless there is a specific provision to the contrary', (Cmnd 7891, 1980, p 6 para 18). A citizen's conduct may be deemed an offence under common law because of past judicial decisions to that effect or become an offence if such conduct is prohibited by statute (Act of Parliament), for example, the provisions of the 1936 Public Order Act. However, it has been pointed out that although Lord Scarman asserted (Cmnd 5919, 1974, pp. 1-2) that 'Amongst our fundamental human rights there are, without doubt, the rights of peaceful assembly and public protest' -

> The history of public order in the United Kingdom is essentially a history of restrictions. There is no guaranteed right to demonstrate. What is asserted by Lord Justice Scarman is not a right in the strict sense, but that peaceful demonstrations are lawful. By contrast in the United States, the constitution guarantees freedom of assembly. This in effect creates a right to use the highway for the purpose of assembly.(10)

Ingraham has argued that during most of the nineteenth century British governments were able to maintain
public order through a policy of 'minimal repression ...'
because '... Parliamentary measures were sufficiently
adaptive to demands for change and reform ... (and) ...
prosperity and progress took a lot of steam out of revolutionary movements which could do little but promise more
of the same'.   However, he points out that during the
twentieth century British governments placed an increased
emphasis on preventive measures exercised with caution.
The aim being to '... repress political crime in order to
avoid head-on collisions which would disturb the tenuous
consensus that prevails among Englishmen of different
classes and political persuasions ...'.   He further
argues that:

> "Prevention" in the modern English sense means
> avoiding the issues raised by the political
> opposition at all costs, shunning direct con-
> frontations wherever possible, smothering the
> opposition in a morass of humdrum regulations,
> harassing them with arrests and prosecutions for
> petty offences, and above all shrinking from the
> glare of publicity.   In this way the English
> have been able to maintain their reputation as
> an oasis of political liberalism in an age in
> which liberalism in the management of political
> crime is dead.(11)

Indeed there is sometimes a different reality in the
management of political crime in Britain shown by the
comments of public figures such as former Home Secretary,
Merlyn Rees' sweeping and subjective statement that the
police Special Branch '... collects information on those I
think cause problems for the state'.   (945 HC Deb 55, Col
650, 2 March 1978)   Furthermore, in 1977 the Association
of Chief Police Officers stated that '... the police can
no longer prevent public disorder in the street', and
called for a new Public Order Act to give the police
greater control over marches etc, '- similar to police
powers in Ulster'(12) (author's emphasis).
    Whilst under common law there are the offences of
causing a breach of the peace, the offences of affray and
unlawful assembly, rout, riot and public nuisance all per-
tain to the maintenance of public order.   Acts such as
the 1936 Public Order Act and the Prevention of Terrorism
Acts (1974 and 1976) are specifically designed to provide
powers to deal with identifiable public order problems,
eg, prevention of marches deemed likely to cause a breach

of the peace, the proscribing of an organisation as illegal and the prohibition on the wearing of political uniforms in public. The Memorandum submitted by the Home Office to the review of the 1936 Public Order Act stated (HC 756-II, 1980, p 11),

> The Public Order Act 1936 marked a watershed in conferring powers to take preventive action in respect of marches which might occasion disorder. It also dealt specifically with the conduct of those who deliberately intend in their activities or behaviour to threaten or insult individuals or sections of the community in such a way as to make a breach of the peace likely.

The same Home Office Memorandum took as its, '... starting point the need to safeguard certain fundamental human rights - the rights of peaceful assembly and public protest and the right to public order and tranquillity,' (HC 756-II, p 2). It is useful to examine under what conditions these rights may be modified or are sought to be modified.

Firstly, with reference to the banning of public processions, the duty to assess that a ban is desirable because of a real risk of serious disorder resides with the chief officers of police. The power to issue a ban rests either with the local authority (ie elected local representatives) or, the Commissioner of the Metropolitan Police in the case of London, with in both cases the consent of the Home Secretary (an elected MP). Thus, in theory, there is an element of democratic control even in public order legislation. In contrast with this essentially decentralised division of power, in the case of the Prevention of Terrorism Acts the ultimate power resides, at national level, with the Home Secretary and much discretionary power rests with the police alone. Because, as Lord Shackleton said in his review of the operation of these Acts, 'Society expects the police rapidly and effectively to detect and prevent acts of terrorism ...' (Cmnd 7324, 1978, pp 48-49). With that statement few would quarrel. However, there is less consensus when one considers the appropriate response to Trade Union strikes or pickets, marches against racialism or 'sit-downs' against cruise missiles, and the fact that one politician's view of who are 'subversive elements' may clash with another politician's view of those same people as legitimate protestors against government oppression or controversial policies. In Britain the official response to public order problems is a product of the policy of the ruling political party and the ability of the police to maintain order by means that are publically acceptable and at a cost in terms of personal risk, that the service is prepared to accept.

The police evidence to the Home Affairs Committee on the law relating to public order contains interesting observations on possible future developments in this area of law. The Police Federation in their letter to the Committee, advocated (HC 756-II, pp 28-9) '... a policy of prohibition of all public marches and demonstrations which in the opinion of the appropriate chief officer of police, are reasonably likely to lead to serious breaches of the law'. This policy the Federation felt was preferable to the consequences '... if chief officers continue to decide the question of whether or not to apply for the prohibition of a march or demonstration, on a professional calculation of how much violence is likely to occur, and the capacity of the police to retain some semblance of control'. The consequence of this policy, the Federation pointed out, was the introduction of riot control training and equipment, '... which were once considered alien to our tradition'. They also advocated a uniform national requirement of seven days' notice of the intention to hold a march or demonstration.

The, then, Metropolitan Police Commissioner, Sir David McNee, submitted a Memorandum to the Committee which outlined what he saw as four main deficiencies in the 1936 Public Order Act. These were (HC 756-II, p 42): 1. The Act did not adequately prescribe all types of public gathering that should be subject to control, eg an assembly or 'picket' designed to change other citizens' actions. 2. A dearth of preventive measures other than a ban or the imposition of conditions upon a march. Sir David suggested a legal requirement of 'notice of intention' to march given within a reasonable time before the march plus more precise powers to control demonstrations. 3. Creation of the specific offence of throwing a missile. 4. An increase in the penalties imposed for public order offences. During the Home Affairs Committee's oral questioning on the above Memorandum, the Metropolitan Police Assistant Commissioner, Mr. Wilford Gibson, made it clear, that whilst the police did possess relevant powers under a variety of Acts such as Section 121 of the Highways Act on wilful obstruction, they would find it simpler to be able to use a more explicit and expanded Public Order Act. Presumably to make it quite clear that a public order problem was deemed to exist, rather like the old requirement for a magistrate to 'read the Riot Act'.

Further police evidence, from the Association of Chief Police Officers, advocated the creation in Britain of provisions similar to those in use in Northern Ireland under the Northern Ireland Emergency Provisions Act (HC 756-II, p 61 & 62). They noted that Section 24 of that Act had substantially reduced the number of assemblies in Northern Ireland. Section 24 states:

> Where any commissioned officer of Her Majesty's forces or any officer of the Royal Ulster Constabulary, not below the rank of Chief Inspector is of the opinion that any assembly of three or more persons may lead to a breach of the peace or public disorder or may make undue demands on the police or Her Majesty's Forces he, or any member of these forces on duty, or any constable, may order the persons constituting the assembly, to disperse forthwith. Where an order is given under this section with respect to an assembly, any person who thereafter joins or remains in the assembly, or otherwise fails to comply with the order, shall be liable on summary conviction to imprisonment of a term not exceeding six months or to a fine not exceeding £400 or both.

Certainly the consideration of making '... undue demands on the police ...' provides a very neat neutral mechanism for dispersing any type of gathering!

Police organisational responses to public order problems

An alternative or complementary approach to public order problems to that of legal restraint is to increase the ability of the police to physically contain public order problems through training, equipment and organisation. Sometimes there is a call from the 'law and order' lobby for the creation of a '3rd Force' (between the police and army) and the French Republican Safety Companies (the CRS) are offered as an example. I have noted elsewhere that 'It is contended that, when the ordinary police are being hard pressed and yet the breakdown of law and order is not such that martial law and the armed forces should take over, some form of paramilitary police may be able to help restore order'. However, '... a true "third force" that is neither part of a police system nor an army unit is quite a rare organisation'.(13) The CRS is an integral part of the French Police Nationale. In Western Europe the only true "3rd Force" exists because of special national circumstances and that is the West German Bundesgrenzschutz (The Federal Border Guard). The Bundesgrenzschutz is neither a unit of the West German Army nor part of the Länder police system. It is an independent force under the Federal Minister of the Interior.

However, whatever their exact organisational status the existence of large, well trained anti-riot forces does not by itself guarantee the acceptable resolution of public order problems in democracies. In an authoritarian state regimes may survive by shooting protestors and in developing countries the colonial heritage may include an, albeit grudging, acceptance that as a last resort the police will shoot. In India this power may be seen as preferable to calling in the army and risking a military takeover of political power.(14) The problems in a democratic state, even with large police reserves like the CRS and Gendarmerie Mobile in France, have been examined by Philip Stead in the context of the riots in Paris when the police had plenty of fire power available but as Stead points out: 'The heart of the problem was to oppose the rebels forcefully without bloodshed. French history is not without examples of protest which over-reaction by the authorities has turned into revolution. If the police had opened fire on the young rebels of May, the consequent martyrdom would assuredly have brought down the regime. During those six weeks the order to fire was never given.'

Moreover, Stead notes that, 'The resolution of the Paris riots of 1968 eventually had to be a political one. General de Gaulle sensed the reaction of the law-abiding population and acted accordingly to bring the disorders to an end.'(15) Although sometimes British police officers may look with envy at some of the continental police equipment and powers and even the police equipment and powers available in Northern Ireland other officers take a different view. Ben Whitaker, cites one Chief Constable as saying 'Paradoxically sometimes a weak police force causes society to come to terms with its problems and take political action which it would be discouraged from doing if the security services were strong'.(16)

There are a number of writers who suggest that Britain already has the equivalent of a "3rd Force" where that equivalent is understood as something distinct from the Army and the traditional forms of police organisation in Britain. They cite, in support of this view, the existence of permanent or ad hoc police support units, like the Special Patrol Group in the Metropolitan Police one of whose functions was to be available to assist with public order problems.(17)

Similar units have also been reported by Chief Constables as existing in 24 of the 52 local police forces. The Metropolitan Police SPG is about 200 strong and, for example, in 1969 the Thames Valley Police formed '... two Tactical Aid Groups of 41 men each, led by a chief inspector, (which) moving quickly to the scene ... (are) supported by dog teams and a special Landrover filled with riot equipment, CS gas and cartridges, rifles and ammunition. They are trained to handle sieges, demonstrations and other confrontations', (Manwaring-White, 1983, p. 44). These units are quite a recent innovation and in their use in public order maintenance form a clear contrast to the older, less formal methods of manpower support within and between police forces supplemented, if necessary, by the use of the small numbers of mounted police maintained by some forces.

Despite the reserve unit developments within the organisation of British police forces it must be pointed out that they do not equate very closely with some continental examples. Firstly, many of the police reserve forces in Western European states are, in British colonial police parlance, barracked police reserves. In other words they are police under training, living in barracks, used as a manpower reserve in public order situations, eg the West German Länder Bereitschaftspolizei, or the reserves form a specially established component of the police organisation, as is the case with the CRS in France.

Moreover, there is a considerable difference in the scale of the reserves available. If one assumes an average of 40 officers in an 'SPG' outside London plus 200 in the Met's SPG this only gives a total of reported permanently established reserve units of about 1,160 or 1.02% of the total police establishment in England and Wales. It may be objected that this calculation does not take account of the ability of police forces to form 'support units' by taking specially trained officers off other duties. However, this is an organisational flexibility one would expect from any type of police force. It is more important to contrast the small scale of the permanently available British police public order reserves with that found in other major Western European countries. In France the permanently established police public order reserve capacity (CRS and Gendarmerie Mobile) is 21% of the total civil and military police forces. Although the size of the British police forces' permanently staffed SPG format units are relatively small by some continental standards, the size and capability of the divisional Police Support Units (PSU) formed as required by officers

on other duties, has increased. Part of the PSU training
is for public order duties. It has been estimated (New
Society, 21-8-1980, p.352), that approximately 11,000
police officers are now trained and available for PSU
duties. Since then the number has clearly grown.
Evidence for the spread of public order training in the
PSU format is provided by the current police deployments
in the miners' strike of 1984. Whilst reference to a
national police force is not factually correct, it is
clear that the organised public order capability of the
British police forces has, regrettably, had to increase to
maintain the rule of law in certain circumstances.

The evolution of British police tactics and equipment
will next be considered in relation to the handling of
public order problems since 1945. In this context the
author fully agrees with a 1982 Home Office Study (No. 72)
that at the extreme of the public order spectrum: 'Ultimately, riot control depends on the restoration of the
moral, rather than physical authority of the police, which
permits ordinary policing to take place by consent.'

MAJOR PUBLIC ORDER PROBLEMS IN BRITAIN SINCE 1945

General Issues

It is very necessary to set obvious examples of major
clashes between members of the public and the police, such
as at Red Lion Square, London, in 1975, St Paul's in
Bristol in 1979, Toxteth, Liverpool and Brixton, London in
1981 against both the long periods of relative tranquility
and the fact that many police force areas are not directly
involved with such incidents. A more recent factor is
that incidents involving rowdy elements at football matches can produce serious public order problems, unassociated
with those public order incidents which may contain a
challenge to the political system.

Also the issue of maintaining public order has always
been particularly complicated in industrial disputes
because such disputes are not necessarily political challenges and there are legal rights for workers to picket.
However, if disputes are seen to threaten 'vital services', such as fuel, transport, water, refuse collection,
fire-fighting or medical services then a government may
take emergency powers and call in the armed forces not as
extra 'police' but to give military aid to the civil
powers, eg, manning auxiliary fire engines, providing
military ambulances and collecting refuse. In such circumstances the police must ensure that the armed forces
can carry out their assigned tasks even if that means

taking action against workers in an industrial dispute.

Even more sensitive and new are the public order problems posed by Britain becoming a multi-racial society without governments being prepared to take proper cognisance or action over the consequent problems of racial ghettoes, race hatred and cultural differences. A very useful and well documented study of this issue is Paul Gilroy's <u>Police and Thieves</u>. In particular Gilroy identifies the undramatic but thoughtful way a 1967 Home Office circular to chief constables emphasised that 'there is little doubt that the most likely cause of friction between police and the immigrant community is the lack of knowledge and the misunderstanding of each other'. Gilroy comments, 'this was the era in which officialdom understood blacks seriously if paternalistically in terms of the problems of the coloured school leaver, outside the syntax of 'mugging', and without reference to racial conflict in American cities'. In contrast Gilroy cites the comments of former Metropolitan Police Commissioner, Sir David McNee who stated in 1979, some twelve years later that, 'policing a multi-racial society is putting the fabric of our policing philosophy under greater stress than at any time since the years immediately after the Metropolitan Police was established in 1829'.(18) When Lord Scarman was asked to look at '... the serious disorder in Brixton (London) on 10-12 April 1981 ...' he notes that:-

> During the week-end of 10-12 April ... the British people watched with horror and incredulity an instant audio-visual presentation on their television sets of scenes of violence and disorder in their capital city, the like of which had not previously been seen in this century in Britain. In the centre of Brixton, a few hundred young people most, - but not all of them, black - attacked the police on the streets with stones, bricks, iron bars and petrol bombs, demonstrating to millions of their fellow citizens the fragile basis of the Queen's peace. (Cmnd 8427, 1981, para B 1.2)

When addressing the issue of the police response Lord Scarman expressed the complexity of the issue with great clarity:

> The policing problem is not difficult to identify: it is that of policing a multi-racial community in a deprived inner-city area where unemployment, especially among young black people,

is high and hopes are low.   It is a problem
which admits of no clear cut solution.   We require of the police that they maintain and enforce the rule of law in our ethnically diverse
society.   Without an appreciation of the needs
and aspirations of the many elements which constitute that society it is impossible to set the
standards for successful policing.   For good
practical as well as logical reasons, therefore,
it is necessary before attempting an answer to
the policing problem to understand the social
problem.

Lord Scarman's last comment underlines what is perhaps the
single most important issue in the maintenance of public
order.   Namely, that on the one hand the rule of law must
be upheld but, equally and in parallel, government must
tackle society's problems so that the disadvantaged can
actually experience some positive benefits.
     Terrorism poses a rather different form of public
order challenge.   There may be an obvious relationship
between, for example, race riots and a terrorist group
threatenting retaliation by bombs or assassinations
against particular racial groups.   In such cases whilst
the terrorist group must be dealt with by the police with,
if necessary, military support if the tactics and equipment required are more normally military than police,
there still exists a requirement for government to act in
relation to the underlying social and economic problems.
     Terrorism's very different public order challenge
arises when the terrorist acts, in this case, in Britain,
not in response to a problem in Britain but as part of a
campaign to affect events in another country.   Paul
Wilkinson has described the type of terrorist campaigns
and incidents, so far experienced in Britain, as 'spasm'
terrorism that is 'a series of attacks of relatively low
intensity and brief duration'.   The police response to
these incidents or campaigns has to cover intelligence
gathering, the prevention of and protection against terrorist acts, and the ability to carry out counter-terrorist operations.   Wilkinson has pointed out that these
tasks are 'closely analogous to those required for combating other serious crimes of violence.   But the tasks
involved require a high degree of specialised knowledge
beyond the scope of normal criminal investigation departments.'(19)
     It is this point of needing to go beyond the 'normal'
or 'familiar' in terms of a police response in Britain
that relates the terrorist incident to the riot in terms

of a public order problem. In both cases the police system has to change. The questions are how and to what extent. A common response in many countries is to form, if they do not exist already, special police anti-riot and/or anti-terrorist groups.

The traditional British police response to crowd control problems was to smother trouble with large numbers of police and a certain amount of toleration. However, numbers and toleration clearly cannot contain people intent on violent confrontation. Therefore permanent reserves, like the Metropolitan Police Special Patrol Group were created in part for public order maintenance and as part of a general reactive police style. In his inquiries into the 1974 and 1981 disorders, Lord Scarman has (Cmnd 5919, 1975 and Cmnd 8427, 1981) both recognised the value of such reserves and cautioned against over-reliance or thoughtless use of such police units suggesting that '... the major part in controlling and managing demonstrations should continue to be played by ordinary divisional policemen'. An approach that the present Metropolitan Police Commissioner, Sir Kenneth Newman, has stressed with his concept of the 'omnicompetent' constable. That is a policeman trained and equipped for all situations. These approaches can work in Britain providing major public order problems are of a relatively short or isolated nature and, providing there is public confidence that new equipment, training or organisational forms are only to be used for approved purposes which are officially and explicitly stated and subject, ultimately, to parliamentary scrutiny.

In this context, in Britain, the contrast between the powers of elected government Ministers, accountable to Parliament and their continental counterparts is very striking. The French CRS were established by a French government and are under the direction of the elected Minister of the Interior. The Home Secretary is not a Minister of the Interior or Police Minister as could be the case in many continental countries. In Britain police reserves like the SPG or Greater Manchester's Tactical Aid Group are created by chief officers of police by the exercise of the powers of their office. No external body, like the local police authority, is directly involved.

Intelligence gathering is another important aspect of the police response to public order problems. In the computer age this has raised many questions about the type and scope of information that could be held by police intelligence computers. Methods of surveillance and intelligence gathering, like the activities of the Special Branch are open to misinterpretation because of unnecessary official reticence. Figures on the numbers of officers in the Special Branch were first made public in 1920s but they were not officially up-dated until 1978. In the context of the response to terrorism the former Metropolitan Police Commissioner, Sir Robert Mark, has admitted (The Times, 12 March, 1976) that the response was too often surrounded by 'needless secrecy' which was more likely 'to provoke than allay social disquiet'.

The Police and Street disorders

1936-1970. If one takes as a starting point the presumptions that in Britain the citizen may peacefully protest in public and that the police will, even if their manpower resources are severely stretched, try to permit processions etc, to go ahead, then in the period from 1936 to 1960 relatively few bans on marches were sought under the 1936 Public Order Act. In London there were 20 bans issued between 1936 and 1950, a number partly explained by the activities of Mosley's Blackshirts in the late 1930s. However, between 1951 and 1960 only 2 processions were banned. Outside London only two bans on processions were issued between 1936 and 1964.

The marches of the Campaign for Nuclear Disarmament after 1958 caused the first serious post World War II clashes between the police and protesting citizens. The police response to this campaign involved both surveillance and intelligence gathering on CND activists by the Special Branch and the use of large numbers of police to control the demonstrations. In April 1961 a CND demonstration in London of about 2,000 people was attended by 3,000 police and 800 arrests were made. In September 1961 another CND demonstration in Trafalgar Square was attended by 4,000 police and 1,300 demonstrators were arrested. At this CND demonstration participants received some rather firm handling by the police in a situation where the police were clearly not overwhelmed by the numbers of protestors. Whatever the reason for these police tactics it is certainly a fact that the government did not welcome CND activists and some of the Committee of 100 were to be convicted on charges under the Official Secrets Act.

By contrast there seems to be general agreement that the British police handled the large anti-Vietnam War protests at the end of the 1960s with exemplary patience. The police tactics were essentially to rely upon policemen providing human barriers. Bowden quotes the then Metropolitan Police crowd control training officer, Chief Inspector James Hargadon, as saying 'We have no riot hel-

mets or visors ... We don't think they are necessary, and
if we did put on riot helmets it might work the crowd up a
bit and cause a spot of trouble.' Commenting on the
October 1969 anti-Vietnam War demonstration Bowden recalls
that:-

> ... more than 30,000 protestors marched through
> the streets. Scotland Yard assigned 8,846 pol-
> ice to control the mobs. The forecasts pre-
> dicted trouble, but the "treat-em-gently" tactic
> paid off. When protestors threw coins at one
> cop he laughed and asked for bigger ones. When
> another bobby was hit by a flying pear he picked
> it up and ate it. At the end of the day there
> were forty-seven civilian casualties... And dem-
> onstrators and police - who had seventy-four
> injuries - sang a chorus of Auld Lang Syne to-
> gether outside the undamaged American Embassy,
> which the extremists had threatened to bomb.(20)

Up to the end of the 1960s there is evidence for both
a 'hard' and a 'soft' police response to public order crises of various types. What is not so well understood is
why there should be such differences. Clearly political
direction by the government in power could play a part.
Also, given the discretion accorded to police officers in
exercising their powers, differences in the forms of response may be explained by the conduct of individual ordinary policemen and from the orders of supervisory grade
officers. Even the nature of the public order crises may
play a part. The 'soft' response to the anti-Vietnam War
demonstration of 1969 may be explained, firstly, by the
fact that the protest was not aimed at British institutions or government policies but at the American Embassy
and American government policy. Secondly, in the aftermath of the riots in Paris and American cities in the
1960s, partly stemming from the Vietnam issue, the British
police may have wished to demonstrate an ability to control protests without resorting to the tactics and equipment found necessary both in France and America.

1970-1983. Bowden has argued that '... at no other time
has the British police structure and response capability
to crisis altered more dramatically than during the past
six years; (1972-8)'.(21) Why did the public order
problems of the 1970s lead to changes in police structures
and responses?
     In his 1982 report the Chief Inspector of Constabul-
ary made the apt comment (HC 15, 1982, p 47) that 'no

doubt the reasons for the comparative lack of trouble on the streets (in 1982) are as complex as the reasons for the earlier disorder' (1981). This seems a very sensible line of argument and this section is not going to attempt any comprehensive account of why serious public disorders occur or do not occur. However, with reference to the period 1970-83 what will be discussed are forms of police response to public order problems and especially why and how the response may be seen to change.

Firstly, there were 'spill-over' effects from the troubles in Northern Ireland, both in terms of IRA terrorist campaigns and the RUC type police equipment and tactics.(22) Secondly, there were some very serious industrial disputes, such as the miners' strike in 1972 and the Grunwick factory strike in 1977 in which the police found it difficult to deal with the pickets. Thirdly, there were the effects of other, non-IRA terrorist campaigns and acts, such as the Angry Brigade bombings. Finally, race relations issues erupted into violent clashes with the police, such as the Red Lion Square demonstrations of 1974, Southall in 1979 and at some of the Notting Hill multi-racial carnivals when police had to use dustbin lids as shields in the riots of 1981.

Before the recent call by Sir Kenneth Newman for more stress upon the 'omnicompetent' constable the police organisational philosophy of the 1970s seems to have been one of increased 'specialisation'. As mentioned earlier there was the formation of anti-terrorist, or bomb squads, a Diplomatic Protection Group (in the Met.), squads of expert marksmen (or as the Americans call them 'SWAT squads' - Special Weapons And Tactics) and, the permanently organised, manpower reserves like the Special Patrol Group. Thus public order problems in the 1970s both partly caused the British police to make available specialised forms of response and they were occasions on which specialised forms of response could be used. However, it must be emphasised that the separate police forces do not and cannot maintain uniform types of response capability. As the Chief Inspector of Constabulary said in his 1980 Report (HC 409, p 6) '... when there is a spontaneous outbreak of serious public disorder, particularly in non-metropolitan areas, large reserves of police are not immediately available to deal with the incident'.

Earlier the term 'riot' was applied to the serious breakdowns in public order in various parts of Britain in 1981. A riot can be defined in general terms as occurring when people in large numbers, and over a prolonged period break a variety of laws, attack the police trying to restore order, loot and damage property. This is clearly a qualitatively different situation to a demonstration which is generally peaceable but which may produce a short-term violent clash with the police. Rioters in both Northern Ireland and in Britain have at times tried to establish 'no-go' areas for the police. This raises the public order problem to a challenge to both the rule of law and a government's powers to govern.

Having defined a riot in the above terms it allows the analysis to divide the British police response to the control of public disorders into two parts. Firstly, few police would seriously quarrel with Lord Scarman's findings (Red Lion Square, 1974, Cmnd 5919, and Brixton 1981, Cmnd 8427) that wherever possible public order problems should be contained by the traditional use of large numbers of non-specially equipped police. Some policemen would also agree with Lord Scarman and others, like former Chief Constable John Alderson, that positive efforts at improving police-community relations and a 'community style' of policing could contribute to reducing the risks of incidents sparking off trouble.

However, there is another police view, within the evidence given to the 1980 Home Affairs Committee inquiry into the Law Relating to Public Order (HC 756-I and II), that the police response should be one of preemptive policing and not reactive policing. It was suggested that Chief Constables should no longer be placed in a position to have to decide if they could contain serious violence if it should break out during a demonstration. Instead Chief Constables, if serious violence was likely, would seek a ban on such a demonstration. This development raises the important general question of to what extent should the ability to protest be protected both as a form of right and as a matter of fact. A right to protest is of little use without the opportunity to exercise it. However, there still remains the issue of how much risk to life and limb is it reasonable to ask of a policeman so that some citizens may protest. In a democracy with a common law tradition it has to be admitted that no finite answer to these issues is possible. Public and political attitudes to police response will remain a variable factor.

The riots of 1981 and their aftermath

It is clearly not within the scope of this section that an attempt should be made to provide a comprehensive discussion of the causes of the 'serious disorders' (Scarman, Cmnd 8427, 1981, p. 3 para 1.10) during April, July and August 1981 in Southall, Brixton, Liverpool (Toxteth),

Manchester (Moss Side) and the West Midlands. These have been discussed, at great length, in many sources.(23) There does seem to be some consensus that the following factors contributed to the outbreaks of serious disorder or riots as many would label the scenes of violence and destruction. The factors identified cover racial tensions and the experiences of relative deprivation due to unemployment or poor living conditions, all of which can be more generally described as associated with the "inner city problem" found in many major industrial societies. None of the above causal factors are a police responsibility but a responsibility for the whole country and, particularly the government in power.

However, within the literature on the 1981 riots there does emerge a form of consensus (albeit somewhat hesitant from some police officers) that the police themselves can be a contributing factor in the outbreaks of serious disorders. Scarman's comments about Brixton are echoed elsewhere and can be cited as fairly representative. On the key point of the breakdown in community relations which makes policing by consent impossible, Scarman identifies police shortcomings as most importantly that of:-

> ... the unwillingness to consult on police operations, and "hard policing" (saturating an area with police for some general or specific anticrime drive) ... (and) ... other factors that helped to build up the image of an unimaginative and inflexible police presence ... notably the conduct of some officers in their dealings with black people, and the formal and complicated system for handling complaints against the police. (Cmnd 8427, 1981, p 66 para 4.71)

These comments raise issues about how police forces are organised, the operational handling of police forces and the relationship of police forces to the communities they serve.

Before these issues are discussed it is necessary to mention, briefly, pre-1981 incidents which caused concern about police attitudes and tactics especially those involving contacts with ethnic minorities. It is also necessary to describe the abnormal policing methods used in the attempts to control some of the riots to try and identify the problems of riot control for an essentially unarmed police force, which has no specific public order unit.

In November 1983 there was published a major in-depth study into the Metropolitan Police, commissioned by Sir David NcNee (when Commissioner) from the Policy Studies Institute. Amongst its findings were those of the existence of racialist attitudes amongst some police officers. Sir Kenneth Newman (the current Commissioner) has generally accepted these and other findings and observed that some of the problems such as improving race relations were being tackled by better training methods. Nonetheless this report does give support to the allegations of racialist attitudes in some police forces which are thought to have contributed to the deterioration of police-community relations. For example, in April 1979 there occurred the death of Blair Peach during a confrontation with police attempts to handle a counter-demonstration against a National Front meeting in Southall and also in 1979 there were widespread protests at the hard-line policing in the Knowsley Division of the Merseyside police area which included allegations of racialism within the local police. Thus at the very least and from whatever cause, some police officers having racialist attitudes or certain ethnic minority groups causing more law enforcement problems than others, police-community relations had evidently deteriorated badly in some urban areas before the outbreak of the riots in 1981.

With that background one can turn to the actual police response to the 1981 riots. In this context it is helpful to identify when a 'serious disorder' can legally be described as a riot. Scarman, reporting on Brixton and referring to the events of Friday, 10 April states:- 'The disorder was not initially a riot. But it had become a riot by 6.36 pm ... The critical moment was when the crowd turned and stoned the police. This was violent crowd action in which members of the crowd were mutually assisting each other in the execution of a common purpose, namely an attack upon the police. It was dangerous and alarming.' (Cmnd. 8427, 1981, p. 42 para 3.98)

In this instance the police managed to contain and bring the riot under control using reinforcements of manpower including the Special Patrol Group, charging the crowds with drawn truncheons (commonly known as a 'baton charge') and by attempting to enhance the capability of each individual officer by the issue of protective helmets and shields. This response did not see the use of any extraordinary tactics or weapons by the police. Nevertheless it had deficiencies, particularly the delay in mustering, rapidly, adequately trained and equipped reserves. A point that police forces were supposed to have been well aware of after the problems in the handling of the disorders in the St Paul's area of Bristol in April 1980. Lord Scarman also noted that some of the equipment available to the police was unsuitable: the protective shields and helmets, when they became available, proved inadequate; the helmets provided insufficient protection to the head; the foam padding at the rear of the shields — themselves heavy and cumbersome — caught fire when petrol spilled over them. Officers untrained in the use of shields or in the command of men carrying them found themselves thrust into the front line. Officers' uniforms were also ignited by the flames from petrol bombs. Police vehicles were totally unprotected from missile throwing mobs. There were difficulties in radio communications between officers deployed at the scene and police control, and between different units of officers on the ground ... (Scarman, Cmnd 4827, 1981, p 71 para 4.91)

In the case of the Brixton disorders it does seem as if the deficiencies in the police handling of the incidents were mostly organisational and technical and of a type that should be capable of being overcome by internal action and Home Office support.

There is here, however, a dilemma for police-community relations. Harriet Harman of the National Council for Civil Liberties (NCCL) has written that the NCCL fully supports ' ... the issue of more effective, protective clothing, helmets and shields to the police, and the introduction of more intensive and more effective training in methods of containing and reducing serious street disorders'. However, Harman (and also Scarman) have noted that protective equipment, like shields, may be used improperly for offensive purposes. More important though is the question of 'balance' as Harman points out:-

> ... equipment which depersonalises police officers, and makes face-to-face contact more difficult or impossible, also makes the tasks of the police more difficult: if police officers begin to look like fighting machines, they will be regarded even more strongly as legitimate targets for attack. Very careful consideration must therefore be given to how most effectively to combine protection for police officers under fire with the maintenance of the traditional police appearance.(24)

A very different set of issues were raised by the nature of the disorders in Toxteth, Liverpool and the police response. The disorders appear to have been of a more violent and large scale nature than those in other parts of

Britain and, in Lord Scarman's terms, capable of being described as a riot. Two particular features of the police response in Toxteth have caused comment. The Merseyside Chief Constable, Kenneth Oxford, as part of his 'positive police policy' of response, firstly used '... protected vehicles deployed into the crowd in order to break it up and wherever possible to arrest the ringleaders ...'.(25) Secondly and for the first time in public order operations outside Northern Ireland CS gas was used. This resort to CS gas was both, in part, improper and also regrettable in the light of known evidence concerning the effects of CS gas. The improper use of CS gas relates to the use of 41 rounds of Ferret CS cartridges whose use was restricted by Home Office instructions to circumstances where penetration of solid obstacles was necessary. The cartridges have a warning that they should not be used against 'any person or crowd'.

Although Chief Constable Oxford could to some extent reasonably seek to justify his actions by arguing, on the use of CS, that this was the 'correct use of minimum force which was necessary and available', there is a more general issue to be considered. Is it politically acceptable that in extreme situations the police in Britain should be the users of these levels of force - CS gas or protected vehicles or some variation such as water cannon and plastic bullets? Or should the armed forces be called in when a certain level of response is needed to avoid the police having to move too far away from their normal equipment and tactics and thus making the return to policing by consent that much more difficult? As Field and Southgate argued: 'the great and often unrecognised problems in controlling riots, and even in stopping incipient riots, argue for control through prevention ... this is ultimately a political point rather than a technical one about the limitation on means of crowd control'.(26)

Here the police and the broader community must come face-to-face because the maintenance of law and order has always been recognised as dependent, in part, upon good relations with the community being policed. In this context the riots of 1981 in so far as concern was expressed at a breakdown of communications between some police forces and their communities gave impetus to considerations about police 'accountability' for their actions.

Now, police 'accountability' is an issue on which very polarised views are expressed. At one extreme are ideas of policing by some kind of 'people's militia', at another the police fear being put under some form of direct control by elected politicians who might attempt to order policing along lines to support policies in party manifestos but not laid down by statute.

Leaving the extremes aside there still remains a substantial and important number of problems concerning police accountability. These can be considered as relating to formal, statutory relations or legal accountability and a more informal type of accountability which can be considered under the heading of police-community relations.

There are two separate but related issues with regard to legal accountability. These are the powers and duties of the local police authorities and apart from the City of London, the fact that the Home Secretary is the police authority for the Metropolitan Police area. Both these topics have been discussed quite well in several chapters in Cowell, Jones and Young (1982). The common features of both topics are whether, how and to what extent police officers should be answerable for their actions not just to the law, or, ultimately and somewhat tenuously to the Home Secretary but also to the locally elected representatives of the people because local authorities meet part of the cost of the police, and how to enable the local representatives to help their community and the local police form a mutually supportive relationship.

The 1962 Royal Commission on the Police noted that a Chief Constable:

> is accountable to no one and subject to no one's orders for the way in which, for example, he settles his general policies in regard to law enforcement over the area covered by his force, the concentration of his resources on any particular type of crime or area, the manner in which he handles political demonstrations or processions and allocates and instructs his men when preventing breaches of the peace arising from industrial disputes ... (Cmnd 1728, 1962, para 89).

and the Royal Commission recommended that, 'Chief Constables should be subject to more effective supervision' (para 405 (5)).

However, the resulting 1964 Police Act did not provide the statutory powers to enable or require local police authorities to carry out effective supervision. For example, Harman has pointed out that:

> Many police authorities have not attempted, as the Royal Commission on the Police intended, to expose their Chief Constable 'to advice and

guidance of which he would be expected to take heed'. A survey conducted by the Association of County Councils and Association of Metropolitan Authorities in 1976 revealed that 10 out of the 41 police authorities did not regularly ask for reports on policing from their Chief Constable, as they are empowered to do ... and in only 10 authorities were reports frequently required.(27)

If one assumes that there would be as much general public unease about local councillors directing day to day operations as there is about the current autonomy of Chief Constables there still remains a "middle" way possible, in which it might be felt desirable and helpful for the local police authority to try and enter into a meaningful dialogue with a chief constable about his policing objectives and methods. But how do lay people question a professional police officer?

The former Home Secretary, William Whitelaw, acknowledged somewhat prophetically the existence of the issue in his James Scott Lecture on 17 September 1980. He said:-

> there is ... a real need to ensure that the views of the public are adequately taken into account in the development of policing policies ... I think it has become increasingly desirable that police authorities should see themselves not just as providers of resources but as a means whereby the Chief Constable can give account of his policing policy to the democratically elected representatives of the community, and in turn, they can express to him the views of the community on these policies.

However, the present government has not made any determined effort to help such a development. As an example of the existing problems Margaret Simey has pointed out that when the Merseyside Police Authority attempted to find another professional source on the activities of the Merseyside Police, other than the forces' own reports none was available. She wrote, the Police Authority turned, '... to our HMI who, on the basis of an annual inspection advises that the Home Office as to whether the force is efficient and merits financial support. Incredibly, custom and practice dictate that his reports are not available to either Chief Constable or Police Authority.'(28)

Some official encouragement has been given to the suggestions for police-community liaison bodies contained in the Scarman Report on the Brixton riots. However, as Bundred has pointed the London '... borough liaison committees established by the Home Office in the wake of the Scarman Report have been denied even the modest powers recommended by Scarman'.(29)

Looking to the Future

Any forward looking analysis must seek to rest its propositions on the most solid bases that can be found. In the context of this chapter it must be admitted that the least "solid" base is likely to be predictions of future public order problems. For example few people would have predicted that protests against cruise missiles at the Greenham Common Air Force Base would have required at times the daily presence of some three hundred police officers under the command of an Assistant Chief Constable. However, it is perhaps not unreasonable to put forward the view that with the large scale protests of the 1960s, the various terrorist campaigns, incidents such as the Red Lion Square disorders of 1974 and the riots of 1981 Britain has recently experienced all the types of public order problems that are likely short of situations of such serious and widespread disorder, which would require emergency powers and the use of the armed forces.

Therefore, looking to the future, it seems that it is not necessary to speculate about possible public order scenarios. Rather one can consider, firstly, the legal and political framework within which public order will be maintained and the citizen's rights protected. Secondly, one can consider the possible lines of development in the structure of the police and methods of policing that may have an impact on the maintenance of law and order.

The 1980 Home Office consultative paper (Cmnd 7891) on 'The Review of the Public Order Act 1936' contains some indications as to the views of the current Conservative government on statutory provisions and the report of the Law Commission (HC 85, 1983) 'Offences relating to Public Order' comments on common law provisions and certain statutory offences. Among the general principles of its approach the Home Office Review believes in a balance between the rights of demonstrators and those of the rest of the public. However, the Review does not take the view that a specific right to demonstrate would be helpful because of the difficulties of adequately defining such a right to suit all possible circumstances. Moreover, the Review holds the view that some specific statute law on public order is necessary to protect citizens and help the police in the execution of the duties.

However, it is stated as the view of the present Government that modern methods of communications do not make it unnecessary to demonstrate it is accepted that 'the freedom to demonstrate one's view in public - within the law - is fundamental to a democracy' (Cmnd 7891 p 11 para 36). Moreover, the Government does not believe that organisations putting forward contentious policies should be proscribed unless there exists, '... the most exceptional circumstances. Proscription has in Great Britain been confined in recent years to organisations openly and avowedly dedicated to violent terrorist acts and to the overthrow of the civil authorities.' (Cmnd 7891, p 11, para 37). The Government has also expressed opposition (Cmnd 7891, p 19, para 65) to ideas which suggest that protestors should meet the costs of policing protests. It accepts that a fundamental freedom should not, in effect, be "taxed".

The police operation at Greenham Common has just provided a good example of an issue resulting from a public order problem particularly related to Britain's decentralised police system. The local Chief Constable had to reduce the police presence to 100 and terminate aid arrangements with neighbouring forces. This action resulted from local pressure against meeting the full costs of a protest directed at national policies, chargeable to the ratepayers of the area. The government then announced a special grant to the Thames Valley Police authority to help meet the costs of policing the anti-cruise protests.

With regard to the issue of banning processions or marches the Government notes that it is necessary to look at the competences of chief officers of police and/or local authorities to initiate bans. In England and Wales initiation rests with the police but in Scotland (under local legislation and the Burgh Police (Scotland) Act 1892) local authorities can initiate a ban. However, the Government clearly favours a situation under which the competent Secretary of State (Home Secretary or Scottish Secretary) should have to approve bans thus allowing the restriction of citizens' rights to be challenged in Parliament.

Because the review of the 1936 Public Order Act reached its preliminary conclusions before the riots of 1981 the government decided to reconsider these conclusions to take account of the 1981 experiences of public order problems and the Scarman report. Consequently, reform of the Burgh Police (Scotland) Act 1892, which was supposed to have occurred in parallel to changes in the

1936 Public Order Act, has proceeded on its own. Whilst the government has warned that the new Act for Scotland (the Civic Government (Scotland) Act 1982, c 45) may have to be amended, when the public order review is complete, the Scottish Act, and its passage does provide some clues to current government thinking on public order legislation.

During the passage of the Act through Parliament government ministers made some interesting observations on public order issues. In particular, in June 1982, the Solicitor-General for Scotland made it clear that the government wanted two types of explicit powers to be available for controlling processions. Firstly, powers to ban or restrict processions because of problems not normally considered to justify the term 'serious public disorder'. The example given was the traffic and police manpower problems that could occur in Glasgow if a procession was scheduled for a Saturday when Rangers were playing Celtic. Secondly, powers to impose bans or restrictions because of legislation akin to the 1936 Public Order Act.

The Civic Government (Scotland) Act 1982 (c 45) gave regional or islands' councils (these being Scottish local police authorities) the powers, '... after consulting the Chief Constable ...' (s 63) to ban or impose restrictions on processions. Those proposing to hold processions are required (s 62) to give seven days' notice, in detail, to the local authority. Contravening a ban or conditions is an offence (s 65) and can be punished by a fine and/or imprisonment.

In terms of other legislative developments the Government takes the view that the law needs better provisions to help the police prevent disorder before it breaks out, that the 1936 Public Order Act is deficient in that it does not cover meetings and demonstrations which can lead to similar public order problems as marches, it also contains a rather stringent test of the ability of police resources before the imposition of a ban and, in relation to that point, the Government supports a national requirement for advance notice of processions and suggested 5 days' notice as a compromise between existing variable time requirements in local legislation. The Government also favours a clarification of police powers 'to deal with a disorderly or unlawful assembly ...' (Cmnd 7891, 1980, p 23, para 81).

On the specific issue of race relations the Government noted that controversy surrounded attempts to prevent the fomenting of racial hatred, eg Sec 70 of the Race Relations Act 1976 inserted a new section (5A) into the 1936

Public Order Act covering incitement to racial hatred. However, no powers existed, or it is felt could easily exist, to proscribe racialist organisations if they did not advocate or practise violent terrorist acts or plan the overthrow of the civil authorities.

In general the Government's view was that the present state of the law is marginally unbalanced in favour of the demonstrator as against the interests of the rest of the public. The Law Commission in its proposals for "Offences Relating to Public Order" (HC 85, 1983) has taken a similar view arguing that 'In so far as these offences are concerned with civil liberties, they are essentially intended to penalise the use of violence or intimidation by groups of people because such violence or intimidation goes beyond legitimate means of a public expression of views and becomes conduct which stifles such expression of views'. (HC 85, p 6, para 2.3).

The Law Commission felt that their inquiry showed that greatest criticism was levelled, on grounds of lack of clarity, at the offences of unlawful assembly and breach of the peace in Sec 5 of the 1936 Public Order Act. Therefore the Commission proposed replacing the common law offence of unlawful assembly with two statutory offences of 'violent disorder' and 'conduct intended or likely to cause fear or provoke violence'. However, they still feel that the offence of riot should remain denoting '... the most serious occasions of violent disorder (for a common purpose) by a substantial number of persons' (HC 85, p 9, para 1.10), but it should be made a statutory offence.

On the basis of the Home Office Review, the House of Commons Home Affairs Committee inquiry (referred to earlier) and the Law Commission's proposals it seems likely that the law relating to public order will remain substantially unchanged. With the exceptions that powers to prevent disorder may be both codified and increased and that a new code of offences relating to public order may be introduced to mark more clearly degrees of disorder and penalise conduct which is not generally accepted as legitimate in the context of an implicit right to protest within the law. However, it must be acknowledged that even this apparently reasonable line of development of the rule of law will not meet all cases. Recently, Christian anti-nuclear protestors have been arguing that their conduct was not civil disobedience but holy obedience! Nonetheless the likely developments in the law relating to public order do seem to be of a kind that will assist rather than hinder the police in the execution of their duties being along the lines recommended by the Home

Office '... of being capable of being enforced by the police and the courts'. (Cmnd 7891, 1980, p 4 para 13).

An important exception to the above is in the area of Trade Union legislation where generally the Trade Unions at the moment seem to be avoiding confrontations with employers and the government; this state of affairs might not last if unemployment continues to rise sharply. The Trade Union and Labour Relations Act 1974 as amended by the Employment Act 1980 provide for and specify what is lawful picketing (prohibition of 'secondary picketing'). However, Supperstone quotes Professor Wedderburn's view that 'the only indisputably lawful pickets ... are those who attend in small numbers near the chosen place and who keep out of everyone's way'. But as Wedderburn continued, '... in practice workers do picket in a rather more effective way ... and sensible experienced police officers often take no action so long as there is no violence or other serious obstruction in fact'.(30) But as disputes such as Grunwick have shown serious confrontations can arise and miners' strikes have shown that the confrontations can be widespread. A major test for the current legislation on picketing has been provided by the NGA dispute at the Stockport branch of the Messenger group of newspapers. During some of the most intense periods of large scale picketing the police used tactics and organisational forms developed since the 1981 riots.

In the 1984 mining industry dispute the police have been able to provide quite an effective response to both massed and flying or secondary pickets. Up to c 8,000 police have been made available from nearly half the police forces in the country. Moreover, the police in some areas have been ready to take a view of their duty to preventing breaches of the peace to include stopping pickets moving outside their own NUM area, one example being the turning back of Kent miners at Dartford on their way to other NUM areas. In consequence it has been quite common, in the 1984 miners' dispute for the police to actually outnumber pickets at pit entrances.

Not surprisingly this time police response has produced political controversy. It has been encouraged by the Conservative government. Sir Michael Havers, the Attorney-General, has urged the police to try and see that the code of practice related to the 1980 Employment Act is upheld. This suggested that, in general, 6 pickets should be sufficient at any works entrance. The Attorney-General also supported the interception of flying pickets well before they reached picket lines. The Labour opposition has concentrated its criticisms of the police action on the infringement of civil liberty inherent in stopping people at considerable distances from picket lines and what they see as an attempt to make the picketing code come into the orbit of the criminal law rather than leaving it clearly as a civil wrong.

As industrial disputes can easily be given a political slant it is inevitable that both the law on industrial relations and the police response to industrial disputes will remain controversial.

The general development of the public order maintenance capacity of the police is now enabling the police to produce quite an effective response to the particularly sensitive public order problems posed by industrial disputes.   In 1972, during a miners' strike, 15,000 pickets were able to prevent 800 police from keeping open the Saltery Coke Depot in Birmingham.   Former Conservative Home Secretary, the late Reginald Maudling felt that in such a situation a government was rather helpless.   The only alternative seeming to be the use of armed troops with the risk that the troops might have to fire on strikers.

However, since that time the police forces have developed their individual capacities through the more formalised public order training given to the PSUs (Police Support Units - each of 1 Inspector, 2 Sergeants and 20 PCs) and their capacity to help each other under the mutual aid scheme laid down in the 1964 Police Act. Typically though, in the traditional British manner of avoiding contentious issues the coordination of the police response has been left to a non-official body.

The mobilisation of police support for the coalfield areas police forces has been carried out by the National Recording Centre (NRC) maintained by the Association of Chief Police Officers (ACPO) at New Scotland Yard.   The NRC was activated in the Spring 1984 miners' dispute by the President of the ACPO, Mr. D. Hall, Chief Constable of Humberside, after informing the Home Office through Sir Lawrence Byford, HM Chief Inspector of Constabulary.   The Home Office has a liaison relationship with the NRC and the NRC acts for police forces as a sort of central despatch service.   However, the NRC has no operational role, reserves always come under the operational control of the Chief Constable requesting their presence.

How will the police respond in the future?   The answer, at the moment, seems to be simple.   They will respond using techniques, equipment and organisational forms developed during the last decade or so.   These reflect a mixture of the autonomous decisions of chief officers of police and those forms of standardisation of response tactics and equipment endorsed by the Home Office.   In July

1983 the Home Office Minister, Douglas Hurd, in a written
Commons Answer stated,

> In England and Wales, police operations to main-
> tain or restore public order, which are primary
> duties, are the responsibility of the individual
> chief officer of police of the area concerned.
> Subject to that, the Department (Home Office)
> and Her Majesty's Inspectors of Constabulary
> maintain close and regular liaison with the
> Association of Chief Police Officers, the Com-
> missioner of the Metropolitan Police and, as
> necessary, other individual chief officers,
> about the maintenance and development of measur-
> es to prevent disorder or to deal with it effec-
> tively should it occur.

Specifically, the Home Office has endorsed proposals by
the Police Training Council for standardised public order
training for all ranks and the proposals of the Working
Party on Protective Clothing and Equipment of the police
(ref. Commons' Written Ans. – 10 HC Deb. 6s, cols 488-9,
30/10/81). This Report made recommendations on protective clothing and anti-riot weapons. However, the actual
provision of these items remains a matter for individual
Chief Officers of police and local police authorities.
Lastly, the then Home Secretary, William Whitelaw laid
down official guidelines (10 HC Deb 6s, cols 30-31,
19/10/18) for the use of CS or Baton rounds. These
stated that:-
1. CS/Baton rounds are only to be used on orders
   from a Chief Constable or his deputy and then
   only under the supervision of a senior police
   officer designated by the officer in charge
   and by trained police officers.

2. CS or Baton rounds are only to be used as a
   last resort where conventional police methods
   have failed or where they would not be effective. The use must also be necessary to
   prevent loss of life or serious injury or
   widespread destruction of property. If possible a public warning of use must be given.

3. Only Home Office approved CS equipment, Baton
   rounds and riot guns may be used.

Also any use of CS or Baton rounds (the latter now stocked
by 14 police forces) must be consistent with the principle

of the 'minimum force necessary' as laid down in S3 of the 1967 Criminal Law Act.

What remain unresolved, with regard to the British police response to public order problems, are the issues of the accountability of the police to locally elected authorities in some format, of which the current police authorities are just one example, and the separate but related issue of how autonomous Chief Constables will set the 'style' for policing in their areas.

FOOTNOTES

1.   Gaskell, G. & Smith, P., "The Crowd in History", New Society, 20th August 1981.
2.   Whitaker, B., The Police in Society, Eyre Methuen, London 1979, pp. 35f., 43.
3.   Manwaring-White, S., The Policing Revolution, The Harvester Press 1983.
4.   Cf. chapter on Eire.
5.   Manwaring-White, op.cit., pp. 20f.
6.   Cmnd. 1728, 1962, p. 165.
7.   Cook, P.M., "Centralisation and Decentralisation of the Police Force: The British Model", Police Science Abstracts 9 (5) (1981), 1-4.
8.   Ingraham, B.L., Political Crime in Europe (University of California Press, Berkeley 1978, pp. 19-26.
9.   Evans, A., "Ordre Public Policy and United Kingdom Immigration Law", European Law Review 3 (1978), 370-381.
10.   Supperstone, M., Brownlie's Law of Public Order and National Security, Butterworth, London 1981, pp. 25f.
11.   Ingraham, op.cit., pp. 218, 288, 314.
12.   Hain, P., (ed.) Policing the Police, vol. II, John Calder, London 1979, pp. 185f.
13.   Gregory, F.E.C., "The British Police and Terrorism", in Wilkinson, P. (ed.), British Perspectives on Terrorism, Allen and Unwin, London 1981, p. 110.
14.   Gregory, F.E.C., "The Indian Police System and Internal Conflict", Conflict Quarterly 2 (1) (1981), 18-23.
15.   Stead, P.J., "The Nature of Police Command", Police Studies 4 (1981), 36-42, pp. 40f.
16.   Whitaker, B., op.cit., p. 51.
17.   Cf. Hain, op.cit., Manwaring-White, op.cit., and Bowden, T., Beyond the Limits of the Law, Penguin Books, Harmondsworth 1978.
18.   Gilroy, P., "Police and thieves", in Centre for Contemporary Cultural Studies, The Empire Strikes Back, Hutchinson, London 1982, pp. 153, 146.

19. Wilkinson, P., _Terrorism and the Liberal State,_ Macmillan, London 1977, pp. 139f.
20. Bowden, T., _op.cit._, pp. 211f.
21. _Ib._
22. Manwaring-White, S., _op.cit._, pp. 25-37.
23. Cf. HMSO publications referred to in _Further Reading._
24. Harman, H., "Civil Liberties and Civil Disorders", in Cowell, D., Jones, T., and Young, J. (eds.), _Policing the Riots,_ Junction Books, London 1982, p. 49.
25. As quoted from Oxford's report to his Police Committee in Cowell, Jones, and Young, _op.cit._, pp. 28f.
26. Field, S. and Southgate, P., "Public Disorder: a review of research and a study in one city area", _Home Office Research Study_ No. 72, HMSO 1982.
27. _Op.cit._, p. 46.
28. Simey, M., "Police Authorities and Accountability: the Merseyside Experience", in Cowell, Jones, and Young, _op.cit._, p. 55.
29. Bundred, S., "Accountability and the Metropolitan Police: A suitable Case for Treatment", in Cowell, Jones, and Young, _op.cit._, p. 74.
30. Supperstone, M., _op.cit._, p. 68.

Further Reading

Government Publications (all published in London by Her Majesty's Stationery Office).
"Royal Commission on the Police - Final Report", (Cmnd. 1728, 1962).
"The Red Lion Square Disorders of 15 June 1974" (an inquiry by Lord Justice Scarman), (Cmnd. 5919, 1975).
"Review of the Public Order Act 1936 and related legislation", (Cmnd. 7891, 1978) (carried out by the Home Office).
"Review of the Operation of the Prevention of Terrorism (Temporary Provisions) Acts of 1974 and 1976" (carried out by Lord Shackleton), (Cmnd. 7324, 1978).
"The Brixton Disorders 10-12 April 1981" (Report of an inquiry by Lord Scarman) (Cmnd. 8427, 1981).
Also various reports published annually by Her Majesty's Chief Inspector of Constabulary (as House of Commons' Papers), by the Commissioner of the Metropolitan Police (as Command (Cmnd.) Papers) and by Her Majesty's Chief Inspector of Constabulary for Scotland (as Command (Cmnd.) Papers).

Parliamentary Publications (also published in London by HMSO)

Reports of the House of Commons Select Committee on Home Affairs:
Minutes of Evidence on 'The Home Office', HC321-i and ii 1979.
2nd Report - "Race Relations and the "Sus" Law", HC559, 1980.
2nd Report - "Racial Attacks", HC.106, 1982.
5th Report - "The Law Relating to Public Order", Vols. I and II, HC. 756, 1980.

Report to the Law Commission (No. 123):
"Offences relating to Public Order", HC. 85, 1983.

On the Civic Government (Scotland) Act 1982:

Scottish Grand Committee: First Sitting, "Civic Government" (Scotland) Bill (Lords), 20 April 1982.
First Scottish Standing Committee: 18th Sitting, "Civic Government (Scotland) Bill (Lords), 24 June 1982.

Books

Alderson, J.C., Policing Freedom, (Macdonald and Evans, Plymouth, 1979).
Alderson, J.C. Law and Disorder, (Hamish Hamilton, London, 1984).
Bayley, D.H. (ed.), Police and Society, (Sage, London, 1977).
Benyon, J. (ed.), Scarman and After, (Pergamon Press, Oxford, 1984).
Bowden, T., Beyond the Limits of the Law, (Penguin Books, Harmondsworth, 1978).
Bunyard, R.S., Police Organisation and Command, Macdonald and Evans, Plymouth, 1978).
Cowell, D., Jones, T. and Young, J. (eds.), Policing the Riots, (Junction Books, London, 1982).
Evans, P., The Police Revolution, (Allen and Unwin, London, 1976).
Hain, P. (ed.), Policing the Police, (Vol. I and II, John Calder, London 1979, 1980).
Ingraham, B.L., Political Crime in Europe, (University of Calif. Press, Berkeley, 1978).
Lea, J. and Young, J. What Is To Be Done About Law and Order? (Penguin Books, Harmondsworth, 1984).
Manwaring-White, S., The Policing Revolution, (The Harvester Press, Brighton, 1983).

Mark, Sir Robert, In the Office of Constable, (Collins, London, 1978).

Pope, D.W. and Weiner, N.L. (eds.), Modern Policing (Croom Helm, London, 1981).

Schaffer, E., Community Policing, (Croom Helm, London, 1980).

Supperstone, M., Brownlie's Law of Public Order and National Security, Butterworth, London, 1981).

Varwell, D.W.P., Police and the Public, (Macdonald and Evans, London, 1978).

Whitaker, B., The Police in Society, (Eyre Methuen, London, 1979).

Williams, D., Keeping the Peace, (Hutchinson, London, 1967).

Wilkinson, P., Terrorism and the Liberal State, (Macmillan, London, 1977).

Articles and Pamphlets

Alderson, J.C., "The Role of the Police in Society", RUSI Journal, Vol. 118, No. 4, 1973, pp. 18-23.

Cook, P.M., "Centralisation and Decentralisation of the Police Force - The British Model", Police Science Abstracts, 9 (5), 1981, pp. i-iv.

Field, S. and Southgate, P., "Public Disorder: a review of research and a study in one city area", Home Office Research Study, No. 72, (HMSO, 1982).

Robinson, C.D., "Ideology as History: A Look at the Way some English Police Historians Look at the Police", Police Studies, Vol. 2, 1979, pp. 3.

Gaskell, G. and Smith, P., "The Crowd in History", New Society, 20 August 1981.

McCullough, H.M., Asst. Chief Const. RUC, "The Royal Ulster Constabulary", Police Studies, Vol. 4, 1982, pp. 3-12.

Stead, P.J., "The Nature of Police Command", Police Studies, Vol. 4, 1981, pp. 36-42.

Tuck, M. and Southgate, P., "Ethnic Minorities", Crime and Policing: a survey of West Indians and Whites", Home Office Research Study, No. 70, (HMSO, 1981).

Chapter 4

THE CIVIL POWER AND AIDING THE CIVIL POWER:
THE CASE OF IRELAND

Trevor C. Salmon

The Historical Perspective and Legacy

It is open to debate whether the period 1916-1922 saw a
'revolution' in Ireland, or whether it was merely a
'coup'. Brian Farrell argues, for example, that in comparison with most definitions of 'revolution', "no such
major change in Irish political culture is perceptible in
the formation years of the state. Certainly a colonial
regime came to an end, there was a transfer of power and
one political leadership was replaced by another. But
this was no more than a 'palace' revolution. The mystery
is that a new regime that set out to change so little in
the Ireland of the twenties was able to survive."(1) The
argument being that the most significant changes were already under way. This is a necessary and important cor-
rective to the conventional wisdom of a radical political
culture of dissent, rebellion and militancy. And yet, the
manner of the pre-1922 struggle has left its mark upon the
Irish Republic, and its forebear, the Irish Free State.
Especially significant, of course, is that, for some, the
business of those years is still unfinished, that irredentism lives. Indeed, the official ideology of the State
endorses this view.

In the area of 'public order' the formative years of
the new Ireland left three particular legacies: (a) it
was a struggle for national liberation fought by the
methods, amongst others, of guerrilla warface and an
attempt to undermine the existing regime by supplanting
it; (b) the struggle and its methods led to the development of a certain attitude to law and order and; (c) for
some the struggle is very much unfinished business, but
importantly this is _not_ just with respect to the six
north-eastern counties, but also as to the very nature and
legitimacy of a twenty-six county state. The nature of

its legitimacy is something of an open question for republicans who claim to be the real heirs of the 'Old IRA' and the men of 1916.

(a) For generations many in Ireland felt impelled to challenge the "illegitimate" British rule in Ireland, often by periodic uprising and other significant signs of disaffection. As "independence" came nearer, this disaffection became more widespread, even popular. By the time of the First World War it was even recognised by the British government. For example, although conscription became law in Great Britain in January 1916, it was not applied to Ireland, although the end of the war perhaps came just before its extension. A wide variety of Irish opinion denied "the right of the British government or any external authority to impose compulsory military service in Ireland against the clearly expressed will of the Irish people".(2)

Even more significant was the creation of the first Dail, elected via the British general election of 1918. It saw that one way to cause the British to evacuate was to make British civil administration and military control untenable. Having secured 73 out of 105 Irish seats (in the whole island), Sinn Fein sought to carry out their fundamental strategy of providing an alternative government in Ireland to the British regime centred on Dublin Castle. In January 1919, the Dail issued a Declaration of Independence which _inter alia_ gave _post facto_ legitimacy to the rising of Easter 1916, claimed that the electorate had endorsed the action in the election of 1918, and ordained "that the elected Representatives of the Irish people alone have power to make laws binding on the people of Ireland, and that the Irish Parliament is the only Parliament to which that people will give its allegiance ...(3) In pursuance of this approach the Dail sought to establish its own machinery of state, its own government, acting under its authority, which was to supplant British administration. This strange government, with no formal government offices, and departments moving from house to house, survived, with some departments, for example, Local Government, being relatively successful. Moreover, for a time, the British machinery of justice was supplanted by 'Dail Courts'.

A further dimension of this policy was the War of Independence 1919-1921, although the extent to which, especially initially, the Volunteers were under Dail authority is not clear. Initially the war "was in essence a struggle between the IRA and the police"(4), but the skirmishes, although numerous, were mostly on a small scale. But gradually it developed, with the appearance of the

Irish flying columns exploiting the tactics of ambush, "the development of guerrilla warfare _a l'outrance_".(5) Ambushes, assassinations, terror and counter-terror became common, most notoriously perhaps epitomised by the Black and Tans on the British side.

(b)   Given the establishment of a rival authority, the attempt to supplant British rule and law, and a war of independence, the local custodians of law and order became crucial targets. The RIC – Royal Irish Constabulary – had in many parts of Ireland been "often the only tangible form of authority which the people knew"(6) especially in rural areas. They were boycotted and attacked. Gradually the RIC was beaten back from large areas of the country-side, leaving behind burnt barracks and severed lines of communication.   The number of stations was reduced by about half. As the position of the RIC became invidious, large numbers resigned, including whole barracks.   The final nail in the coffin was collaboration with the Black and Tans. The RIC had always had a difficult task, having to investigate and suppress 'disaffection' of every kind, quelling outbreaks of agrarian violence, and reporting on Fenians etc., and so had attracted a good deal of odium. Importantly law and order was not something to be respect-ed. There was then, in this struggle a moral cost. Viol-ence, hatred and killing etc. became patriotic, even hero-ic, whilst disrespect for law and authority became legiti-mate.   For many, law-breaking, sabotage and even murder, became the norm.   In addition, with the RIC retreating, there was a wave of crime and lawlessness which overflowed into "landgrabbing, anarchy and sheer criminal lawless-ness".(7) There was a sharp increase in crime, often ac-companied by intimidation or violence, and often under a 'political/military' guise.

It is not too far-fetched to argue that this attitude to the upholders of law and order to some extent has en-tered the Irish psyche, so that a casual disregard for the law became deeply embedded, and common. There is today a casualness to upholding law in everyday life that is very prevalent, manifesting itself in attitudes to motoring offences, TV licences etc.

(c)   The national liberation struggle was for a thirty-two county Republic, and few republicans seriously contemplated any other situation. For many, the settle-ment of 1921-22 could _never_ be satisfactory or acceptable. Given the _post facto_ legitimacy accorded to 1916 (of pro-found significance to subsequent Irish history), physical force to do something about Partition was for this group acceptable, necessary and, indeed, it possessed a certain legitimacy. It was those who had accepted, and captured,

the government of the twenty-six counties which was illegitimate, having violated their oath to 'the Republic'.
For those taking this view, 'the Republic' established in
1916, and endorsed in 1918, could not be dis-established.
This was to mean, of course, that both (a) Stormont and
(b) Dublin 'governments' were illegitimate and, therefore,
legitimately open to attack. Disagreement over the treaty
settlement of 1921-22, led, of course to the civil war of
1922-23. Peace only came, not because the anti-treaty
forces accepted the settlement but because in de Valera's
words "The Republic can no longer be defended successfully
by your arms ... Military victory must be allowed to rest
for the moment with those who have destroyed the Republic.
Other means must be sought to safeguard the nation's
right."(8) Some would not, and have not, accepted "other
means".

It was in this climate and context that the Garda
Siochana was brought into existence in 1922. Initially
the task of finding a replacement force for the RIC was
not accorded a high priority, partly because the political
leadership on the pro-Treaty side had more pressing problems - working out the details of taking over the British
administration, and the continuing internal debate. In
addition, there was not sufficient awareness of the complexity of the task, whilst what attention there was given
to the problem was fragmented and inadequate.(9) Michael
Collins, who was the senior politician involved, relied
very heavily upon advice from contacts with experience,
and service in the old RIC and Dublin Metropolitan Police,
this leading to mutiny among some of the new force within
a matter of months, when these individuals were given high
rank in the new force. For the most part the Garda
Siochana differed little from the RIC in things like basic
ranks etc. But it was remarkable that given the situation
in the country it should be decided, albeit after initial
doubts, that the Free State would have an unarmed police
force, a notable difference from the RIC and the RUC being
set up in Ulster. The force was to be non-political in
its administration and composition, although it should be
noted that initially recruitment was purely upon the basis
of personal recommendation, there being no public announcement nor advertisements, since the anti-treaty forces
had said such a police force would be 'unauthorised' and
provocative. Despite this careful recruiting, the force
did not become simply the partisan agent of government in
a civil war situation. This is perhaps the more surprising given another crucial initial decision. The new force
was to be administered by a Commissioner who was not to be
responsible to an independent police authority, but rather

was directly responsible to the government. Given the strong emphasis accorded the British model, this is perhaps strange, less so, however, given the civil war context. It has, however, left a powerful legacy, reaching down to events even in 1982.

The Guards had many early problems internally, but there was an effort to get them out into the country quickly. Some problems, such as the RIC influence, were only resolved after mutiny and just before the civil war opened. Essentially the Guards fulfilled a defensive function during the civil war i.e. patrolling railway lines etc. and were not mobilised as a fighting force. Fortunately, the anti-treaty forces decided not to seek to kill the Guards, although they wished to make their life uncomfortable.

Being in the country, the Guards did contribute to a restoration of normality and of policing in the community. They also did become non-political in that gradually they became willing to accept whatever government was elected by the Irish people, so that in 1932 they accepted a government headed by de Valera. In those ten years the Guards had much to learn. In 1922 there was little effective training, little or no knowledge of crime investigation, and little known about professional police duties. Much training was initially by post and magazine!

As noted, the transfer of power in 1932 did go smoothly, although the Commissioner of ten years' standing, General Eoin O'Duffy, had considered a coup to prevent a de Valera victory. However, even the Cumann na nGaedheal (pro-treaty) government had become unhappy with him by 1931. O'Duffy was forced out by de Valera and went on to form the "Blueshirts",(10) partly as a defence against a 'communist IRA'. The new government reacted by recruiting the "Broy Harriers" i.e. Fianna Fail men who were duly recruited directly by the new Commissioner. However, the overwhelming majority of the force was, in any case, ready to support the new government, however much they despised it. But even if the Guards accepted the transfer of power, even if de Valera was now in power, the IRA itself was not so reconciled by events, and remained determined to continue in the campaign against both Stormont (principally), but also _any_ twenty-six county government.

The Emergency

Contemporary Ireland is still marked by these historical wounds. All have affected the Garda Siochana, attitudes to the state and the problem of 'public order'. The most significant manifestation of this legacy is that for over forty years Ireland has been under a "state of emergency". Initially stemming from the outbreak of war in 1939, "the emergency" was not allowed to lapse with the ending of war. This anomalous situation was only regularised in 1976 when the Oireachtas (Parliament) determined "that, arising out of the armed conflict now taking place in Northern Ireland, a national emergency exists affecting the vital interests of the State".(11) The actual catalyst for this was the murder of British Ambassador Ewart-Biggs, plus explosions at the Special Criminal Court, whilst in May 1974 there had been bombings in Dublin and Monaghan, and since then a number of kidnappings, and an exponential rise in armed bank robberies etc. within the Republic. The 1976 "emergency" was linked to the passage of the Emergency Powers Act and the Criminal Law Act of 1976, but even before this, in 1972 a Fianna Fail government had issued a proclamation declaring that the ordinary courts were inadequate to secure the effective administration of justice and the preservation of public peace and order. This had led them to activate Part V of the Offences Against the State Act (1939) and to establish the Special Criminal Court. Whilst this Act is of most current significance, it should be remembered that previously the Irish Free State had introduced a whole litany of draconian measures to deal with challenges to the public order, especially from republicans. The 1939 Act of the de Valera government dealt with offences against the state ranging from usurpation or obstruction of the powers of the government and its agents to publication of seditious matter or disturbing the peace. Most noticeably, it provided for the setting up of a Special Criminal Court when the government was satisfied that the ordinary courts were inadequate. The government admitted at the time that it could not bring forward evidence to convict that would satisfy an ordinary court, whilst it remained convinced that certain people were engaged in hostilities against the State. There was also legislation allowing for internment of aliens, which was quickly amended to cover Irish citizens too. President Hyde sent this to the Supreme Court to test whether internment was repugnant to the Constitution. The answer was no, and significant numbers were interned during the war.

Further action had to be taken as a result of the IRA's "border campaign" of 1956–62. Throughout this period, and since, successive Irish governments have reiterated that under the constitution only the Oireachtas can raise and maintain an army, that it forbids any other forces to be raised or maintained.(12) They have seen what they regard as unlawful military activities as a challenge to rightful authority of the Oireachtas and government, and to the democratic rights of the Irish people. In July 1957 this conviction led to the re-introduction of internment, which lasted until March 1959, during which time 206 detainees had been interned. Most had been tried but refused to recognise any "twenty-six county" court. The charges involved membership of an illegal organisation, illegal possession of firearms etc. and failure to give accounts of their movements - still widely used charges against IRA suspects. Early on internment faced them on completion of their initial prison sentence, but during the latter half of 1958 they were not tried but sent direct to internment.

Whilst internment was ended in 1959, illegal activity continued, so that eventually the Special Criminal Court was reactivated. Citing fear of intimidation of juries, the Minister of Justice, Mr. Charles J. Haughey, was responsible for reactivating the practice which had been dormant since 1948, although still on statute book.

As noted earlier, 1972 saw this legislation reactivated again. This followed an acquittal on a charge of possessing arms to endanger life. The opposition had serious doubts about the 1972 action, but it was they, when in government, who took the action in 1976. Again, an Irish President decided to test the validity of some of the measures by sending the Emergency Powers Act to the Supreme Court. The interesting question raised by the Emergency Powers Act 1976 was whether the mere invocation of the formula specified in Article 28(3)(3) of the Constitution(13) put all matters, including the existence of a national emergency, affecting the vital interests of the state, beyond scrutiny by the courts. The legislation was allowed to stand. Incidentally, this action by President O'Dalaigh had a bizarre side-effect, in that it led to the Minister of Defence, Mr. Donegan, calling the President, who is also Commander-in-Chief of the armed forces a "thundering disgrace" in a speech to the army. O'Dalaigh resigned and Donegan was moved. O'Dalaigh resigned on the grounds of the integrity of the Presidency being called into question. An odd episode, involving a senior government minister undermining the constitution the new emergency was supposed to uphold.

More importantly in the longer term, the measures taken by successive governments have added up to a formidable arsenal against the IRA. The 1976 measures partly backfired in that since the penalties for membership of an illegal organisation were very substantially increased, up to 7 years, some IRA members began to recognise the Special Criminal Court and to challenge the word of the Garda Chief Superintendents, which previously (since it was unchallenged) had tended to be regarded as proof of membership. The increase in punishment was perhaps the main feature of the 1976 changes. Some have argued that the new powers in the 1976 legislation were actually rather slight, and that the act of declaring a new emergency was a political response to the Ewart-Biggs murder. Nonetheless, as a result of the 1976 legislation, the Garda could now hold in custody for up to seven days, instead of the previous forty-eight hours, persons suspected of serious offences or thought to have information concerning them. Moreover, the army was empowered for the first time to arrest people for certain clearly defined terrorist offences, plus having equal powers of search to those of the police. These new powers of arrest would require a request from at least a Garda Superintendent, and any person so arrested had to be handed over to the Garda within six hours. The government sought to emphasise that they were not altering the basic role of the Defence Forces in security since "They will continue to act in aid of the civil power assisting the Garda Siochana who will continue to have primary responsibility for internal security."(14) The 1972 government had considered similar measures but were particularly concerned apparently about giving "the powers of arrest and search to people who are not subject to police discipline", whereas the gardai underwent a detailed course of training, especially with regard to arresting and searching people. Army training was regarded as very different and there was even a suggestion that army discipline was too.(15)

It must be emphasised that the threat is and is perceived to be against the institutions of the twenty-six county state and not merely 'the North'. Thus Prime Minister Cosgrave, in introducing the 1976 collection of measures after dealing with the North, went on to say "These are all considerations of the highest importance. But over-riding all of them is our concern with the public safety and with the preservation of the State".(16) It was clear that the outrages had been carried out "by an illegal armed organisation dedicated to the overthrow of the institutions of this State."(17) In the battle against this activity since 1972 the real mainstay of legal action has been the institution of the Special Criminal Court in May 1972 and the Offences Against the State Act (Amendment) Act at the end of 1972, which made membership of the IRA illegal. In the period 1972-80 more than 1500 persons appeared before the Special Criminal Court, of whom more than two-thirds were convicted.

Other dimensions of "the troubles"

The threat to the Republic has taken many forms,(18) not
least of which has been the continuing threat to the lives
of the citizens of the Republic. In an important document
issued on 3 November 1983 by the Forum for a New Ireland
on 'The Cost of Violence arising from the Northern Ireland
Crisis since 1969'(19) it was noted that since 1972 some
'45 people have been killed in terrorist explosions in the
South and 8 members of the Garda Siochana have been murdered by terrorist activity'. In fact, later that month,
that figure rose to 9. A further impact has been the economic drain of the violence upon one of the less-develop-
ed economies of Western Europe. The Forum document reported that on the financial plane, "For the South it is
estimated by the relevant Government Departments that the
extra security costs arising from the violence amounted in
current prices to IR £724 million between 1969 and 1982 or
IR £1,050 million in 1982 prices. These extra costs were
incurred by the Defence Forces, the Gardai and the Prison
Services". In 1982 prices that is, roughly, £850 million
(sterling). The following figures give an indication of
the vast increase in security costs in the South: total
expenditure on security for 1969-70 = IR £31 million; for
1983 the total was, IR £506 million. Similarly, extra
security costs due to violence for 1969-70 = IR £2 million; for 1983 the figure was, IR £134 million. (Forum,
Table 6). In addition, the Forum report highlights a number of other costs, including the cost of compensation for
injury and death, damage to property, the general economic
impact of violence, and the damage to the tourist trade
etc. It attempts to give an approximation of the direct
and indirect costs of the violence. Whilst admitting
"elements of arbitrariness have been unavoidable in esti-
mating some components of this aggregate figure ... it is,
however, a reasonable approximation to the order of magnitude of the total cost of the violence". The figures
are: Exchequer costs to the South since 1969 (in 1982
prices) on extra security, IR £1050 million. When other
costs are added, such as damage to tourism (IR £1130 million), the total economic cost to the South over the period
is put at IR £2255 million (Forum, Table 20). The Forum
report concludes "Combining the estimates for direct and
indirect costs, North and South, gives an overall estimate
for the cost of violence arising from the Northern Ireland
crisis over the period from 1969 to 1982 of IR 11,840
million (stg £11,064m.) in 1982 money values."

For over a decade now, there have been periodic riots
in the South over the North, perhaps the most notorious

both involving the British embassy. On the first occasion it was burnt down in February 1972 after "Bloody Sunday" in Londonderry, with allegations that the gardai did not intervene forcefully enough, and even allegations that it was allowed to happen to act as a public safety valve to very high emotions. Then in July 1981 there was a full-pitched battle to stop demonstrators on a National H-Block/Armagh Committee march from gaining access to the embassy. The rioting involved about 500 demonstrators out of 13,000-15,000 people on the march, and over 1500 gardai were involved, some in riot gear. Stones and petrol bombs were thrown at the gardai, especially those forming a physical block across the road. Having stood their ground, the police went on the offensive with a baton charge to disperse the crowd, leading to many allegations of over-reaction and brutality. Over 200 people, including gardai received treatment. One result of those events was a feeling that Gardai training for civil disorders was inadequate. Given 1972, the Emergency Powers Act and the Offences Against the State legislation this was perhaps a rather odd omission in their training. For most guards such training amounted to only a few lectures. It was also apparent that the bulk of guards were ill-equipped to protect themselves from missiles. Not all had proper protective clothing, and most had to rely on helmets, face visors and short shields. As of 1981 the force did not have CS (tear) gas, plastic or rubber bullets or much of the associated equipment available to their European counterparts.

The police could, in the event of failing to control the riot, have called in the army, of which about 100 soldiers, with a number of vehicles, were on duty nearby. In fact, they played no part, although the army had been on full alert to "come to the aid of the civil powers" ever since the wave of demonstrations over the H-blocks began. If necessary the senior garda on duty could directly request of the army such aid. In addition, of course, the government does possess the power to ban marches.

It appears that in thinking about the events of the summer of 1981 the Garda Siochana did decide that it needed to re-vamp its tactics and its training in this field. There was, for example, to be a greater emphasis upon the use of 'snatch teams' and armoured vehicles. The blanket baton charge was to go, but there was still a feeling that CS gas and plastic bullets were not needed.

The Permanent Defence Force (PDF) does, of course, have a significant involvement in internal security matters, deriving from the role of rendering aid to the civil

82

power, which in practical terms means the police. They are involved in military escorts, bomb disposal, protection of installations of national importance, provision of guards at civil prisons, as well as having in custody certain civilian prisoners, the protection of banks and cash movements, the border area and as a physical back-up to the gardai in certain situations. Thus in the mid-1970s, it was not unusual, in any one year, for the PDF to supply over five and a half thousand military parties for checkpoint duties, plus a further 14,000 or so joint Garda-Army checkpoints. In any year there were of the order of 800 escorts for explosives and 600 bomb disposal requests.

The main area of activity and cooperation, of course, is the border. In 1981 the PDF supplied 14,145 military parties for border checkpoints, and the number of Garda-Army patrols on the border was 10,537. In 1982 both figures significantly increased: 21,032 military parties supplied for Border checkpoints, and 11,244 joint patrols. This level of activity appears to have been maintained. Although slightly down again now, in the mid-1970s the PDF was up 70% in size compared to the figure at the end of the sixties. Expenditure also rose, partly to pay for the increase in personnel, but also to buy armoured personnel carriers, more helicopters and better communications equipment. Whilst before 1969 there had been no permanent military bases north of the 'Galway-Dublin line', by the early eighties there were ten.

As well as aiding the civil power in this area, the PDF is also concerned with 'showing the flag' and establishing the authority of the government. They do not regard their role as merely providing back-up for the gardai. They are there to defend the sovereignty of the national territory. Partly this relates to the possibility of northern Protestant forays across the Border, but it is also relevant that between 1973 and 1976 there were some 304 minor border incursions by the British Army into the Republic. Such incursions did not end in 1976, and many in the Republic feel affronted by such incidents. In 1982 there were some 2,000 troops on the border out of a total army of 15,000.

A further specific response of the army to "the troubles", specifically the Herrema kidnapping in 1975, was the creation of a highly secretive 'Ranger' corps within the PDF. The Rangers have much in common with similar commando-style, highly trained specialist units in other West European countries, and in Ireland number about one hundred. They were used both in response to the Tidey kidnapping in 1983, and were also sent to occupy the British Embassy in 1981 when it was under seige by rioters.(20) It now looks as if they will form the core of future responses to kidnapping operations etc.

The Garda Siochana is directly involved in the border problem and has made a number of responses to it. There is clearly close cooperation with the PDF, although certain problems existed for several years. For example, in a chase, there was no radio communications between the Garda and Army vehicles involved. Now apparently, a couple of soldiers go in the gardai car. Another response by the police was the creation in 1979 of a Special Garda Task Force to act in terrorist emergencies and against serious crime. Originating from discussions at European Community interior ministers' meetings, this specially trained group has to some extent been based on the German GSG9 - given Irish perceptions of the SAS role in Ulster, the SAS was not a suitable model. The group now has some personnel stationed in different border stations. Several are permanently cruising in cars, armed with hand guns and Uzi submachine-guns. The unit is different from any other in existence in the Garda Siochana. It is also responsible for dealing with Herrema-type situations. Given the serious crime now committed in Dublin (see below), some of the task force have recently been moved to Dublin to deal with crime there.

Even more significant regarding the border is the cross-border cooperation between the ruc and the Garda Siochana. in fact, this is not new, although for several years it went into serious decline. Older generation policemen on both sides of the border can recall previous relatively cordial relations, when RUC arrest warrants were accepted by the gardai and prisoners hauled over at the border for criminal charges. More recently, individual officers have again struck up some personal relationships. Some are wary, so as to avoid the taunt of 'collaboration' but especially in the Special Branch area, relations are good. The police on the ground still remain in many ways at arms length, and the very psychological barrier imposed by the sheer presence of the border should not be under-estimated. At the highest level there are now regular meetings of the Garda-RUC Coordinating Committee established in about 1977 to deal with 'operational security matters' involving the two forces. These monthly meetings take place secretly, alternately in north and south.

The key factor in improving relations was the Sunningdale meeting and agreement in December 1973, particularly the involvement of the SDLP in the power-sharing executive. The fact that Unionists no longer controlled the RUC was crucial. In addition, the Republic was increasingly aware of a deteriorating security situation south of the border, with bank raids and cross-border gun battles. The improvement has been quite remarkable given the virtual collapse in the relationship between 1969 and 1972. Now these high-level meetings are attended, it is believed, by divisional border commanders of both police forces and by one or two officers from each side of assistant chief constable or deputy garda commissioner rank. After this development the next step was to improve regular communication by the use of scramble-phones and after 1973 land-lines as well. Therefore, direct telephone connections have existed between stations on both sides of the Border for many years. Either side can pick up the phone and talk directly to their counterparts on the other side. Direct radio contact in May 1975 was a real improvement. RUC Border Commanders can now make a speedy and private contact with the appropriate Garda Superintendent. Now each side monitors each other's radio communications and there are exchanges of confidential files on criminals and suspects. Virtually every Garda vehicle now has two roof aerials - one for Garda radio signals and the other for RUC communications.

The PDF, restricted as it is to aiding the civil power, was not able to talk directly with the RUC or the British Army. Nor could the British Army talk to the gardai. But radio contact has eased the four-way link-up across the border, except when the mountains get in the way. There is a vastly improved level of interforce communication. When a border incident now occurs, the radio officers on duty at RUC area headquarters almost immediately alert the gardai, and the gardai and PDF can arrive at their side of the border very quickly. This has reduced the number of border gun battles, as has the presence of the PDF. Previously the unarmed gardai could do little. Cooperation, then, is now good, although occasionally things can go wrong, and friction may occur, particularly at senior levels, over particular incidents. Nonetheless, these occasions do not appear to have undermined the generally close relations that have been established, especially among middle-rank officers. Both forces realise they face a common enemy, and the consequent need for joint action.

There are, however, limits to cooperation, thus the mooted idea of allowing members of the RUC into the Republic to interrogate suspects for up to forty-eight hours has proved too politically sensitive, even though it was to be joint questioning of suspects under specific conditions by both police forces. The Garda's middle-ranking officers do, however, appear to support the idea.

Generally the cooperation is good and the Chairman of the Police Federation of Northern Ireland has been, as recently as April 1982, fulsome in his praise for the level of that cooperation. It is worth noting that perhaps some 11-12% of the Garda Siochana is on the border!

Most recently, the notion of cooperation has been taken further, at any rate in the realm of ideas with the Garret FitzGerald proposal for some kind of all-Ireland police force. This idea was under consideration by the first FitzGerald coalition government in 1981, although it was not fully worked out. Indeed, even in the now famous Dimbleby lecture of May 1982 FitzGerald was not very specific. This was to prove a problem since it led to all sorts of speculation in the Republic, such as whether the RUC would patrol in Dundalk. In fact all that FitzGerald said in May 1982 was that two lots of courts and police, "divided by a Border which only the terrorists can cross with impunity,is a recipe for anarchy". He went on "Surely, we could put aside our differences and come together, under whatever umbrella of authority may be the most effective for this purpose, whether Anglo-Irish or North-South, in order to face an all-Ireland terrorist movement with an all-Ireland judicial and policing system. No obstacles of constitutional theory or political prejudice in either North or South should stand in the way of such a potentially effective step towards restoring peace in the island."(21) Nonetheless, the response has not been widely enthusiastic and the practical difficulties are immense. The actual idea seems to be some kind of island security-zone, with an all-Ireland court and the all-Ireland police complementing not replacing the work of the gardai and RUC. It does appear that some element of governmental power in Ireland would have to be transferred to some kind of external authority, presumably manned equally by the British and Irish governments. That might indeed require a constitutional amendment. It was precisely on the grounds of sovereignty and the constitution that Fianna Fail opposed the proposal. The new force would be small, probably fewer than 250 men, whose task would perhaps not be dissimilar from those officers in both forces who already collate information from various sections of their own forces. These officers would not be under either Garda or RUC authority. Most comment on the proposal has suggested that it must inextricably be linked to an all-Ireland Court, although given the Criminal Law Jurisdication Act of 1976 this might not, in fact, be necessary. Already people accused of certain offences in Northern Ireland can be tried in the Republic. Thus, despite not initially being invoked (something the Irish

Government accused the British of, in response to British criticisms over extradition), more recently action has been taken under it. Most conspicuously, perhaps, in the arrest, trial and sentencing of Gerard Tuite, and of two escaped prisoners from Crumlin Road prison in Belfast. Whilst in 1982 a Northern Ireland judge sat briefly in the Dublin Special Criminal Court to hear evidence in a case proceeding at the time in Belfast.(22) Perhaps the key problem, alongside the concern with sovereignty, is the feeling that far-reaching, if only small scale, moves towards some kind of all-Ireland police force would require widespread support in both North and South. Therefore, it may be thought not to be imminent! More specific proposals, for example, joint Garda-RUC patrols in say, South Armagh, have not been proceeded with.

A related issue is the vexed question of extradition, or rather the lack of it for "political offences" from the Republic. For years the Republic has argued that to do any such thing would be "unconstitutional", but it is important to remember that there is no specific constitutional prohibition on extradition in the constitution. The article that the argument hinges upon is Article 29.3 which states "Ireland accepts the generally recognized principles of international law as its rule of conduct in its relations with other States". It is argued that one of those principles is no extradition for political offence and this understanding was written in to the Irish Extradition Act of 1965. That act, incidentally, also stipulates that extradition should be refused if, though the offence with which the accused is currently charged is not political, there is a substantial danger that if he were returned, he would be charged with a political offence. The Republic has tended to fear that any Catholic returned to the North would not receive a fair trial. In practice, of course, there are severe difficulties in determining what is "political" i.e. is a bank raid in Belfast to obtain funds for the IRA "political"? It must be said that there has been a lack of consensus upon what constitutes 'political' and certainly in Ireland up until very recently the law was not clear on this point, although motive appears to have been regarded as the key criterion.

Recently there have been two developments which have changed the situation somewhat. The first was the European Convention on the Suppression of Terrorism 1977 which significantly reduced the scope of international law. It was initially felt that Ireland might sign it, although along with Malta ultimately it did not. It should be noted that the Convention did provide that if extradition was refused the refusing state could put the accused on trial in their own jurisdiction. There has, of course, also been a European Community agreement. Even more significant, and perhaps not sufficiently reported was the McGlinchey decision of the Irish Supreme Court in 1982 which made a significant change in the Irish law of extradition.(23) In essence, by invoking the concept of the "reasonable man" the Court side-stepped the problem of definition. Would a "reasonable man", a civilised man, regard the act as political? Furthermore, the Court declared that terrorist acts are "often the antithesis of what could reasonably be described as political". Thus Ireland came much closer to the original idea underlying a 'political offence' and came almost into line with the 1977 Convention although it still has not signed it - partly because of the emotive connotations involved in this area.

Reference has already been made to the number of bank raids in the Republic and this is largely yet another aspect of the troubles in the North. Notwithstanding this, many in the South feel that the raids have reached such a level that the foundations of the state are being threatened as state authority, its law and order, is so blatantly challenged. In 1969 the Garda Siochana recorded something less than 26,000 indictable crimes throughout the country. Ten years later more than 40,000 such crimes were being committed in Dublin alone, with in 1981 89,400 in the country as a whole, a figure which rose further in 1982 to 96,000. At the same time, over the ten year period, the detection rate has decreased over two-thirds to one-third. Cash stolen rose from about £30,000 per year to over £2 m. during the same period. In that period "serious crime" rose by 137%. In the 1970s there were over 2,000 "incidents" involving firearms, excluding cases on or near the border, whilst guns were used in over 1,000 cases. The number of murders a year increased ten-fold from a yearly average of two or three. Crime used to be something of a novelty, yet in an editorial headed "Black Fridays" on 16th October 1982, the Irish Times could by then write "Friday is the day for robbing post offices". Much of this does have to do with spill-over effects from the troubles, and in some Dublin stations 80% of the force is tied up on miscellaneous duties in one way or another connected with Northern Ireland. There is also the problem of the number of gardai on border duty (as noted above, some 11-12%). In addition, as the gun has become more common, so 'ordinary' criminals have been prepared to use it, and to imitate those who whilst on the run because of IRA involvement seek to make a living from crime. Some

88

raids, of course, are to raise money for the IRA and their various activities. The following figures indicate something of the problem:

1975	153 armed robberies	£ 759,483 taken
1976	185 armed robberies	£ 627,339 taken
1977	298 armed robberies	£ 919,521 taken
1978	287 armed robberies	£ 2,196,508 taken

whilst in 1981 there were 306 armed robberies. Perhaps indicating the success of government measures, the figure dropped to 158 in 1982.

It is important to note, however, that the rising crime rate in Ireland is not all connected with the North. Indeed, for many parts of the Republic the slogan "law and order" does not conjure up concern with the institutions of the State or terrorists. Rather it concerns ordinary public safety. Things such as the stealing of hand-bags on the passenger-seat, whilst the car is being driven by a sole woman driver and is stationary at traffic lights. Events such as the "riot" in Limerick on Christmas Eve 1982 when there was window-smashing and looting, albeit by a small crowd of teenage drunks. There has been a general deterioration in the law and order situation, and whilst the racial and cultural problems of Toxteth etc. are missing, there are parts of Dublin - Sean MacDermott/Gardiner Street areas - where the social conditions are conducive to alienation of the young. In 1982 the Minister of Justice was moved to refer to parts of Dublin as "bandit country". There have been a number of responses to these developments: (i) increasing the strength of the gardai (a) in terms of numbers and (b) in terms of their powers; (ii) increasing the strength of the armed detective force to more than 300; (iii) calling in the army to provide additional armed protection for large cash consignments in transit, and a greater degree of armed protection to banks and post offices and; (iv) a greater police presence on the streets. Other measures involving greater use of computers and better organisation have also been taken, and it is to the structure and development of the Garda Siochana that attention will now be addressed.

Development and Structure of the Garda Siochana

Most of the previous discussion relates to (a) problems emanating from the 'unfinished' question of the border and (b) problems emanating from the doubts held by some concerning the legitimacy of the twenty-six county state, but the Irish police force has, and has had, other concerns and pre-occupations in its sixty year history, and even in the post-war period.

Up until the border campaign of 1956-62 there was little crime in the Republic, little political violence and little overt evidence of subversive activity. In this environment the Garda Siochana found itself in an almost unique position among West European police forces. Its strength was allowed to decline below the authorised establishment which is outlined by the Oireachtas. There were economies in manpower, and a substantial reduction in the number of stations, whilst even today many of those that remain are not in good condition. The basic structure, which is still unwieldy, had changed little from the 19th century model of the RIC, for example, with respect to the basic system of districts and divisions outside Dublin. In addition the hierarchical structure had developed and then ossified. Furthermore, given the relative lack of activity and a succession of weak Commissioners, control shifted somewhat away from the force itself to the Department of Justice. This subservience to the Department also resulted from a resistance to change within the force. Early in the sixties, in the autumn of 1961, young gardai took action over a pay claim, eventually after the so-called 'Macushla Revolt', working to rule. One consequence was the already tough internal discipline within the force was tightened even further, but this was occurring against a background of an Ireland which was experiencing rapid socio-economic change, a thriving economy, and a breaking of the mould of old values. The gardai became more organized and better able to argue their case. By 1968 the discontent was again serious and further industrial action took place. Large numbers failed to turn up for work, or pleaded illness etc. The major result was the establishment of the Conroy Commission which reported in January 1970, and after which it can truly be said that nothing was quite the same again. The Commission "took the widest possible view of its own brief, examining everything from recruitment and training to the relationship between the Commissioner and the Department of Justice".(24) It was, apparently, appalled by the internal administration and workings of the force, particularly the tight and detailed control exercised over it by the Department of Justice. In particular, they cited "evidence of an unclear definition of roles as between the Department of Justice and the Garda Siochana. Specifically there was a vagueness, causing uncertainty and ineffectiveness about the relationship between the Department and the Commissioner. There seemed to us to be a lack of delegation from the Department to the force. This lack of delegation permeated the force."(25) But despite these insights the Commission's findings had one result, which is now almost universally regarded as a disaster, namely the introduction of overtime. The more structural aspects of the report, and those of the Ryan Report in 1979, plus a report by a team of management consultants, appear to have been ignored, but the old-fashioned style of blanket-policing ended when overtime came in. Before Conroy, leave had been regarded as a privilege and overtime was unheard of. With overtime, cost became a much more crucial element in police thinking and police work. Overtime pay has led the force into disarray. No new planning system accompanied the introduction of the new system. It has led to strengths varying widely, and districts being left without police cover when the money ran out. On occasion, police cordons etc. have not been called into operation if the overtime allocation is spent. In addition, because there is very little or no civilianisation about 25% of the force are engaged in what might not strictly be regarded as police work, namely being employed as mechanics and clerks etc. Leaving aside the Border and Dublin, there may only be about 5,000 gardai available for the rest of the country. Given holidays, a three x eight hour shift system, and illness etc. there may be less than 1,000 gardai actually on duty. Limerick, a city of over 60,000 had 32 gardai on duty on the night of the Christmas riots, but only 9 were mobile. In addition, of course, since the Conroy Commission the work of the gardai has multiplied several times over.

By the late seventies it was necessary to have another report, principally to examine the pay structure but originally envisaged as embracing a re-assessment of administration and productivity. One idea floated at the time was the need to attract a higher quality of recruit into the force. For a number of years the force had been finding it difficult to get good applicants, and educational requirements were not particularly high. There was, then, discussion of "split-level" entry, with future officers going in as cadets, and also of the need for accelerated promotion on the basis of talent, as against what appeared to be the case, namely having to be of a certain age before receiving advancement. The Ryan Report would have led to a better standard of recruitment and training, partly by the use of psychological testing, in-service training to be enhanced etc., but generally successive governments have been slow to accept the recommendations on recruitment, training and promotion. Some movement has, however, taken place in this area. For example, at the end of the decade it was announced that

there would be a new training college for higher ranks –
i.e. above inspector. This was to revolve around a number
of short courses. More recently, links have been established with educational establishments such as the
National Institute of Higher Education in Limerick for
training in personnel management etc. There has been a
growing consciousness of the need for change, even if the
change has only been introduced slowly. One clear reason
for change in structure and organisation is the very great
changes the force itself has undergone in the period since
1969. Within a year or so, it will have doubled in size,
it has a new radio and telex system, greater computerisa-
tion and new forensic laboratories and technical bureaux.
So far, the force has failed to adapt its structure and
some critics suggest that there is a great, top-heavy,
over-centralized bureaucracy in its Phoenix Park headquarters, with little or no organizational response to the
crime wave of the 1970s.(26) One problem has been the
mushrooming of ad hoc specialised units, that perhaps
specialisation has been carried too far, with there being
a particular overlap between the Special Branch, Crime
Task Forces and Crime Ordinary. Even more generally, relatively simple operational tasks can be nightmarish as a
result of a proliferation of units, and the problems associated with overtime, especially financial. Recently
efforts have been made at rationalization, but the power
of successive Commissioners is weakened by (a) the fact
that the Department of Justice is the de facto police
authority, determining police policy and principles and
(b) the growing strength and professionalism of (i) The
Garda Representative Association and (ii) The Association
of Garda Sergeants and Inspectors.

Although the largest concentration of crime is in
Dublin, the city possesses no Serious Crime Squad i.e. a
central group to investigate such offences. Each of the
41 Garda stations in the Dublin area has a group of
detectives who deal with crime investigation in their
areas, but coordination of work/knowledge between areas
could be better. There is also a Central Detective Unit
at Dublin Castle, which comprises five sections – fraud,
drugs, stolen vehicles, criminal intelligence and crime
prevention. They have a particular responsibility to
back-up local detectives. There is also now, relatively
recently formed, a detective unit attached to Garda HQ at
Phoenix Park which has nationwide responsibilities. Every
Garda division, as part of the renewed fight against
crime, had up until recently been in the process of getting an armed Crime Task Force, which was intended to
concentrate on short-term assistance where the volume of

offences had suddenly and significantly risen. More recently these divisional task forces have now been integrated with the Special Branch. The government claims that their manpower and firepower has remained the same, but critics have argued that the forces have lost their distinctive role. In addition, some of the units and groups mentioned do still feel that they face bureaucratic obstacles and organizational problems – that there is a certain lack of freedom, initiative and equipment.

One area where there does appear to be a degree of freedom and scope for initiative is for the re-named Garda Siochana Special Branch, now known as Intelligence and Security, Dublin, although its broad functions remain the same. It has about 600 detectives in it (roughly the same size as the old Special Branch). The Special Branch dates back to the pre-independence Oriel House CID, which after independence continued to play an active and controversial part in the fight against violent republicans. It was in 1925 that Crime Ordinary and Special were officially distinguished, the latter becoming known as "the Branch". Recently, in 1982, Intelligence and Security, Dublin was brought directly under the control of the same Assistant Commissioner, Joe Ainsworth, as that of the existing overall Intelligence and Security Branch. This re-organisation may well now be under further review given Ainsworth's resignation in the wake of the "Liffeygate" scandal. The Intelligence and Security Branch has a number of different sections – Security, International Liaison, Special Detective Branch, Security Task Force, Intelligence and Divisional Task Force. There may be 1,000 men involved altogether.

Generally the Garda Siochana is proud of its sixty-year tradition of being unarmed, and this remains the strong preference of the bulk of the members of the force. Gradually, however, more and more gardai are being armed, albeit not the guards on "the beat". Hand-guns are now carried by all plain clothes Garda detectives in Dublin, a decision taken after a ballot amongst them, and after they had suffered the loss of colleagues through murder and wounding. In the winter of 1983-84, the question of arming the police force again came up after the Tidey kidnapping, search and release (during which a young garda recruit and a soldier were killed) and unfortunate confrontations with Dominic McGlinchey. In addition, there have been cases of unarmed gardai being ambushed and humiliated by armed gangs. In the short-term these events have led to more gardai being armed, and, for example, as a temporary expedient, an attempt to ensure that at any garda check-point there is at least one armed garda or soldier. In January 1984, during a special Dail debate on security (which in itself shows how seriously the situation was viewed), a former Minister of Justice and still leading Fianna Fail figure, Dessie O'Malley, called for a second Garda force organized on paramilitary lines, and armed, since "no ordinary civilian police force" could deal with "ruthless, vicious, professional anarchists and criminals".(27) This idea was rejected by the Minister for Justice and met a cool reception from Garda representative bodies. The Garda has generally also reacted with restraint in the face of the violent attacks upon it in recent years, but there have been a number of allegations of brutality and even of a "heavy gang" to undertake such activity on a quasi-organized basis.

In looking at the structure and development of the force it is necessary to mention the continuing problem of "political interference". Ever since that original decision on ultimate political control this has been an issue. The original argument put forward by Kevin O'Higgins and others was the Civil Guards were the people's police, and that the people controlled them through the government they had elected, that the police were answerable to the people through the minister responsible. The problem is that of the lack of clarity in the relationship between gardai and the Minister of Justice touched upon by Conroy. Recently the whole question has come to the fore with a number of specific allegations concerning recent Ministers of Justice interfering on behalf of constituents. A recent Minister, Mr. Sean Doherty, in December 1982 claimed it was his duty as a TD (MP) to "communicate the views of constituents to any area when requested to do so ... The fact that I become Minister does not necessarily mean that I have to become silent regarding my constituents." He emphatically denied applying pressure on gardai to drop particular cases, but it has been claimed he actively sought the transfer of a Garda Sergeant who had sought to pursue an after-hours drinking case.(28) Even more worrying for some is that appointments to the rank of Superintendent and above are solely the preserve of government, and indeed the question is discussed at Cabinet meetings. Moreover, it is not unknown for certain appointments to be made by an outgoing government in the interval between the election results and the new Dail meeting to elect a new government. Thus Mr. Ainsworth was appointed to the rank of Deputy Commissioner in this manner in December 1982. The incoming Fine Gael-Labour coalition have plans for a judicial inquiry into political interference with the gardai, but there is some feeling in the country that no party has completely clean hands in this area. The most notorious case of political involvement, of course, involved the aforementioned Mr. Ainsworth and Mr. Doherty. These were two separate but related incidents. In one Mr. Ainsworth received a request from Mr. Doherty to supply a tape recorder to the then Minister of Finance, Mr. Ray MacSharry. It is alleged that this minister used it to tape a conversation by telephone with another colleague, Martin O'Donoghue, and that via the good offices of Mr. Ainsworth this tape was transcribed by a Garda office and then returned to Mr. Doherty. It is alleged that the conversation transcribed related solely to party political issues concerning the governing Fianna Fail party and included nothing which could be thought to relate to matters of concern to the Garda Siochana. The other incident also involved the tapping of the phones of two journalists — Bruce Arnold and Geraldine Kennedy — who were writing detailed accounts of intra-Fianna Fail splits. Instead of the initiative for tapping coming from the Garda Siochana as it should, it is alleged that it came from Mr. Doherty, and that Mr. Ainsworth succumbed to that pressure. As a result Mr. Ainsworth and his Commissioner, Mr. Patrick McLaughlin, were allowed to retire.

Too many of these incidents were simply the tip of the iceberg, and the various garda representative bodies had for a period of years previously been complaining about political control, even over the daily operation of the force.

Apart from the short-term impact of these cases, which was considerable, they may well have a significantly longer term effect, namely the setting up of a Garda Siochana Authority. The magazine of the Association of Garda Sergeants and Inspectors, Garda News, said in the autumn of 1982 (i.e. before the 'bugging' revelations) that "There is now an urgent necessity for such an Authority, and it may well be that its establishment should take precedence over the establishment of a commission to examine the role of the force. Such a role can never be clearly defined until the operational management of the force is removed from the sphere of political influence. Plans for a 'new' Garda Siochana can only be made under the aegis of an independent controlling body which has no other desire or object than to provide a police force sufficient in numbers, adequately paid, equipped, housed and administered so that it can effectively police the country."(29) They were keen to emphasise the distinction between overall policy and direction being a legitimate government concern and direct involvement in day-to-day operational affairs. Interestingly, before the election at the end of 1982 both Fine Gael and Labour had committed themselves to an authority. It will be interesting to see what happens. The AGSI has been seeking such an authority at least since November 1978, and in 1981 submitted proposals to the Department of Justice. The essential aim being that the responsibility for the management of the police would be vested solely in the authority.

The Agenda

Clearly the main priority for the Irish police force remains the battle against subversion whether directed against the six north-eastern counties (or from it) or against the twenty-six county state. As has been shown, a number of measures have been taken in the last decade or so to attempt to deal with this problem. It must be emphasised that the Irish are committed to this battle, if only because they themselves are threatened. This concern took on a new edge during 1983 given the kidnapping of Mr. Tidey, and indeed 8 other known kidnappings in that year. In 1982 there had been 6 abductions, whereas previously such incidents had been isolated. In 1983, it has been alleged that two ransoms may have been paid. Kidnapping where ransom has been the primary motive first appeared in July 1979. In 1983 it also took on another dimension with the kidnapping of Shergar, the Derby winner. In addition to these problems, but coinciding with them, has been the inability to apprehend McGlinchey, and renewed concern at attempts to destabilize the state. Indeed, given that two members of the security forces were shot during the Tidey release, concern arose that the Provisional IRA might have changed their traditional policy of not shooting members of the Republic's security forces. In the early 1980's, the authorities of the Irish Republic have again had to focus attention on the threat to the institutions and authority of the state. In early 1983 a number of responses were under consideration: (a) the introduction of internment has been called for by Dr. Conor Cruise O'Brien, a former Labour T.D. and Minister, and regarded as an unfortunate possible necessity by senior Fine Gael and government back-bencher (and Forum member) Paddy Harte T.D. Dr. O'Brien was keen to emphasise the selective nature of the internment he proposed, perhaps a dozen or couple of dozen people.(30) Mr. Harte spoke in the context of options running out, that whilst he had opposed internment all his life, "we have reached the situation that we might not have any alternative". He was clear that "The people who continue to commit acts of criminal violence and who have no respect for the democratically-elected parliament of the State, nor for the lives, limbs and properties of fellow Irishmen and for the gardai, and people who are hell-bent on pulling down the institutions of the State will have to clearly understand that this ultimate step by the Government may have to be faced."(31)

The Taoiseach, Dr. FitzGerald, ruled out internment in the immediate future, but noted it might be necessary as a "last resort". The general tenor of his remarks, in fact, emphasised this last resort aspect.(32) Notwithstanding this it appears that a document on the possible introduction of internment and the proscription of Sinn Fein may have been put to the Irish Cabinet in January 1984. Factors against it are (a) is the hostility generated in the South by the use of internment in the North; (b) the possible arming of greater numbers of gardai; (c) following several security reviews in 1983 and early 1984, a new policy of giving the army control of operations against known armed terrorists. If implemented, the Rangers might be given a greater role. Whilst the army's role would remain that of aiding the civil power, such aid would be requested earlier, and the army would now assume a predominant role in specific actions against armed subversives. This shift has evolved from both _intra_ and _inter_ Garda-Army discussions, and has Cabinet support. It does relate, of course, to the desire to avoid arming widespread numbers of gardai permanently; (d) an examination of the ways to strengthen the laws against incitement to violence and hatred, a course that may be preferred to proscription. Interestingly, however, the leader of the Opposition, Charles J. Haughey (Fianna Fail) has committed his party to supporting both proscription and tightening the laws on incitement, if the government felt it necessary, "with the full knowledge of the security situation".(33) Such action would be, presumably, applied to Sinn Fein, given its links with Provisional IRA, and the reported remarks of the Sinn Fein President, Gerry Adams M.P. that those involved in killing the garda and soldier during the Tidey release "were in a position where they were doing their duty".(34); (e) a general review of tactics, procedures and performance, especially communications, the manning of check-points and security cordons, the distribution of weapon-carrying trained men, the training of Special Task Forces, and equipment etc.

Secondly, there is the business of political interference, and the possibility of a Garda Authority, although given the nature of Irish society, its smallness and its 'fixer' mentality that may not prove to be a panacea.

Thirdly, there is the continuing fight against crime, the cost of crime being estimated at some IR £250 m. in

1983. Given the increasing problem with crime, a number of decisions were pending in the winter of 1983-84, particularly the passage through the Dail of a new Criminal Justice Bill, which was announced in October 1983 and debated in the Dail early in 1984.

Prior to the publication of the Bill there had been a number of suggestions in this area. The gardai themselves had spoken of having increased powers to stop, search and question (without arresting) when reasonable grounds for suspicion existed, the gardai themselves determining reasonable. In addition, there were calls for changes in 'Judges' Rules', for example, in the nature and timing of the caution given to a person under questioning, and some argued that the right to remain silent should not be absolute. There were also calls for the conditions attached to the granting of bail, and the granting of bail itself, to be more restrictive. On the other hand, civil rights groups pointed out that under measures connected with "the emergency" the police already possessed very extensive powers, and instead of extending such powers they called for a complaints tribunal.

In the measures proposed in the autumn of 1983 the overall balance clearly favoured the gardai, but Mr. Noonan, the Minister for Justice, did make it clear in announcing the new Criminal Justice Bill, that the new legal powers would not be invoked until after a new, and independent, complaints procedure had been established to deal with allegations of abuse against the gardai. The provisions of the new Bill included: (i) the courts would in future be entitled to draw inferences from the failure of the accused person to offer an explanation to the gardai while he was being questioned. inferences could also be drawn from the refusal of the accused to account for his presence in a certain place or his possession of certain objects; (ii) majority verdicts in criminal cases (except where the death penalty is involved) and a number of changes in trial procedures, for example, notification of alibi and the right of a defendant to make an unsworn, non-cross-examined statement would be abolished, and in future all such statements to be sworn and liable to cross-examination; (iii) increased powers of detention, in fact, for up to 20 hours or for two 6-hour questioning periods on the authority of a chief superintendent, although a solicitor etc. is to be notified as soon as possible; (iv) the powers of detention, strip-searching, finger-printing and photographing of suspects were being provided in cases of serious crime; (v) where offences committed while on bail, consecutive sentences of up to two years could in future be imposed and; (vi) life sentences rather than fourteen-year prison terms for certain firearms offences, which will bring the Repbulic's legislation into line with that of Northern Ireland.

In presenting the Bill to the Dail, Mr. Noonan made it clear that the government believed the measures to be fundamentally right in principle, although they were willing to consider detailed amendments during the committee stage of the Bill. Most reaction to the Bill saw it as something of a curate's egg, a mixture, moreover, of the mundane and sensible, the radical and the controversial and dangerous. The Gardai generally welcomed the Bill, especially the provisions relating to bail and trial proceedings, but were disappointed that they were not given greater powers to search, and felt that it did not go far enough, although a number of weaknesses exploited by law-breakers in the past were being removed. None doubted that it would increase Garda powers. The Fianna Fail opposition agreed to support the Bill in principle.

Widespread disquiet about certain provisions was evidenced by the Irish Council of Civil Liberties, the Incorporated Law Society of Ireland and the Association of Criminal Lawyers. Although each of these groups, and others, had its own particular complaints, in essence the general criticisms were: (i) the perceived attack on the presumption of innocence until proven guilty, given the crucial link between it and the right not to say anything or to remain silent in the face of one's accusers; (ii) and related, what many saw as the effective abolition of the right to remain silent, since the possibility of inferences being drawn would constitute an attempt to compel that person to speak; (iii) this, plus the increased periods of detention, might allow the police to trade upon the inherently coercive atmosphere of police custody; (iv) the above would lead to such testimony being less reliable; (v) the related possibility of what, in effect, would be 'investigative detention' and; (vi) the introduction of majority verdicts.

Such criticisms were by no means confined to anti-establishment groups, with even the chairman of the Bar Council (albeit speaking in a personal capacity) having objections, particularly with reference to erosion of the right to remain silent. Indeed, he, and others, hoped that President Hillery would send the Bill to the Supreme Court to pronounce upon its compatability with the constitution before it became law.

Fourthly, there is the debate about "community policing" with the AGSI being strongly in favour, and regarding it as an attempt to check the causes of crime rather than simply concentrating upon its effects. They have proposed a pilot scheme to be launched in the major cities.

Finally, a whole series of questions about the organization of the force – the future of small country stations, the degree of centralization, whether there should be an unpaid and voluntary reserve which would release full-time gardai to fight crime, by undertaking clerical work, certain traffic functions and some control at sporting functions etc. (This Fine Gael proposal contains an echo of the 1974 proposals for a similar type of force to act as the eyes and ears of the gardai with respect to car bombings etc.) Such a reserve would also provide an alternative to the pressure which exists for there to be vigilante groups, particularly in Dublin. A final item on the agenda perhaps is whether there really needs to be another commission to examine the role of the Garda Siochana. It depends, perhaps, on whether such an inquiry would really come to grips with ensuring that the role, function and organization of the force is geared to meeting the demands of the day in a rapidly changing society. It also depends upon whether any action would follow such a commission. Previous experience is not encouraging in this regard.

FOOTNOTES

1. Brian Farrell, The Founding of Dail Eireann Parliament and Nation-Building, (Dublin, Gill and Macmillan, 1971) p.xiv.
2. Dorothy Mcardle, The Irish Republic, (London, Corgi edition, 1968) p.233. Originally published in 1937 with a Preface by Eamon de Valera, Miss Macardle's book might be said to represent a 'republican' viewpoint.
3. Ibid. p. 253.
4. F.S.L. Lyons, Ireland Since the Famine (London, Fontana, 1974) p. 412. This work is perhaps the most widely respected study of modern Irish history.
5. idem.
6. Conor Brady, Guardians of the Peace, (Dublin, Gill and Macmillan, 1974) p.21. This is the only major study of the Irish police force, and is particularly useful on the formative years of the force and its origins. Conor Brady, Conor O'Clery and Peter Murtagh (three Irish Times journalists) have produced a number of authoritative articles for their paper on the matters under review in this chapter.
7. Ibid. p.24.
8. Macardle, op.cit. pp.781-2, this is the famous 'Soldiers of the Republic, Legion of the Rearguard' mes-

sage of 24 May 1923.

9. Brady op.cit. p.40 ff is excellent on this period.

10. M. Manning, The Blueshirts, (Dublin, Gill and Macmillan, 1971) is the classic work on this episode.

11. Dail Debates volume 292: column 3 ff for the debate on the resolution.

12. Bunreacht na hEireann (Constitution of Ireland), 1937, Article 15, Section 6, "The right to raise and maintain military or armed forces is vested exclusively in the Oireachtas." - "No military or armed forces, other than a military or armed force raised and maintained by the Oireachtas, shall be raised or maintained for any purpose whatsoever."

This clearly reflects earlier, and continuing difficulties with certain groups claiming the legitimacy of "The Republic" for their actions.

13. "Nothing in this Constitution shall be invoked to invalidate any law enacted by the Oireachtas which is expressed to be for the purpose of securing the public safety and the preservation of the State in time of war or armed rebellion, or to nullify any act done or purporting to be done in time of war or armed rebellion in pursuance of any such law. In this sub-section "time of war" includes a time when there is taking place an armed conflict in which the State is not a participant but in respect of which each of the Houses of the Oireachtas shall have resolved that, arising out of such armed conflict, a national emergency exists affecting the vital interests of the State ..."

14. Dail Debates op.cit. 292: 14-15.

15. Ibid. 292: 88 ff, for the speech by Mr. Dessie O'Malley, who had been Minister of Justice in 1972.

16. Ibid. 292: 8-9.

17. Ibid. 292: 16, emphasis added.

18. One T.D., Oliver J. Flanagan, incidentally very briefly Minister of Defence 1976-77, spoke in August 1982 of the possibility of a coup. He argued that the country was becoming ungovernable, disillusionment with the State was growing and economic depression becoming more severe. "I am not saying the Army, who have always been loyal to Government would ever take over, but the possibility exists in every democracy as history has taught us. The location of the defence forces in this country make it an easy task. In Dublin all that is required is to take over Government Buildings, all public offices, RTE etc., and the other locations at Cork, Galway, Athlone, Kilkenny, Dundalk, Monaghan, Letterkenny, etc. make it possible to take over without the firing of one single shot and with-

out the loss of even one life. I am convinced it is on the way and every day that parliament fails is a day nearer to the end of democratic rule as we now know it". Irish Times 13 August 1982.

Mr. Flanagan has a somewhat eccentric reputation and is prone to the use of colourful language, but several prominent parliamentarians are worried about the effectiveness, or rather lack of it, of the Dail and a growing disillusionment with politics.

For a discussion of the general problems of Irish defence see the author's 'The Changing Nature of Irish Defence Policy', World Today, November 1979 and on the basis of Irish security policy, the author's 'Ireland: A Neutral in the Community?' Journal of Common Market Studies, March 1982.

19. New Ireland Forum. The Cost of Violence arising from the Northern Ireland Crisis since 1969. See Ireland Today - supplement - No. 1,003 November/December 1983 Bulletin of the Department of Foreign Affairs. The Forum also issued 6 December 1983, The Economic Consequences of the Division of Ireland since 1920. See Ireland Today - supplement - No. 1,004 January 1984. The Forum was initially the idea of John Hume MP, leader of the Social and Democratic Labour Party of Northern Ireland (SDLP). The SDLP principally represents minority opinion in Northern Ireland and has been keen to pursue the "all-Ireland" dimension.

In the Dublin government statement of 11 March 1983 on the creation of the Forum, the Irish government spoke of the "establishment of a forum for consultations on the manner in which lasting peace and stability can be achieved in a new Ireland through the democratic process".

All who had representatives in (or eligible for) either the Irish Parliament or the Northern Ireland Assembly could participate, as long as they rejected violence.

It was hoped to report "on possible new structures and processes through which its objective might be achieved". See Ireland Today No. 997 April 1983. The first meeting of the Forum was on 30 May 1983. In addition to an independent chairman, it is composed of: 9 Fianna Fail members, 8 Fine Gael, 5 Labour and 5 SDLP. A number of parties in Northern Ireland refused to acknowledge or participate in it.

20. Dr. Herrema, a Dutch managing director of the Ferenka plant in Limerick was held by two dissident republicans in Monasterevan, Co. Kildare in the autumn of 1975. The house was surrounded by the police for over a fortnight. Mr. Don Tidey was kidnapped by members of the IRA in November 1983 and held for 22 days. A British business

executive, Mr. Tidey, was released after a gun battle, but his abductors managed to escape whilst two members of the security forces were killed.

21. The text of the Richard Dimbleby lecture of 20 May 1982 was printed in the Irish Times, 21 May 1982.

Nearly a year later controversy still surrounded the proposal, when in April 1983 Garret FitzGerald's Minister of Justice, Mr. Noonan, (Fine Gael by that time in government again) ruled out any possibility of an all-Ireland police force while the Border remained in existence, and emphasised no plans for such a force existed in his department. He also declared that "An all-Ireland police would be subsequent to an all-Ireland State". There is speculation that this means the proposal is now dead. cf. Irish Times, 30 March 1983.

22. The Criminal Law Jurisdiction Act of 1976 was based on the report of the Anglo-Irish Law Enforcement Commission set up after the Sunningdale agreement of December 1973 which inter alia led to the power-sharing Executive in Northern Ireland. The act provided for the trial in courts on either side of the Irish border of scheduled terrorist offences committed in either the Republic or Northern Ireland, and for some offences in Britain. Tuite was sentenced at the Special Criminal Court in Dublin in connection with the possession of bomb-making equipment in Greenwich (London). He had escaped from prison in London while on remand, but was subsequently arrested in the Irish Republic, and tried there. In May 1983 the Court of Criminal Appeal in Dublin dismissed his appeal and refused him permission to appeal to the Supreme Court.

23. See 'The Politics of Extradition' by David Gwynn Morgan, Irish Times, 22 December 1982 for an excellent analysis of Irish attitudes and the McGlinchey case's importance. However McGlinchey absconded whilst on bail while the extradition proceedings were under consideration. Since that time it is alleged that he has been directly involved in a number of particularly violent terrorist activities, for example, the Darkley chapel murders in November 1983. It does appear, however, that given the Supreme Court decision he could now be extradited immediately without going before a 26-county court again. However, it appears that by now he may have committed serious offences within the Republic, and therefore, might be tried for those there.

24. Brady, op.cit., p.243.

25. Ibid., p.244.

26. See, for example, Conor Brady, 'A powerful case for reorganisation' in the Irish Times, 26 September 1979,

who argues that these are the real problems of the force rather than a lack of powers or legislation. He argues "It is not exaggeration to say that the Garda Siochana have at their disposal now, more sweeping police powers than any force outside the Communist bloc, with the possible exception of certain turbulent African states. Certainly, they are way ahead of any other police force in the Western world in this respect."

27. Dessie O'Malley in the Dail on 24 January 1984, reported in the _Irish Times_, 25th January 1984.

28. Mr. Doherty was speaking on the RTE Radio One programme "This Week" on 12th December 1982. The representative associations of the gardai have repeatedly complained about detailed political interference. Of a number of cases one other that aroused particular interest, apart from the case of Sergeant Thomas Tully of Boyle Station, Co. Rosecommon (Mr. Doherty's constituency) who successfully appealed to the Garda Review body against being transferred, and the "Liffeygate" episode, is the so-called "Dowra affair". Mr. Doherty's brother-in-law was charged with assault, but on the morning of the case the chief prosecution witness was arrested by the RUC, and was unable to attend the hearing, leading to the case against Mr. Doherty's relative being dismissed. The RUC brought no charges against the man they arrested. Ever since this episode in September 1982, a number of questions have been asked about Garda-RUC contact, and who initiated it. It has not improved RUC-Garda relations.

29. _Garda News_, October 1982. _Garda News_ is the magazine of the Association of Garda Sergeants and Inspectors.

30. See _Irish Times_, 21 December 1983 for Dr. O'Brien's remarks from a radio interview the previous day.

31. Paddy Harte T.D., speech reported in the _Irish Times_, 6 January 1984.

32. As reported in the _Irish Times_, 24 December 1983.

33. Radio interview of 18 December 1983, reported in _Irish Times_, 19 December 1983.

34. Reported in _Irish Times_, 19 December 1983.

Further Reading

Conor Brady, _Guardians of the Peace_, Dublin, Gill & Macmillan 1974.

H. Manning, _The Blueshirts_, Dublin, Gill & Macmillan 1971.

Glossary

A.G.S.I. – Association of Garda Sergeants and Inspectors.

Black and Tans – Additional recruits, from England, to the Royal Irish Constabulary in 1920, taking their name from their distinctive uniforms. They were not a special force, but were distinctive, numbering about 7,000.

Blueshirts – Paramilitary, superficially Fascist, associated with Fine Gael in early 1930s.

Coalition – Ireland has experienced a number of coalitions, in recent years between Fine Gael and Labour, but in earlier years rather more elements were involved.

Dail – First Dail elected in the British General Election of 28 December 1918. The Sinn Fein candidates were pledged to withdraw from Westminister if elected and form a constituent assembly. On 21 January 1919 this First Dail met.

– Dail Eireann is the lower, popularly elected House of the Irish Parliament.

Eire – Ireland post-1937.

Fianna Fail – Soldiers of Destiny, founded in 1926 by de Valera out of anti-Treaty factions prepared to opt for the parliamentary method. It has been in government for long periods since 1932: 1932-1948, 1951-1954, 1957-1973, 1977-1981, 1982.

Fine Gael – Family/Tribe of Gaels, formed in 1933 principally out of pro-Treaty forces, especially, but not exclusively Cumann na nGaedheal. Since that time it has been a dominant force in coalition governments of: 1948-1951, 1954-1957, 1973-1977, 1981-1982, 1982– .

Garda Siochana – Civic Guard, the Irish police force.

Garda Representative Association – Members of the gardai below rank of sergeant organisation.

Irish Free State (IFS) – The state for the 26 counties (the South) formed as a result of the treaty of 1921. It became Eire in 1937.

Irish Republican Army (IRA) – Old IRA, the army of the Irish Republic proclaimed Easter 1916. It grew out of the Irish Volunteers, becoming transformed and popularly known as the IRA shortly after the foundation of the First Dail in 1919.

– Official/Provisional IRA – always prone to division between a primary emphasis upon 'nationalism' and 'socialism', the successors to those who refused to follow de Valera in 1926, split in the winter of 1969 into 'Official' and 'Provisional' IRA, with parallel Official and

Provisional Sinn Fein. Generally, the 'Officials' have been more socialist/Marxist in orientation, seeing the need to appeal to more than 'nationalism', and in recent times have played down violence.

The 'Provisionals' (Provos or PIRA) take their name from the Provisional Government announced in 1916, and have concentrated upon nationalism and violence, although even among the Provisionals tensions exist between those who believe nationalism per se is enough, and those who see a need to have a socio-economic (and socialist) programme as well. This latter group may now be in the ascendancy.

Northern Ireland - Ulster, but not the old Province of nine counties, rather the artificial entity created in the 1920-22 period, and comprising six counties (the North).

Oireachtas - Irish Parliament comprising Dail and Seaned Eireann (and constitutionally, the President).

Royal Irish Constabulary (RIC) - the police force throughout the island before independence, and disbanded in 1922.

Royal Ulster Constabulary (RUC) - the Northern Ireland police force.

Seaned Eireann - Upper House of the Oireachtas, constitutionally largely vocational in composition but, in practice, largely party politicians.

Sinn Fein - 'Ourselves', sometimes mistranslated as 'Ourselves Alone'. Originally founded by Arthur Griffith in 1906, it was re-vamped under de Valera's leadership in 1917. Although its members held a variety of views, it stood for a sovereign, independent republic. Some refused to follow de Valera in 1926 in recognising a 26 county state. Sinn Fein has always been closely associated with the IRA, reflecting its concerns, tensions and divisiveness.

"The Republic" - Proclaimed in 1916, and encompassing all 32 counties on the Ireland. For some, no 26 county decision can dissolve this almost mystical Republic, and the election of 1918 result is held to give it legitimacy and popular endorsement, a fact important to the IRA today.

It is not to be confused with the republic declared by Eire in 1949 covering the 26 counties.

Taoiseach - Prime Minister.

Teachta Dala (TD) - Member of Dail Eireann.

Treaty - "The Articles of Agreement for a Treaty", signed 6 December 1921 by British and Irish delegates. On 7 January 1922 the Dail voted 64 votes for the Treaty to 57 against.

Chapter 5

THE FRENCH POLICE(1)

John Roach

History(2)

France has a tradition of policing going back to the
Middle Ages which has been characterised over the years by
its overriding concern with the maintenance of public order, 'le maintien de l'ordre' and 'l'ordre public' being in
practice synonymous. Another feature of the evolution of
the French police lies in the close association of the
police and the state, a symbiotic relationship which has
provoked many tomes of commentary by jurists, as J.P.
Stead puts it, 'The evolution of the French police is an
inseparable process in the evolution of the French
state.'(3) That evolution is marked by a relentless move
towards centralisation and the policing of individuals,
groups, ideas as much as crime.
    Louis XIV's drive towards the creation of a single
state through the imposition of central control resulted
not only in the creation of Versailles as instrument and
symbol of that centralisation, but also the creation of
the first quasi Minister of Police with the establishment
of the post of Lieutenant-General of Police for Paris in
1666. The first incumbent, Nicolas de la Reynie, was to
prove himself the first police technocrat. His brief was
wide, from overseeing food supplies, controlling prices,
weights and measures, inspecting markets, hostelries and
lodging houses, to apprehending criminals and, above all,
establishing a system of surveillance of individuals and
groups who might be thought to endanger the state. This
duality of police functions between administrative tasks
and judicial tasks (investigating crime and. apprehending
criminals) persists to this day,(4) when French citizens
still have to go to the police commissariat to obtain,
among other things, driving licences, passports, identity
cards and the police still have to carry out many of the
tasks laid down during the time of la Reynie. The admini-

strative tasks of general policing are often a source of
frustration with the police, who complain that they are a
misuse of their time and also act as an unnecessary source
of conflict with the public, especially as the environment
of the Commissariat is not always welcoming.   In his
statement to the Commission des Lois on the Projet de
Finances for 1983, M. Defferre, the Minister of the Interior, stated that the Prime Minister and he hoped to relieve the police of such tasks as the delivery of visas,
identity cards, passports; as a consequence he estimated
that between 5,000 and 7,000 policemen could be back on
'active' service.   This has not yet happened.   Similarly, just as the many and diverse tasks given to the police
have persisted to the present day, so too has the general
practice of appointing administrators, i.e. non-profes-
sional policemen, as head of the police force at national
and prefectoral level.   Today not only is a politician,
the Minister of the Interior, in charge of all the police
services, 'flic numéro un' (the boss cop) but almost all
the heads of the important Directorates are political appointees drawn from the prefectoral corps, the magistrat-
ure or some other senior branch of the administration,
(for
   details of Directorates cf below under 'Organisation').
Furthermore at departmental and regional level, the
administrative agents of central government, appointed by
it, the Prefects, are responsible for the maintenance of
law and order, especially public order, within their
designated territorial limits.(5)
   A subsequent Lieutenant-General of Police, Nicolas
Berryier, who held the post from 1747 to 1757, introduced
the 'Bureau de Sûreté' which acted as a centre for the
collection, sorting, collating and filing of reports and
information received from agents and other sources.   Indeed, in the eighteenth century the main thrust of police
work was largely concerned with surveillance and intelligence gathering.   The police were active in carrying out
directives of the state in such matters as censorship,
opening the mail of suspects (an early variant on phone-
tapping) and the use of the infamous 'lettres de cach-
et'.(6)   Interestingly the use of the 'lettres' was often
resorted to in order to protect the 'good name' of important individuals or families, on the grounds that to allow
a scandal to become public would lessen confidence in the
regime by eroding respect for its finest representatives -
a concern which has not altogether disappeared.
   Broadly, over the period 1666 to the Revolution, a
police structure and a bureaucracy were established which
were essential to the administration of the State and it
was a police which progressively became an instrument of

surveillance, of control and of repression. For all that, the police of the Ancien Régime failed to anticipate the intensity of the events which precipitated the Revolution and brought down the monarchy which it served. The Declaration of Rights of August 26, 1789, denounced the arbitrariness of the police and the abuses committed by it, and declared the police to be an instrument for the suppression of liberty. The office of Lieutenant-General of Police was abolished, similarly the 'maréchausée' was disbanded, to reappear in 1791 as the Gendarmerie Nationale, while in Paris the task of maintaining order was given to the National Guard, a somewhat motley crew, ill-adapted to the demands of Revolutionary Paris.

The great transformation in policing came with Napoleon who saw the creation of an efficient police system as indispensable to his creation of a centralised state. Furthermore, the circumstances of the French Revolution clearly demonstrated the need for a police force whose primary function would be the maintenance of public order, the events of 1789 being clear evidence of the way in which public order disturbances could quickly become a revolution. Thus, paradoxically, one of the consequences of the Revolution was to inspire subsequent régimes to create a police apparatus which would protect them from revolution. In much the same way as today, international terrorism has resulted in states developing police forces and extending police powers to an unparalleled extent. It may be part of the terrorist groups' grand strategy of polarisation, but the development must be a cause for concern in democratic societies. Napoleon created a Minister of Police and named as his Minister a man who is perhaps the most celebrated of policemen, Joseph Fouché, later Duke of Otranto. Fouché not only played an important role in the coup of 18 Brumaire (9 November 1799) which brought Napoleon to power, and remained at the head of the police during virtually the whole of the Napoleonic period, but he also went on to run the police during the Restauration. Fouché concerned himself with what he called 'la haute police', that is, a political police whose business was the security of the state. His aim was to set up a network of spies and informers to gather information in order to enable him to act against all enemies of the state from whatever quarter. The essence of Fouché's system was information gathering and secrecy of action. Thus there were no trials which might attract too much attention and stir-up opposition. He declared that, 'to my mind, the police should be etablished in order to forestall and prevent crimes and check any which the law has not yet foreseen.' These principles established the police as the arbiter of the public good and that meant being the master of public order. To achieve this he set up a vast bureaucracy and coupled it to Napoleon's administrative restructuring of France and the establishment of a new system of law through the Code Napoléon, principally the penal code and the code of criminal procedure. The police and the administration came together in the Ministry of the Interior and in the administrative structure Napoleon created. Briefly, this consisted in dividing France into 'départements' and subdividing these into 'arrondissements' and 'communes', with central government appointees at each tier so as to set up a chain of command leading from and back to the Ministry of the Interior in Paris: at the head of the department was the Prefect, at arrondissement level, the sub-prefect (4 or 5 per department) and in the commune the Mayor. All of these were agents of the Minister of the Interior, bound by and acting in the name of his authority, and they in turn had authority over the police forces in their areas, especially in matters of public order when they could call upon the services of the Gendarmerie which, then as now, was a part of the military but which in its operational policing role came under the Minister of the Interior.

The nineteenth century saw developments in police structures and procedures, especially the extension of urban police forces and the creation of the uniformed police, the 'sergents de ville' in 1829, renamed in 1871 'gardiens de la paix'. The police continued to be primarily concerned with security, the growing fear of popular unrest brought about by the economic, social and ideological upheavals of the century. Following the coup d'état of 1851, in which the police played an active role, Napoleon III sought to establish a police state,(7) by resurrecting a Minister of Police and appointing central commissaires in all large urban areas under the authority of the departmental prefect. In 1855 an imperial decree created the 'Police Spéciales des chemins de fer' with a network of agents all over France, whose task was not so much to police the railways, as to frequent stations and trains to gather information about anyone or any movement or organisation which might be a danger to the security of the state. They were the forerunners of the present day Renseignements Généraux, the internal intelligence agency.

Following the fall of Louis Napoleon, the violence of the Commune and the establishment of the Third Republic, a Direction of the 'Sûreté Nationale' was set up under the authority of the Ministry of the Interior in an attempt to co-ordinate the various branches of the nationwide police forces (Paris and the Seine were excluded). The consequence was to create a highly politicised directorate which changed with virtually every change of government. In 1899, in the throes of the Dreyfus Affair, the counter-espionage service was removed from the army and placed under the Ministry of the Interior as a police service, the 'Surveillance du Territoire' (now the 'Direction de la Surveillance du Territoire'). In 1903 a decree established the main principles of organisation for the Gendarmerie, placing it under the authority of the Ministry of War (now Ministry of Defence) and defining its role as a local, then largely rural police force, always in uniform and available to provide a mobile force in support of the civilian police forces in cases of public disorder.

The next major organisational change in the police came during the Occupation and was introduced by the Vichy government. A law of 23 April 1941 established the structure of the police for the next 25 years. Briefly, the law created a General Directorate of the 'Police Nationale',(8) which was subdivided on the lines of the Préfecture de Police of Paris into three operational sections: 'Sécurité publique' (urban police): Police judiciaire (plain clothes, criminal investigation police): Renseignements Généraux (internal intelligence service). Perhaps more importantly, the same law placed the police in all towns with a population of over 10,000 under the 'régime d'état', that is, policemen became civil servants, and were the responsibility of the state, recruited by and paid for by the state. The Gendarmerie was retained but a further public order force was created, the 'Gardes Mobiles de Réserve'.(9) These were disbanded at the time of the Liberation but reconstituted in 1945 as the Compagnies Républicaines de Sécurité (C.R.S.), which were to be specialised mobile units expressly concerned with public order, under the direct control of the Minister of the Interior and the Prefects.(10)

The troubled years of the Fourth Republic did little to improve the morale, efficiency or structure of the police. Indeed, rapidly evolving social, economic and political circumstances made increasing demands of the police, most especially in their public order tasks. Strikes, lock-outs, manifestations, marches were frequent and often violent and the situation was further exacerbated by the outbreak of the Algerian war in 1955 and its impact on metropolitan France. Conflicts between pro and anti-war factions, a mounting climate of plots and counter plots, the presence on French soil of great numbers of Algerian-Arabs, mostly concentrated in urban, industrial areas, and the activities on French soil of the rebel organisation the 'Front de libération nationale' (F.L.N.), all of these factors and others such as discontent about pay and conditions, led to serious breakdowns of discipline in the police and to multiple abuses especially in matters of public order. Ironically, one of the most serious breaches of public order was by the police, when in March 1958, 3,000 policemen marched on and laid siege to the French parliament. This massive demonstration clearly expressed the contempt which the police (at least in Paris) felt for the government and their action was an open defiance of its authority. There can be little doubt that this demonstration was an important factor in discrediting the government yet further and that as such it contributed to the collapse of the Fourth Republic. In Algiers two months later there were riots by the settlers demanding the return of General de Gaulle. He obliged, the Fourth Republic fell and the Fifth Republic was established with a new constitution designed to extend the powers of the executive through the President. As part of the design of increasing executive authority the new constitution added to the already considerable powers of the state in circumstances of any serious breakdown of public order. As previously, the government could declare an 'état de siège' or an 'état d'urgence', a power which came into being during the Algerian crisis. The 'état d'urgence' is less extreme than the 'état de siège' but still gives the government and its agents considerable powers. For example the Prefect, amongst other thin can prohibit all movement of traffic at certain times, forbid all gatherings and demonstrations, close all public places, instigate day and night searches, censure the press, radio and so on. To these powers the Constitution of the Fifth Republic added Article 16. This may be invoked only by the President of the Republic when he judges that the nation and its institutions are in peril. He then has virtually unlimited power to rule by decree. Article 16 has been invoked once, in 1961 following four Generals' attempted putsch in Algeria. As a result of the O.A.S. outrages('Organisation de l'armée secrète', French North-African terrorist group), de Gaulle set up the 'Cour de Sûreté de l'Etat' (15 January 1963) after the 'Conseil d'Etat' had judged illegal the Special Military Courts created in 1961. This use of the legislative process to create a special court to by-pass the established judicial procedure was denounced as anti-democratic, not least by François Mitterrand who declared that with the passage of the law setting up the court: 'civil liberties have been put back 100 years'. The Cour remained operative until M. Mitterrand became President and abolished it. It is a good example of the way in which 'exceptional' measures in times of crisis can become institutionalised.

During the highly volatile years from 1958 to the end of the Algerian crisis (1962) and faced by the terrorist activities of the O.A.S. which was violently opposed to the Algerian peace settlement, the police became more overtly politicised and individuals were often involved in highly dubious activities with the so-called 'parallel' forces.(11)   Habits were formed which were to be difficult to lose over the next twenty years.   Matters came to a head with the Ben Barka scandal in 1965.(12)   Ben Barka was a leading Moroccan dissident, kidnapped in front of the Brasserie Lipp on the Boulevard St. Germain and presumed murdered.   Investigations showed that there had been active collusion and collaboration by agents from various sections of the police, principally from the 'Préfecture de Police'.   Faced with public outrage, the government introduced a law in July 1966 which sought to abolish once and for all the separate status of the 'Préfecture de Police' by creating a single police force, the 'Police Nationale'.

Police Nationale

Organisation.   Since 1968 the Police Nationale has increased by 25%.   There have been two major recruiting periods in the last twenty years.   The first after 1968 when M. Marcellin saw force of numbers as the way to crush any public order troubles and thus prevent another May '68; for him: 'Public order is the precondition for all other liberties'.   The second great recruitment drive has come with the advent of the Socialists in 1981, since then some 9,000 extra policemen have been brought into the service.   The majority of them are destined to be 'gardiens de la paix' (constables) (13) with the aim of increasing the number of police on the beat and extending community policing ('îlotage').

To meet these objectives the socialist government has proceeded not only to increase numbers but also to re-equip the police with guns, ammunition, vehicles, bullet-proof vests and other forms of hardware.   Altogether some 7,200 new vehicles have been purchased since 1981: also 17,000 Manuhrin 357 Magnum and 38 Special pistols which are intended to replace the traditional Unique 7.65 mm: plus over 1,000 carbines and other rifles: as well as 2,000 bullet-proof vests.   In all the government aims to renew some 60,000 hand guns over five years.   In 1981, 9 million francs were allocated to ammunition; in 1982, 12.3 million, an increase of 37%.   This meant that trainee policemen could fire an average of 200 to 250 rounds per year and members of the force 60 to 80, a considerable increase over the number in previous years.(14)   The aim, of course, was to make the police more competent, less 'trigger happy' and reduce the alarming incidence of 'bavures' ('accidents'). (15)

Numbers in the P.N. now stand at around 120,000 made up of uniformed police, 'gardiens de la paix' (constables), 'officiers' (inspectors) 'commandants' (superintendents), and plain clothes police, 'enquêteurs' (investigators), 'inspecteurs' (inspectors), 'commissaires' (superintendents).(16)   To these must be added a few thousand in the covert police services, the 'Renseignements Généraux' and the 'Direction de la Surveillance du Territoire'.   To the numbers in the P.N should be added 88,000 members of the Gendarmerie Nationale who, though members of the Army, have an operational police function.   There are also 7,000 or so Municipal Policemen, in towns with less than 10,000 inhabitants, appointed by the Mayor under the authority of Prefect and paid for by the municipality. The grand total means that France has one of the highest police densities in Europe.

One of the major concerns of the present socialist government has been to improve the quality of the police service by better training.   To this end, in 1983, the government proposed to establish two more training centres to add to the 14 already created in 1981-82.   These were to offer retraining courses with the aim of providing courses for 10 days a year for a third of the P.N. every year.   These centres are in addition to the 10 training colleges which already existed and to which go recruits to various grades of the police.   They range from the prestigious 'Ecole Nationale Supérieure de la Police', for intending 'commissaires' who are recruited on 'concours' (competitive exam: entrants need not be serving officers) and whose training lasts 2 years; to the six schools scattered over France which are responsible for the 9 months, training (4 operational) for the 'gardiens de la paix'.

The government intends to extend training periods for all ranks but especially the 'gardiens de la paix', the aim being to give a police officer not simply a technical training but also, and especially, to 'educate' him about the socio-economic realities of the society in which he will operate;   to give him a sound grasp of his duties under the law; to lay stress on police responsibilities rather than on police powers.   Police training, it is proposed, should be 'open', that is, those involved in the training should not be restricted to professionals, and people from all sectors of society should be brought into it. The object is to create better understanding, better relationships between the police and the citizens, thereby reducing conflict. To this end the government set up a commission under the Socialist deputy, Jean-Michel Belorgey. The commission's brief was to put forward proposals for reforms which would achieve a rapprochement between police and citizen. The report was delivered to the Minister of the Interior in April 1982. It has not yet been implemented, either in its proposals for structural and operational reforms (e.g. the creation of smaller, more localised 'commissariats' and 'bureaux de police'; the need to extend some judicial police powers to uniformed police; the need to exercise greater control on phone-tapping and data files; its proposed 'déontologie policière' (code of police ethics). Indeed, one must suppose that the report has been shelved to be superceded by the, as yet still awaited, report begun in July 1983 by the Director of Training, Jean-Marc Erbès. Plus ça change ... or, more generously, all this may simply be an example of the extent to which any reform of the police runs into intractable difficulties since there are so many demands to satisfy from so many conflicting factions, both within and outwith the police service. It is far easier to re-equip and increase numbers than to change attitudes ('mentalités') and practices: to the great disappointment of many, not least among them policemen, who anticipated much more profound reforms from the present government.(16)

The Ben Barka scandal which precipitated the structural reforms of 1966 was the excuse rather than the reason for the reforms. The quasi-autonomous position of the Paris Préfecture of Police had long been a cause for concern and already in 1963 the government had introduced measures which aimed at the long term integration of the service into the then 'Sûreté Nationale'. The 1966 restructuring sought to bring the Préfecture of Police within the complete authority of the national force under the Minister of the Interior.(17) This intention was confirmed by a decree of 29 September 1969 which established a Directorate General of the 'Police Nationale' responsible to the Minister of the Interior and controlling a wide range of Directorates. In 1982 the Socialist government created a new post, the Secretary of State in charge of Public Security whose responsibilities are to oversee all police matters. The decision was taken following a wave of terrorist bombings culminating in the machine gun attack on a Jewish restaurant in the rue des Rosiers in Paris on 9 August 1982. The President appointed a close aide to the new post, M. Joseph Franceschi who until then had been Secretary of State for the Aged.(18)   At the same time President Mitterrand announced that he was creating a new post attached to his personal staff: Technical Adviser for Co-ordinating Information and Action Against Terrorism, the post was given to Christian Prouteau, head of the elite anti-terrorist squad, the G.I.G.N. (cf. below in the section on the 'Gendarmerie Nationale'). The creation of the two new posts may have been determined by the need to reassure public opinion, but the terrorist activities may also have been an opportune moment to resurrect what amounts to a Minister of Police.(19) Whatever the reasons, the Police Nationale now had a new supremo in M. Franceschi and alongside him is the Director General of the P.N.(20) who controls the following separate major police directorates.

Polices Urbaines. This service is responsible for all police matters in towns of 10,000 or more inhabitants; its duty is to 'maintain law and order, public safety, security and salubrity'.   The traditional organisational structure of the police had been based on the 'commissariat' and the 'bureaux de police'.   These have been retained, but in 1969 a larger administrative unit was created, the 'circonscription de police' (area unit).   The date of the reform is significant since one of the objectives of the restructuring was to strengthen the capacity and efficiency of the P.U. as a public order force following the events of May 1968.   This was especially evident by the creation of 'Forces d'Intervention des Corps Urbains' (F.I.C.U.), these are specially trained police intervention groups located at district level and co-ordinated at departmental level.   Their function is to provide a rapid response to any public order situation.   The logic of the restructuring was thus clearly inspired by public order considerations.   It was felt that the traditional units were too small and ill-adapted to public order needs and that the larger 'circonscription' would facilitate the formation of specialised groups (21) of trained personnel whose operations would be better co-ordinated at departmental level under the authority of the Prefect, who is, of course, as agent of the central government, ultimately responsible for public order.   The reform exemplified the high priority given to public order policing and for many commentators it represented a radical move away from traditional preventive policing to a more repressive coercive form of policing.   'Today it seems that the police functions in matters of public order are steadily taking over from all other duties.'(22)   These duties include investigating crime and bringing criminals to trial, this is the task of the P.J.

Police Judiciaire. Article 14 of the Penal Procedure
Code defines tasks of the P.J. as being, 'to investigate
all breaches of the law, to gather evidence and to bring
the perpetrators before the tribunals empowered to try
them.' The primary function of the P.J. is to deal with
'délits' (offences) and 'crimes', it does so, however,
under the authority and surveillance of the Magistracy,
carrying out the instructions of a 'Procureur de la République' and acting in his name.(23) In matters of investigation and arrest not all French policemen have the
same powers and within the P.J. there are two categories
with quite distinct powers. (1) 'Officiers de Police
Judiciaire' (OPJ), such officers are entitled to sign a
'procès-verbal', a written police report which is used in
evidence; they may also impose a 'garde à vue' (police
custody) for 24 hours which may be extended for a further
48 hours with the agreement of the judicial authorities.(24) They are empowered to arrest and take in suspected persons for identity checks and they can search.
Those who have the powers of OPJ are: Mayors, their deputies, Prefects: police officers in the P.N. holding the
rank of 'commissaire' and above; plain clothes officers
with the rank of 'inspecteur principal' and 'inspecteur
divisionnaire'; all officers and senior NCOs of the 'Gendarmerie', and 'gendarmes' with at least 5 years' service
who have passed a statutory exam. This category does not
apply to members of the two specialised public order forces, the C.R.S. and the 'Gendarmerie Mobile', their officers are in the category of (2) 'Agents de Police Judiciaire', which is in turn divided into 1st and 2nd class
categories. 'Gendarmes mobiles' are in the 1st class,
C.R.S. are 2nd class. All uniformed inspectors of the
P.N. are 1st class. The distinction is essentially in
that those who are 1st class can sign 'procès-verbaux' and
carry out preliminary enquiries; 2nd class officers can
only submit reports. The distinction between OPJ and APJ
is more important, no APJ may impose a 'grand à vue' nor
does he have any of the other powers of the OPJ. These
distinctions and divisions create operational difficulties
and there is considerable pressure from the police to extend the title of OPJ beyond the present categories, if
only to regularise the fact that the fine distinctions in
powers are often ignored and most frequently so in situations of public order troubles when, for example, the
restrictions on the powers of certain policemen in matters
of stop and search, of arrest and detention often fall by
the wayside.

The Renseignements Généraux. The R.G. branch is basically a political police whose task is to gather information on individuals and groups whose activities may constitute a danger to the state. It operates in every department, reports to the Prefect and transmits its information to the central R.G. directorate in Paris whose task is 'to collect and centralise information on all matters relating to political, economic and social order, which are essential to the government'. To this end the R.G. collects information from newspapers, radio, television, from informers, by attending meetings, by infiltrating groups and organisations, by intercepting mail and phone-tapping (though this is only legally permissible if a judge grants a warrant). The R.G. has a number of specialised services which concentrate on specific sectors and individuals, for example, students and leading politicians. To build up dossiers the service undertakes 'enquêtes individuelles' and 'enquêtes générales'. The former may indeed be on an individual person but often the investigation will concentrate on an organisation, a firm, a movement etc. The 'enquêtes générales' are investigations of political groups or parties and trade unions. Their aim is to present a complete profile of the leaders, the numbers, resources, activities, ideas, projects etc. The information is then collected at Departmental level, passed on to Paris where it is collated and filed. Thus the R.G. provides the government of the day with a continuous stream of information on all manner of activities which might be thought to be a cause for concern. The R.G. with its specifically political tasks and its direct connection with the Prefect are the first source of information pertaining to any possible public order problems. That indeed is their primary function, to forewarn the government. Such is its usefulness that the Socialist government, whose members were for many years the subject of R.G. investigations (and probably still are), has done little to curtail, let alone abolish, the R.G. which was often denounced as 'a political police working in the interests of the Right' during the years in opposition. Nor have the Socialists done much about another surveillance agency attached to the police, the Direction de la Surveillance du Territoire.

The D.S.T. is concerned with the surveillance and suppression of all persons and groups acting in the interest of foreign states on French soil. A fine distinction is used to define its activities: 'It is a service which deals in matters which are secret: it is not a secret service.' But of all the police services it is the most shadowy in that little information is available about its activities, resources or even its numbers (thought to be about 1200). What is known is that it is highly central-ised, has competence over the whole of France with one section concentrating on Paris and 8 others over the rest of the territory. As with the R.G. the D.S.T.'s task is to provide information in order to prevent any danger to the security of the state or which might be a threat to public order.(26)

When public order does break down the front line is usually manned by the C.R.S. These 'Compagnies' were created by a decree of 8.12.1944 from what had been the Vichy government's 'Groupes Mobiles de Réserve' (G.M.R.). Fundamentally the C.R.S. are riot squads, mobile, special-ly trained units which can be rapidly deployed under the authority of the Minister of the Interior through his de-partmental agent the Prefect. Though organised and trained on military lines the C.R.S. are in fact civilians and part of the P.N. They are distributed over the whole of France through 10 territorial group commands, each one with a 'commandant' and a general staff. The territorial groups comprise 61 companies of around 250 men, divided into command and service sections (30 men), four general service sections (45 men) and a motorcycle section. The 61 companies are based around urban or industrial areas, but they may be moved at any time to anywhere. Mobility is essential to their function of rapid response and of bringing reinforcement to the other branches of the police. The training and duties of the C.R.S. are dic-tated by public order considerations. They exist in order to prevent and/or quell disorder. Their presence is designed to have an intimidatory effect and their often brutal interventions makes them a much feared force. It may be a sign of the times that since 1968, the C.R.S. with his riot helmet and military combat uniform, has re-placed the officer with the képi and the cloak as the image of the french police.(27)

Gendarmerie Nationale

As well as the multiple services within the P.N., France has another police force much concerned with maintaining public order, the 'Gendarmerie Nationale'.(28) The Gen-darmes are soldiers, and their service comes under the Minister of Defence. They are controlled by a Director-General who is usually a Prefect, i.e. a political ap-pointee. Basically the Gendarmes provide the police force for all towns with less than 10,000 inhabitants. Over the years this delimitation has caused difficulties

in view of the shifts in population and the growth and
spread of towns and cities. The problem has become one
of policing powers in overlapping territories between the
G.N. and the P.N., since Gendarmes with the appropriate
rank and training are O.P.J.s and A.P.J.s and are thus empowered to investigate and arrest in the same way as their
counterparts in the Police Judiciaire. The consequence
is often a wasteful use of manpower and resources, as well
as rivalries which lead to operational inefficiency.

The G.N. has two major sections the 'Gendarmerie Dé-
partmentale' and the 'Gendarmerie Mobile'.(29) The former are involved in all police matters within their territory. Housed with their families in barracks, they are
always in uniform when on duty and continually on patrol.
Not only do they patrol and investigate, but they also act
in matters of surveillance and information gathering, the
results of which they communicate to the Prefect and to
the G.N.'s 'Service Technique de Recherches Judiciaires et
de Documentation' at Rosny-sous-Bois. There it is collated and put on their computerised filing system. Given
their long history and their systematic collection of information it is no surprise that the central data bank is
estimated to hold over 200 million entries on individuals,
groups, organisations etc.

The 'Gendarmerie Mobile' is a specially trained and
equipped public order force on permanent stand-by. Its
function is to respond to circumstances causing or likely
to cause a breakdown of public order, riots, strikes,
manifestations, gatherings, disasters of any kind (fire,
floods etc.) There are some 18,000 G.M. distributed over
France in 24 'groupements', broken down into units of 130
squadrons made up of 134 men. Unlike the G.D. the G.M.
have no territorial limitations and are frequently on mission away from their base. They do not perform local
policing tasks, their role is entirely geared to public
order duties. As such they are the Gendarmerie's equivalent of the C.R.S. Their training and their equipment is
in fact superior. They have all the usual personal protection at their disposal: helmets, visors, riot shields,
batons, tear gas and offensive grenades, rifles and hand
guns. To this impressive armoury they bring in addition,
machine guns, water cannons, armoured transport vehicles,
armoured combat vehicles, armoured personnel carriers
(some equipped with bulldozer blades and cranes to clear
barricades), helicopters and light tanks. There is even
a parachute squadron based at Mont-de-Marsan. What is
significant in all of this equipment is that it represents
the operational 'tool' of a force which is expressly designed to act on matters of public order, and furthermore

that as a public order force the G.M. is under the authority of the Prefect.(30)

Just as the events of May 1968 led to a rapid increase in the manpower and resources of the P.N. and the
G.N. with a high priority given to their public order
functions, so the Munich massacre of 1972 and the activities of terrorist groups all over Europe, led to the creation of élite squads of anti-terrorist forces.   In France
this took the form of the creation of the 'Groupe d'Intervention de la Gendarmerie Nationale' (G.I.G.N.).   In
theory this élite group is attached to the G.N. of the
Ile-de-France, but in practice it is under central government command, if not control, since it has often acted in
a quite independent way.   At the present time its image
is somewhat tarnished following the disclosure that the
arrest of three Irish terrorists on 28 August 1982 involved planting evidence and the subordination of witnesses, offences for which those in charge of the action are
currently on trial.(31)   Nevertheless, the founder and
commander of the G.I.G.N., Christian Prouteau is still on
President Mitterrand's staff.   Also, over the years the
G.I.G.N. has undoubtedly become involved not just in
covert operations but in covert information gathering as
well.

It is interesting to note that, up to the present
time, the Socialist government has tended to look favourably on the G.N., considering it to be a more disciplined,
less political force than the P.N.   Not only has President Mitterrand put Prouteau on his staff, but he also
gave the task of presidential protection to the G.N. and
put a gendarme into what had hitherto been the exclusive
domain of the P.N., the security of 'Voyages Officiels'
(security of foreign dignitaries and Presidential visits).

There can be little doubt that the G.N. has greatly
extended its policing over the last 10 years and that the
greatest thrust has been towards those areas of policing
which are most closely concerned with public order.   One
striking example of this may be seen in the fact that
whereas in 1972 there were 13,000 'gendarmes mobiles' and
15,000 C.R.S., by 1978 the ratio stood at 17,000 to
15,000.   The reason for this is largely due to political
considerations in that the C.R.S. have a much higher public profile than the G.M. and more often than not the
C.R.S. bear the brunt of public odium in public order
troubles, consequently any increase in their numbers would
be much more politically sensitive, as would the introduction of the equipment and resources available to the G.M.
Thus the specialised public order branch of the G.N. has
continued to grow and since in matters of public order the

121

Prefect, i.e. the government, reigns supreme, it is clear that the growing strength of the G.M. reflects the growing governmental preoccupation with public order over the last fifteen years, a preoccupation which shows no sign of declining.

Public Order Procedures

The police may intervene whenever they judge that there is a danger to 'l'ordre public', that is, when there is or is thought to be a threat to 'la sécurité, la tranquilité ou la salubrité publique', thus the concept of 'ordre public' is a flexible one and in reality it means that the police may intervene when they choose to. If they were right to do so may be subsequently tested in the courts. How they do so is subject, in matters of public order, at least in theory, to certain laid down procedures. It will be remembered that a distinction is made between a police function which is said to be 'administrative' and that which is 'judiciaire'. The former involves surveillance and the maintenance of order where there is no breach of the law, the latter involves investigating an offence and apprehending the perpetrators. In matters of public order the distinction is a fine one and what may begin as 'police administrative' almost invariably and very quickly becomes a 'police judiciaire' matter. It is in this perspective that the various procedures considered below have to be viewed.

'Manifestations' are a way of life in France. Following the violence of the thirties and especially the events of 6 February 1934, a law was passed, 23 October 1935 which requires the authorities to be informed prior to the occurrence of a 'manifestation'. Anyone who wishes to organise a manifestation must make a declaration of intent to the Prefect or the Mayor at least 3 days and at most 15 days before the event. This statement must include the names and addresses of the organisers, three of whom must sign the statement. Details must also be given about time, place, route, numbers expected and the purpose of the demonstration. If the Prefect or the Mayor decide that there is a threat to 'l'ordre public' they can forbid the demonstration, thus in 1979 following violent clashes in Paris, the government gave directives that all manifestations should be banned from town centres if there was the slightest risk to public order.

Getting clearance from the Prefect or Mayor is essential because without it the 'manifestation' becomes an 'attroupement' (crowd, mob) thus allowing the police to intervene as best they judge. Since 1960 all gatherings, meetings, demonstrations in public places (streets, parks, cafés etc.) are considered to be 'attroupements' unless the procedure for authorisation has been followed. Thus by a nice piece of French logic while all citizens have the right to demonstrate, they can only do so within the law if they have been allowed to do so by the authorities. There is, however, a nuance in that not all 'rassemblements' (gatherings) are necessarily 'attroupements', they only become the latter when there has been a breach of the peace ('tranquilité publique'). Furthermore an 'attroupement administratif' only becomes an 'attroupement pénal', that is, a matter of 'police judiciaire' when the authorities have given the orders to disperse and these have been ignored, or if violence breaks out. Thus crowds at sporting occasions are not 'attroupements' unless and until they fail to comply with orders from the police.

Article 104 of the Penal Code prohibits 'attroupements' in public places but leaves a wide measure of discretion to the police in determining what constitutes an 'attroupement' (no specification is given as to numbers). For many people the lack of specificity opens the way to arbitrary actions by the police, for others it allows for necessary operational flexibility. The Article states that any 'attroupement' is forbidden 'qui pourrait troubler la tranquilité publique' ('which might disturb the peace'). The use of the conditional is significant because it leaves the decision to the police, to their perception of the circumstances.

The Code Pénal defines those who have the authority to give an order to disperse. They are, a Prefect or sub-Prefect, a Mayor, a 'commissaire de police', or an 'Officier de Police Judiciaire'. The order to disperse is known as a 'sommation' and is given by one of the above named, clearly identifying himself; in the past this meant wearing the tricolour sash, sounding bugle calls and drum rolls; today loud-hailers and flashing lights may also be used. From the moment a 'sommation' has been given calling upon people to disperse or face intervention by the forces of order, those who fail to do so are in breach of the law. Even if the 'manifestation' had prior sanction, it becomes an 'attroupement' when a 'sommation' is given, and those participating who do not comply with the order to disperse become liable to a fine or a prison sentence of from 2 months to 3 years, 5 years if an individual is found to have an offensive weapon.

The reasons for issuing a 'sommation' are many and varied so that even when a 'manifestation' is entirely within the specified regulations it can very quickly become subject to an order to disperse. Violence is ob-

viously the most common reason, but exactly what constitutes violence is multifarious, furthermore when violence occurs the forces of public order may intervene
without going through the 'sommation' procedures. Apart
from the obvious acts of violence or threats of violence
(a more difficult area to determine) demonstrators may
also be guilty of 'rébellion, violences ou outrages à
agents', any one of which justifies intervention. 'Rébellion' is basically failure to comply with an order or
resisting arrest; if there is physical assault that is
'violences' (pushing may be 'violence'). 'Outrages' is
an all-embracing category, ranging from giving cheek,
offensive gestures, insulting banners, verbal abuse to
physical assault. Clearly there is no lack of justifi-
cations for intervention by the P.N. or the G.N.

Following the first 'sommation' if the demonstrators
have not dispersed, there is a second 'sommation' where-
upon the public order forces may use truncheons and tear
gas grenades since these are not considered to be 'armes'.
Recourse to arms may follow a third 'sommation'. The
general rules governing the use of firearms is different
for members of the P.N. and those in the G.N. Policemen
may only fire in self-defence or in the defence of a third
party, and weapons may only be used in cases of extreme
gravity. It goes without saying that these instructions
are not always scrupulously followed, hence the great number of 'bavures'. The Gendarmes may use their weapons
other than in self-defence, e.g. when under attack and
there is a likelihood of being overrun, or when having
cried 'Halte Gendarmerie!' the person or persons fail to
comply with the order, or when there are no other means of
stopping a vehicle. Some policemen, but by no means
all, would like to have the same rights as the Gendarmes.
In March 1982, M. Defferre caused widespread consternation
when he suggested that the Police might be given the same
guidelines as the Gendarmes. For the present, however,
the situation governing the use of firearms remains unchanged.

In the wake of May 1968, the government introduced,
in June 1970, what was called the 'loi anti-casseurs'.
Though ostensibly aimed at those responsible for the
wanton destruction of property, the law was in fact a public order measure with far reaching consequences for all
forms of protest, with the government declaring that the
'sommations' procedure was ill-adapted, too cumbersome in
the face of this new form of delinquency . Furthermore,
the law created the notion of collective responsibility,
thus departing from the established principle that individuals can only be held responsible for their own ac-

tions. The government sought to justify this by claiming that the procedure was a response to the difficulties in obtaining judgements against those arrested during demonstrations. Thus with the 'loi anti-casseurs' the action of some engaged the responsibility of all and the public order forces could thus arrest anyone on a demonstration regardless of whether they had actually participated in the violence. Not only was this seen as greatly increasing the possibility of arbitrary arrests but it was also condemned as opening the way even more to 'agents provocateurs', though, ironically, the law proposed severe penalties for those who might subsequently be condemned as 'provocateurs'. In fact during the lifetime of the law (it has been abrogated by the Socialist government) very few 'provocateurs' were brought to trial. It seems that many of the 'provocateurs' were closely connected with the forces of public order. Mitterrand, then a Deputy, condemned the government for using the excuse of the actions of a few to deny the rights of citizens to 'réunion' (assembly) and to hold 'manifestations'. He denounced the 'anti-casseurs' law as 'an anti-student, anti-worker, anti-shopkeeper, anti-farmer, and above all an anti-democratic law'. The government defended the 'loi anti-casseurs' as a measure aimed at curbing the anti-social activities of politically inspired vandals but it was seen as a measure which threatened the rights of unions and even the right to strike. Very clearly it was a highly repressive piece of public order legislation through which the government greatly extended its area of control.(33) Without the 'loi anti-casseurs' a person may only be arrested in a public place or in the street in the following circumstances: if they are committing an offence ('délit') considered to be 'flagrant'; if they are the subject of a warrant issued by a 'juge d'instruction' (examining magistrate); or when the person has been sentenced to a term of imprisonment. The first two are the most pertinent in the context of public order. As we have seen, assemblies, meetings, demonstrations may become an offence for a wide range of reasons, which trigger-off the intervention of the public order forces. (34) According to the law (Article 73 of the Code of Penal Procedure) an arrested person must be taken as quickly as possible to the nearest OPJ who alone can proceed with the arrest. In public order circumstances, not only is this procedure not easy but it is frequently ignored. Since 1968 a practice has developed of what are called 'interpellations' (holding for questioning). In reality these are no different to arrests, but the change in vocabulary allows for procedures which are not as clearly defined in law as those pertaining to arrests. Consequently 'interpellation' has been seen as a practice which greatly increases arbitrary actions by the forces of the police. Writing in Le Monde (21.2.1970) Maître Leclerc stated:'The practice of 'interpellation' became habitual during the events of 1968 ... demonstrators were arrested, placed in vans and taken to police stations or detention centres ... what were then measures taken in response to exceptional circumstances have subsequently become institutionalised'.(35)   The law 'Sécurité et Liberté' introduced in 1980, among other punitive measures, greatly extended the powers of the police in matters of stop and search and especially 'contrôle d'identité'.(36)   The law stated that 'anyone whose identity it is deemed necessary to verify must there and then give proof of his or her identity'. 'Interpellations' and/or 'contrôles d'identité' have consistently been used in the maintenance of public order.(37)   The Socialist government abrogated the 'loi sécurité et liberté', but it limited itself to issuing directives to the police to curb the excessive use of 'interpellations', 'contrôles' and 'vérifications d'identité'.   There seems to be little evidence to suggest that the practice has greatly diminished.

Police, Politics and Policies

France's long tradition of civil disorder has produced a vast police apparatus organised through a highly centralised system within which a high priority has been given to public order police functions.   Over the last twenty five years there has been a great increase in the allocation of resources in terms of manpower, equipment, training and organisational procedures, to public order functions of policing.   The two specialised public order corps, the C.R.S. and the Gendarmerie Mobile were reinforced and in the case of the latter the numbers were considerably increased.   At the same time, after 1968, special groups were created within the PN, specially trained for public order duties; in Paris these were known as the 'Compagnies de District' and in the provinces, the 'Forces d'Intervention des Corps Urbains' (F.I.C.U.).   Such developments reflect the acute anxiety on the part of the authorities about public order.   Hard line Ministers of the Interior like Marcellin and Poniatowski made public order their number one concern and they set about applying and extending the already wide range of laws available to governments in matters relating to public order.   Thus they systematically used the legislation against public protest (decree law of 23 October 1935 which gives Prefects and

Mayors powers to ban marches and demonstrations); against organisations considered to be a threat to the state (law of 10 January 1936 which allows the government to ban all associations and groups which are held to be advocating the use of force against republican institutions); against aliens ('ordonnance' of 2 November 1945, which gives the Minister of the Interior the authority to order the expulsion of any foreign national whose presence is considered to be a danger to public order); France's long tradition of giving refuge to exiles and political refugees was attenuated by a 'circulaire' of 2 July 1974 stipulating that all those given asylum must not be involved in any activity which might prejudice the internal or external security of the nation,; and, as we have seen, the 'loi anti-casseurs' of 1970, was clearly intended as a counter to the events of May 1968, even though the immediate justification was claimed to be the activities of the so called 'autonomes'.(38)

Throughout the Giscard presidency governments systematically exploited issues of law and order, fanning the flames of 'insécurité', as a political strategy by which to embarrass the opposition parties who were castigated as soft on crime, 'laxistes'. At the same time the aim was to intensify public concern about delinquency and criminality thereby creating a climate of opinion favourable to the introduction of repressive measures and practices which were designed to reinforce police powers in the context of public order rather than facilitating the fight against crime. As a measure of the government's concern the Minister of Justice Alain Peyrefitte (now a frequent editorialist on law and order issues in the _Figaro_) commissioned and presided over a report which set out to analyse the causes of the malaise and put forward proposals for reforms.(39) In the event, perhaps not surprisingly, the conclusions and recommendations were mainly those most welcome to the authorities, namely the need for greater firmness, more interventions by the police (i.e. controls), an increase in the number of police and that there should be a policy of firmer sentences (Poniatowski, as Minister of the Interior, frequently deplored the leniency of judges). In the wake of this report the government developed the law 'Sécurité et Liberté' (the word order is significant) which was widely condemned as repressive and as a threat to civil liberties by extending police powers in such matters as stop and search and detention. The intentions of the law are best summed up by a government 'circulaire' of 7 February 1981 which stated that the object of the law was to achieve, 'a rapid and thus exemplary repression'.(40)

Throughout the seventies, in response to government policy the police adopted a much higher profile in public order matters. Not only were they present in much greater numbers and with the full panoply of their equipment highly visible, but the interventions were also much more aggressive. This was the strategy laid down by Marcellin who believed in the effectiveness of numbers and the use of force, the intention being to intimidate those present and to discourage others.(41)   As part of this philosophy, the authorities throughout the seventies seemed prepared to give unlimited cover to police operations and actions which were frequently of a very dubious nature, such as the abusive surveillance of individuals, phone tapping (as in the celebrated case of the Canard Enchaîné), excessive stop and search operations (as in Poniatowski's vaunted 'coup de poing' operations: in one such operation covering 80 departments, 30,000 police and gendarmes were mobilised to carry out checks on 1 million individuals, 434,000 cars, 30,000 buildings).(42)   Even more serious was the cover up of 'bavures'. A typical incident occurred on 23 July 1975 at Charenton, when members of a 'Brigade de Recherches et d'Intervention' (B.R.I.) opened fire with machine guns killing a suspect who turned out to be a plain clothes policeman, and also injuring two postmen.   The investigation set up by Poniatowski came to no serious conclusions.   Such incidents, and the complacency with which they were treated, created a great deal of suspicion and hostility towards the police and indeed provoked considerable resentment from many members of the police who objected to being associated with actions they disowned and who were opposed to what they considered to be the government's exploitation of the police for political ends, as instruments of repression rather than agents of prevention.(43)   One consequence of the cover-ups was that confidence in police accountability was low and so too was belief in the integrity of the investigations against the police.   The section responsible for this, the Inspectorate General of the Police, 'the police of the police' fell into public disrepute, so much so that in proposals for police reforms Belorgey stated that the investigations against the police should be placed in the hands of the judiciary.

There is little doubt that the political continuity from 1958 to 1981 created an unhealthy relationship between the police and the political authorities.   It was felt that, especially in Paris, the police were agents of government policy.   Even more damaging, given the connections between the PJ and the Judiciary, were the contentions that the judicial process was often under pressure and at times unduly influenced by the close rapport between the police and the government, so that in matters judged to be politically sensitive, the judiciary could be relied on to act with discretion and in other instances, when exemplary sentences were required, they would be delivered.(44)

When Gaston Defferre became Minister of the Interior in 1981, he declared that 'under the preceding regime the police were especially concerned with actions against workers, strikers ... in certain areas of some of our cities, given the policies of the Right-wing government, the police were involved in racism, antisemitism and race riots ...'.(45)   There is no doubt that police reforms were, and continue to be, a matter of great concern for the Socialist government which has declared itself committed to developing a police of prevention rather than repression.   To this end it set-up the Belorgey commission and the Bonnemaison commission (46) and created a new Central Directorate for the training of members of the PN. In spite, or perhaps because of, their commitment to reforms, practical realities have meant that the government has still a long way to go before its intentions are realised.   The Belorgey report delivered to the Ministry of the Interior in January 1982, has not been implemented. As we have seen, in the first few months of its existence the Mauroy government gave police matters a high priority and sought to obtain the confidence of the police by heavy recruitment, re-equipment, meeting old grievances, better pay, better conditions, better training and career prospects; by promoting senior policemen into administrative posts and attaching serving policemen to the Office of the Minister of the Interior.   All of these measures were welcomed by the majority of the police but there was also resentment at what was thought to be the removal of an essential protection, the death penalty, and the policy of liberal sentences advocated by the Minister of Justice, as well as the restrictions imposed on stop and search and the proposed reorganisation of the service with the intention of achieving what Berlorgey called 'transparence', i.e. less secrecy and greater accountability.   Structural reforms were met not only with resentment but also by direct opposition.   The Socialist government has found that the police system and especially the senior police establishment, 'the state within the state', has not been amenable to structural changes. Faced with police opposition and economic difficulties resulting in mounting public order problems, the government has been unwilling to take on the police 'state'.   Its welcomed ameliorations of service conditions were more than offset by the displeasure caused when the government not only abolished the death penalty, but also abrogated the 'loi anti-casseurs', the 'loi Sécurité et Liberté' and terminated the 'Cour de Sûreté de l'Etat'. Such measures were seen as weakening the position of the police by denying them an essential deterrent and protection as well as gravely reducing the means available to the police in their combat against crime and subversion. The government was immediately condemned for being soft on crime by sections of the police and by the political opposition.(47)   Within the police this hostility reached fever pitch in the gross indiscipline of the Lyons (17 November 1981) and Paris (3 June 1983) police demonstrations against government policies on law and order. But such overt cases have not been the only incidents of police opposition.   There are indications that even in the handling of public order situations, strategies have been employed which are calculated to cause the government great political embarrassment. One such instance occured in Paris during the May-June 1983 student protests against proposed university reforms. There were violent clashes between the students and the public order forces which resulted in 251 injured (of whom 131 were police).   Reporting the incidents with pictures of the violence, <u>Paris Match</u> (10 June 1983) deplored what it called the excessive brutality of the police and the C.R.S., it claimed that there was a complete disregard for the procedural requirements of 'sommations' and alleged that motorcycle squads made up of PE instructors from the Paris police deliberately drove into the demonstrators. Such was the brutality that, according to the report, the forces of public order were 'disgusted by what they were being asked to do'.   The report concluded that, 'the authorities have lost control of their praetorian guards.' Similarly, Rémy Halbwax, head of the 'Syndicat Indépendant de la PN' (the right wing union which on 3 June 1983 spearheaded the police march on the Ministry of Justice) declared that, 'those in charge at the Ministry of the Interior are no longer senior administrators who know how to run things; they are ideologues ...'.   The inference that readers were meant to draw was obvious: violence broke out because there was a crisis of political leadership, the police have no confidence in the political hierarchy and the government is to be condemned for its 'laxisme', its inability to govern, unlike the previous regime ...   Whether or not the above incidents were deliberately orchestrated to damage the public's confidence in the government, there is no doubt that the events highlight the problematic nature of the relationship between the police and the present government, especially in matters of public order. Indeed relations got steadily worse and came to a head with the demonstrations of 3 June 1983, following which a government spokesman declared that the honeymoon was over and the authorities proceeded to discipline those held to be responsible by transferring, demoting or sacking them. One consequence was that the police got a new Director, the tenth in ten years.(48)

In spite of the hostility of certain services and sections of the police (especially the Police Prefecture in Paris) the Socialist government has embarked on a programme of reform since 1981 which is designed to change the image and the practice of the police from that of an essentially repressive force, secretive and lacking in accountability, to a preventive and 'dissuasive' force, closer to the people it serves. The government hopes to achieve this by a process of modernisation, laying great stress on quality recruitment, improved training and continuous training, not only to improve operational efficiency but also to create a more socially aware force; by modernising the 'commissariats' (police stations) making them less daunting places and also better and more efficient places for the police to work in; by extending judicial powers to the 'gardiens de la paix'. There are proposals for a reorganisation of the structures of the 'commissariats d'arrondissement', by breaking them down into smaller, local units, the reasoning being that this will have to take place if the policy of bringing the police closer to the people, if the strategy of 'îlotage' (a French version of 'community policing') is to be effective. This means that within the PN the emphasis is to be directed towards efforts to combat delinquency and the whole gamut of petty crimes which plague the life of the average citizen and generate the sense of 'insécurité'. If this is achieved it is felt that the PN will have become a 'service public' much more than a public order force. To this end the government has declared its intention of getting the C.R.S. more closely involved in general policing duties. However, despite Ministerial declarations to the contrary, the C.R.S. continue to be deployed as a front line public order force and companies are moved around the country as and when the authorities deem it to be necessary (in December 1981, 35 companies were on active service away from their home base). Certainly there is no indication that the C.R.S. are to be disbanded in the near future. The government's desire to see the C.R.S. as a 'normal' police force will not be easy to achieve; forty years of public order duties have produced a police corps whose training, structures and ethos are hardly in tune with the community policing the government envisages. Having been created as a repressive force and more often than not used as the aggressive arm of policing, it will take time for a change of image to come about, especially as the government continues to feel the need to use the C.R.S. to control demonstrations, manifestations, strikes, marches. The Gendarmes Mobiles have been maintained at the same high level and their equipment and operational use has not been modified. Indeed, the Socialist government have tended to favour the Gendarmerie, considering it to be a more reliable, less politicised and better disciplined police force. This in turn has created resentment and suspicion within the PN towards the government and the Gendarmerie, as well as intensifying the already damaging rivalry which exists between the two services.

The traditions, structures and practices of the French police make any reform a highly sensitive political issue, this is expecially the case when reforms touch on matters of public order, for in this context the accusation of 'laxisme' carries a strong political weight. Furthermore, in such a highly centralised system, it is difficult to reform one part without affecting the whole, and it is perhaps impossible to introduce an overall reform without provoking a conflict between government and police and within the police services, which might destabilize not only the government but also the state. There can be little doubt that in France 'The police is first and foremost a political fact.'(49)   As Maurice Grimaud writes, 'From time immemorial and whatever the regime, governments have been unable to resist the temptation to make the police an instrument of policy, rather than a public service. Even within our own liberal regime, the government manifests an irresistible need to withdraw police matters from the legitimate areas of control: Parliament, the Judiciary, and public opinion.'(50)   In the present political climate and given its difficult experiences with the police over the last three years (repeated changes in senior posts, from Director General to members of the Ministerial Cabinet and including serving officers, changes which all reveal a continuing search on the part of the government to find politically reliable men for key posts) the Socialist government will be very wary in dealing with its 'police d'état'.   Yet there have to be bold political decisions and measures beyond administrative adjustments and musical chairs at the top, if the government is to bring about its goal of creating 'a new police, made up of protectors of liberties rather than defenders of order'.(51)   This will mean moving away from a police tradition which has made

public order its first priority.   Fouché, the eponymous
French policeman, declared that 'The police have only one
task, to preserve the social order.'   But who decides
what the social order is or should be and how best to
preserve or change it?

FOOTNOTES

1. Acknowledgements: I wish to thank the following
persons and institutions for their help in preparing this
study: M. Soulier, Director of the Ecole Nationale Supérieure de la Police, at Saint-Cyr-au-Mont d'Or, members of
his staff and the librarian, Madame Dajoz, for welcoming
me and allowing me to use their resources.   M. Bernard
Wallon of 'La Ligue des Droits de l'Homme'.   M. Bertrand
Delanoë, Deputy, 'Conseiller de Paris' and Reporter for
the 'Commission de Lois' on the 'loi de Finances' with
regard to the police; to the staff at the Bibliothèque of
the Préfecture de Police.   To Madame Paula Jojima at the
French Embassy for arranging a 'Séjour d'Etudes' which enabled me to carry out work in France, and to Madame Annick
Stalla-Bourdillon at the 'Bureau d'Organisation et de Co-
ordination' in Paris for her help.
2. P.J. Stead, The Police of France, London, Macmillan, 1983, chapters 2 to 7 give a full historical coverage.
3. Ibid., p.158.
4. The administrative police function is concerned
with surveillance, the maintenance of public morality and
welfare and public order.   The police acts in its judicial
capacity, in its repressive function, in the investigation
of offences and the apprehending of the perpetrators.
When acting in a judicial function, the police are subject
to the state magistracy.   In practice, especially in
matters of public order, the administrative function
invariably becomes a judicial function.
5. As part of their decentralisation reforms the
present government have changed the title of Prefect to
'Commissaire de la République'.   Since their authority in
matters of public order is unchanged, I shall continue to
refer to them as Prefects, if only in the interest of bre-
vity.   An indication of the political importance of the
Prefects is given by the fact that some 60 Prefects were
replaced within months of the Socialist Party's electoral
victory in 1981.   For details of Prefectoral powers see:
B. Chapman, The Prefects and Provincial France, London,
George Allen and Unwin, 1955, especially pp. 177-81.   H.
Machin, The Prefect in French Public Administration, London, Croom-Helm, 1977, pp 114-119, which gives good ex-

amples of the Prefects in their public order role.

6. See Stead, op. cit. p. 30.

7. See B. Chapman, Police State, London, Pall Mall, 1970. A clear exposition of the subject in the series, 'Key Concepts in Political Science'.

8. For obvious reasons, after the war, though the structure was kept the title was changed to the pre-war name 'Sûreté nationale' which was retained until 1966.

9. There was also the 'Milice' a political police whose leader, Joseph Darnand, took the title of Secretary-General for the Maintenance of Order. See, J. Delpierre de Bayac, Histoire de la Milice, Paris, Fayard, 1969.

10. The fear at the end of the war was that there would be severe public disorder as scores were settled and the struggle for political supremacy was engaged. In the event the most severe troubles came in the wake of the political crisis of 1947, when there was a wave of strikes, often accompanied by violent demonstrations. The socialist Minister of the Interior, Jules Moch, sent in the C.R.S., the Gendarmerie, the police and elements of the army. The emergency was quelled. On M. Moch's staff at the time was a man, Raymond Marcellin, who, twenty years later became Minister of the Interior in the wake of the events of May 1968. He was rabidly anti-left, saw a danger to the security of the state in any opposition and he was convinced that May 1968 only occurred because of the lack of force on the part of the government. Consequently, he saw to it that there was no lack of force, he increased the police by some 8,000 and engaged in a systematic and brutal repression of anything thought likely to disrupt public order. As such he set the pattern of policing in the seventies.

11. A major such force was the S.A.C. (Service d'Action Civique) a Gaullist strongarm association which persisted after the end of the Algerian war and to which, overtly and covertly, many policemen of all ranks were affiliated, as revealed by the: Rapport de la Commission d'enquête sur les activités du S.A.C., Rapport No. 995, 1982; Part IV, 'Les activités de Police du S.A.C.'. As a result of this enquiry the socialist government banned the S.A.C.

12. For full details of the affair see: P. Williams, War, Plots and Scandals in Post-War France, Cambridge, University Press, 1970, pp. 78-125.

13. For a schematic description of the French Police see: 'Note d'Information' DOC/LUN/9/82, available from: The French Embassy, Service de Presse et d'Information, 58 Knightsbridge, London, SW1.

Much fuller treatment can be found in: J. Aubert and R. Petit, La Police en France: Service public, Paris, Berger-Levrault, 1981.

The Commission des Lois no 1169, op.cit. p.19 gives the following breakdown of recruits for 1982: 97 Commissaires; 615 Inspecteurs; 254 Enquêteurs; 123 Officiers et Commandants; 6284 Gardiens de la Paix.

In addition to increasing numbers, the government signalled its good intentions by granting the police certain longstanding demands, such as, better provisions for pensions; giving full pension rights to widows of officers killed in service; promising a review of pay, conditions and career structures, epecially for the uniformed branch ('la police en tenue'); a decree of 30.12.1981 created a Directorate for the Training of Police Personnel. It may seem paradoxical that a Party which, during its 23 years in opposition, frequently denounced the police as an instrument of repression, should now vastly increase police numbers and equipment. The government's aim is to refute the Opposition's charge of 'laxisme' (soft on law and order): to demonstrate their goodwill to the police and thus obtain their co-operation: to satisfy public opinion which over the past twenty years has been fed increasingly alarmist propaganda about the increase in crime and the threat to personal 'sécurité': to focus attention on preventive policing rather than coercive and repressive policing such as had been the practice in the previous twenty three years.

14. Commission des lois, op.cit. pp. 23 and 28. See: D. Langlois, Les Dossiers noirs de la police française, Paris, Seuil, 1973.

A. Harnon and J.-C. Marchand, P ... comme police, Paris, A. Moreau, 1983. Chapter 6, 'Bavures'.

15. The translations are by way of an indication of rank since it is not possible to give an exact equivalent due to the difference in systems and functions. For a full comparative list see: J.R.J. Jammes, Effective Policing: The French Gendarmerie, Bradford, M.C.B. Publications, 1982.

16. Members of the P.N. are 'fonctionnaires' (civil servants), as such they have the right to be unionised but they are forbidden to strike. Some 70% of policemen belong to a syndicat. (As army personnel the Gendarmes do not have union rights.) For the uniformed branch there are two major organisations, the 'Fédération autonome des syndicats de police' (FASP) which is the largest and whose leadership is close to the socialist government; and the 'Union des syndicats catégoriels de police' (USCP) which is closer to the opposition. There is a small (2.8% of

police) but extremely militant right-wing union the 'Fédé-ration professionnelle et indépendante de la police' (FPIP) which is especially active in the Paris police and which led the massive police demonstrations in Lyons on 7 November 1981 and in Paris on 3 June 1983. The 'inspec-teurs' and 'commissaires' have their own autonomous asso-ciations, which are extremely active in maintaining hier-archical authority and privileges. There has been a long history of police demonstrations over the last 26 years: 13 March 1958: 19 December 1961: 9 September 1971: October 1976: 20 January 1979: 7 November 1981: 3 June 1983.

17. There is little doubt that though in theory 'in-tegrated' in the P.N., the Prefecture of Police in Paris, popularly known as 'la Grande Maison', continues to be a source of friction between government and police. The demonstration of 3 June 1983 was a serious breach of dis-cipline, a political act of open defiance against the authority of the government. Above all it was a grave breach of public order! Several thousand policemen march-ed on the offices of the Minister of Justice, M. Badinter, shouting such slogans as, 'Tueur de flics' (the killing of two officers was the pretext for the protest march against the abolition of the death penalty) and 'Badinter, étrang-er, hors de France' (the Minister is Jewish). As they stood in front of the ministry, Place Vendome, the police-men were joined by the leader of the extreme right-wing party, Le Front National, Jean-Marie le Pen. Other police forces did not intervene. Following the demonstra-tion a number of senior administrators, officers and men were dismissed, suspended or demoted. Since then rela-tions with the government have been strained, to say the least.

18. M. Franceschi, an academic by training, had been in charge of Mitterrand's personal security during the presidential campaigns of 1974 and 1981.

19. Another reason may have been to relieve the load of the Minister of the Interior, M. Defferre who also had the contentious issue of 'decentralisation' on his plate. However, M. Defferre had kept a very close contact with police matters. This is perhaps best illustrated by his success in maintaining budget allocations and his success in retaining the police's power of systematic 'contrôles d'identités' (identity checks) which had been suspended when the government abrogated the law 'Sécurité et Liber-té'. This concession had led to a very bitter conflict between M. Defferre and M. Badinter.

20. For the full range of Directorates see: J. Aubert and R. Petit, op.cit. pp. 110-181.

21. The practice of creating specialised groups spread throughout the police force from local to national level. There was a mixture of operational logic and public relations in these developments. The theory was that specialised units would be more efficient in combatting their particular sector of crime and this was often true with regard to major and organised criminality. But at local level it often meant a response to some specific public disquiet which it was thought could be pacified by the creation of a special squad. For example, crimes in the métro in Paris led to the not very effective creation of special patrol groups. Generally the multiplication of special squads, as many as 16 in some areas, often weakened the effectiveness of the police by creating confusion and conflicts between the many groups; it encouraged rivalries and the need to justify their existence by results led to abuses and 'bavures'. In July 1982, M. Defferre issued a directive to disband the specialised units, except for motorcycle and bicycle units but it seems that though the names may have gone the practice continues, especially in Paris.

22. J.-J. Gleizal, La Police nationale, Grenoble, P.U., 1974, p.324. (my translation).

23. There are many who argue that the P.J. should be removed from the P.N. and the Ministry of the Interior and placed under the authority of the Ministry of Justice. The argument being that this would remove the present dualism which often involves the judiciary in dubious collusion with the police. For a brief, clear discussion of this issue see: J. Hayward, Governing France: The One and Indivisible Republic, Weidenfeld and Nicolson, London, 1983, Chapter 5.

24. The Socialist government has put forward proposals to abolish the much criticised 'garde à vue' and bring in a form of 'habeas corpus'.

25. The Commission 'Informatique et libertés' which aims to safeguard the possible abuses of computerised data banks, wished to place a restriction on the information gathered by the R.G. for the recently (1982) opened special file on terrorism. In November 1982 the Commission agreed to limit the file to 600,000 names and proposed that: 'It would be contrary to the principle of freedom of conscience to seek out information about the political, philosophical or religious opinions of individuals who were being investigated'. After much behind the scenes lobbying the wording was amended, 'to seek out' ('rechercher') was replaced by 'to instance' ('faire état'). The 'nuance' was crucial since it officially allowed the R.G. to collect such information provided they did not record

it for the Prefect ...

26. The D.S.T. has a military counterpart (under the control of the Minister of Defence but usually headed by a civilian), the Service de Documentation Extérieure et de Contre-Espionnage (S.D.E.C.E.) now renamed but otherwise unchanged, the Direction Générale de la Sécurité Extérieure (D.G.S.E.). These intelligence services are supposed to collaborate but there is considerable rivalry. See: N. Fournier and E. Legrand, Dossier E ... comme Espionnage, Paris, A. Moreau.

27. Some companies also have mountain, sea rescue sections attached to them. At holiday times the C.R.S. patrol roads and beaches. They also often supplement the PAF at airports. The Socialist government has expressed its desire to see the C.R.S. integrated with the uniformed branch of the P.N. i.e. become 'normal' policemen. For the moment the intention has not gone beyond the 'desire' stage.

28. For a full history and a detailed study of the G.N. see: Jammes op.cit. For a more polemical view see: H. Lafont and P. Meyer: Le Nouvel ordre gendarmique, Paris, Seuil.

29. There are also specialised branches, the best known being the ceremonial 'Garde Républicaine' (2000 men) based in Paris. Others include the 'Gendarmerie maritime': 'Gendarmerie des Transports Aériens'. (civilian airports): 'Gendarmerie de l'Air' (military air bases).

30. The G.N. and the C.R.S. participate with the Army in the programme of the 'Défense opérationelle du territoire', co-ordinated by the Prefects of the defence zones. The aim of D.O.T. is to establish contingency plans and strategies to meet any breakdown of public order or threat to the state which may arise from nuclear war or subversion. The government has thus an added reserve to meet national contingencies.

31. The G.I.G.N. had a somewhat more glorious past through its involvement in spectacular actions, over 200 in France and overseas, such as the freeing of 31 French children held as hostages in Djibouti and their intervention to help the Saudi authorities end the occupation of the Great Mosque in Mecca.

32. The most celebrated, or infamous, proven case of such 'provocateurs' occurred during the demonstration of steel workers from Lorraine on 23 March 1979. Violence broke out when the marchers reached the Place de l'Opéra. One hundred and twenty-one shops and cafés had their windows smashed, some shops were looted, a variety of objects were hurled at the police. It emerged from subsequent investigations that those responsible for the initial

violence were members of the SAC who had infiltrated the march. Clear evidence of this was the fact that the march-stewards seized one of the people hurling nuts and bolts at the police, and he turned out to be a police officer. See: C. Picant, Le 23 mars 1979, Paris, Jean Picolles, 1981.

33. The 'Casseurs' offence was a 'délit' rather than a 'crime'. The distinction is important because it meant the trial would not go before a jury. It would be up to judges, state appointees, to pass sentence. They might be thought to be more susceptible to the government's expressed desire to see severe sentences handed down.

34. Before a demonstration the authorities (usually the Prefect) may order 'arrestations préventives', if the security of the state is thought to be threatened by the persons concerned.

35. In J.J. Gleizal op.cit. p. 140.

36. Contrary to what is popularly believed, French citizens do not have to carry their identity papers at all times.

37. 15 November 1969, 3,000 people who had taken part in a demonstration against the war in Vietman, were rounded up by the public order forces and taken to outlying detention centres for 'contrôles d'identité'. They were released in the early hours of the morning with no public transport available. 11,500 people took part in the 'manifestation'; M. Marcellin the Minister of the Interior sent in 12,000 police.

38. The 'autonomes' should not be confused with the 'autonomistes' a term which refers to members of separatist movements claiming for e.g. Breton or Corsican independence. The 'autonomes' claimed to be unattached to any political group. Their strategy was to cause maximum disruption and to provoke a violent riposte from the forces of order, to achieve this they would break the windows of expensive shops or restaurants, set fire or smash cars, hence the term 'casseurs' (breakers).

39. Réponses à la violence, Paris, La Documentation Française, 1977. 2 vols.

40. J.R. Frears, France in the Giscard Presidency, London, George Allen & Unwin, 1981. Chapter 11 'Civil Liberties' pp. 175-197.

41. James Sarrazin, La Police en miettes: le système Marcellin, Paris, Calman-Lévy, 1974. For Marcellin's own views see his: L'Ordre public et les groupes révolutionnaires, Paris, Plon, 1969; and, L'Importune vérité, Paris, Plon, 1978.

42. _Revue de la Police Nationale,_ No. 95, October 1974, p. 7.

43. Gilles Hauser et Bernard Masingue, _Etude auprès des personnels de la police,_ Paris Editions Interface, 1982.

44. Denis Langlois, _Les Dossiers noirs de la justice française,_ Seuil, 1975. Philippe Madelin et Jean-Pierre Michel, _Dossier J... comme Justice,_ Paris, Moreau.

45. In an interview on Radio Monte-Carlo, 28 November 1981.

46. Jean-Michel Belorgey, Socialist Deputy for the Allier, was president of a commission set up by the Minister of the Interior to report on proposals for police reforms. 22 May 1982, the Prime Minister, Pierre Mauroy, set up a 'Commission of Mayors to Inquire into Insecurity', to be presided over by Gilbert Bonnemaison, Deputy-Mayor of Epinay-sur-Seine. The report was handed in on 17 December 1982. Out of the 64 proposals put forward by Bonnemaison as means of reducing delinquency, 12 were rejected outright, 28 were sent for further study, 21 were accepted with a view to implementation, though no specific date was given.

47. M. Chirac, leader of the majority party in the opposition, the R.P.R. (Rassemblement Pour la République) and Mayor of Paris, has played heavily on the 'sécurité' issue, exploiting law and order incidents as evidence of the government's inability to govern. He has welcomed the association 'Légitime Défense' headed by François Romério an ex-president of the Cour de Sûreté de l'Etat. One of M. Chirac's right-hand men at the Hôtel de Ville, is Robert Pandraud who was head of the PN from 1975-78; while at the headquarters of the R.P.R., in the rue de Lille, several senior ex-policemen are to be found, including Jacques Chartron, head of the DST in 1976. c.f. _Les Nouvelles,_ 14-20 September, 1983, pp. 70-77.

48. Following the resignation of M. Mauroy in July 1984 and the formation of a new government led by Laurent Fabius, it may be that there will soon be a twelfth head of the police when the new Minister of the Interior, M. Pierre Joxe, has settled into his post. It is noticeable that there is no mention of a new Secretary of State in Charge of Public Security; the first and perhaps last holder of the title, M. Franceschi, having returned to his post of Minister of State with Responsibility for the Aged and the Retired.

49. Yves Lemoine et Jean-Pierre Mignard, 'Le corps intouchable', in _Le Monde_ 27 June 1983.

50. Maurice Grimaud was Prefect of Police in Paris in 1968. In 1981 he was recruited by Gaston Defferre to be

his adviser on police matters (he has since been replaced). c.f. M. Grimaud's book: La Police malade du pouvoir, Paris, Seuil, 1980.

51. Gerard Monate, Le Matin, 5 January 1982.

Further Reading

J. Aubert and R. Petit, La Police en France: Service public, Paris, Berger-Levault, 1981.

Casamayor, La Police, Paris, Gallimard, 1973.

P. Cerny, 'France: Non-Terrorism and Repressive Tolerance', in J. Lodge (ed.), Terrorism: A Challenge to the State, Oxford, Martin Robertson, 1981, pp. 91-118.

P. Demonque: Les Policiers, Paris, Maspéro, 1983.

J.-J. Gleizal, La Police nationale, Grenoble, Presses Universitaire de Grenoble, 1974.

M. Grimaud, La Police malade du pouvoir, Paris, Seuil.

A. Harmon and J.-C. Marchand, P...comme Police, Paris, Alain Moreau, 1983.

J. Hayward, Governing France: The One and Indivisible Republic, London, Weidenfeld and Nicolson, 1983.

J.R.J. Jammes, Effective Policing, The French Gendarmerie, Bradford, MCB Publications. 1982.

M. Le Clère, Histoire de la Police, Paris, P.U.F., 'Que Sais-je?' No.257, 1973.

L. Mandeville, J.-L. Loubet del Bayle, A. Picard, 'Les forces de maintien de l'ordre en France', Défence Nationale, July, 1977, pp. 59-76.

R. Le Texier, Les C.R.S., Paris, Lavauzelle, 1981.

C. Monate, Flic ou gardien de la paix?, Paris, Seuil, 1980.

P.J. Stead, The Police of France, London, Macmillan, 1983.

Chapter 6

POLICE AND PUBLIC ORDER IN THE FEDERAL REPUBLIC OF GERMANY

Jurgen Thomaneck

The parameters

West Germany is similar in size and population to the UK, approximately 96,000 sq. miles (250,000 sq. km), and with a population of about 60 million. There are no sizeable indigenous minorities, but foreign workers (Gastarbeiter) make up a sizeable proportion of the population, especial- ly in some of the conurbations. These 4.6 million for- eign workers come- very often with their families - from predominantly southern rural parts of Europe and Asia, such as Turkey, Yugoslavia, Spain, Portugal, Greece, and Italy. West Germany is a federal state consisting of ten lands (Länder): Schleswig-Holstein, Hamburg, Bremen, Lower Saxony, Northrhine-Westphalia, Hesse, Rhineland-Palatin- ate, Saarland, Baden-Wurttemberg, Bavaria. The West Germans like to consider West Berlin as an eleventh land, but politically speaking it has a separate, special stat- us, and is still occupied by the three Western Allies - Great Britain, the United States, and France. Each land has its own parliament and government headed by a Minister President, and the police is one of the domains of the land ministers of the interior. Although it would be an exaggeration to speak of eleven different police systems, it is nevertheless true to say that a certain degree of divergency exists. Any account of the West German police must therefore operate with this parameter of federalism. The Federal Republic of Germany was created in the immediate post-war years and formally came into existence in 1949. It is yet another state in the course of German history whose creation was neither determined by ethnic criteria nor the notion of a nation state nor "natural" geographical boundaries. The Federal Republic of Germany resulted from the global political conditions prevailing at the time. It was created out of the three western zones of occupation - the American, the British and the

French.(1) Even its federal constituent parts are arbitrary and artificial in the sense that most of them had no
historical and political tradition and were entirely new
creations.   Only Bavaria, Hamburg and Bremen have a long
constitutionally autonomous history.   After the dissolu-
tion of the Land Prussia in 1946, Prussia's western provinces became separate Länder such as Schleswig-Holstein,
or parts of newly-formed Länder.   For example, Northrhine-Westphalia is the result of a merger between the
former Prussian Rhine province and the province of West-
phalia.   Baden-Wurttemberg came into being on the strength of a plebiscite in 1952.   The Saar Territory (under
French Rule) became part of the Federal Republic in 1957.
Such an artificial creation of a new state both as an entity and in respect of its constituent parts gives rise to
the question of the legitimacy of such a state.   Initially, this problem was tackled by the propagation of the so-
called continuity theory, which saw the Federal Republic
as the constitutional successor to pre-1945 Germany(2),
and the propagation of the Alleinvertretungsanspruch.
The Federal Republic claimed the right to speak and act in
the name of the whole of Germany.   Germany was defined as
the Germany which existed in 1937 (before the Austrian
Anschluss).   Yet, with the advent of Brandt's Ostpolitik
the legitimacy problem could no longer be solved along
those lines, since this Ostpolitik resulted in the de
facto recognition of the German Democratic Republic and
the new borders of 1945.(3)   Legitimacy problems of a
state always have a direct effect on its forces of law and
order.
     The economically and politically extraordinarily suc-
cessful West German phoenix rose out of the ashes of the
Nazi holocaust.   Hitler's Germany itself had been the
direct result of the failure of Germany's first venture
into western parliamentary democracy.   This heritage of a
failed democracy with its ensuing reign of ideological and
genocidal terror, brought about, in 1949, a very delicate-
ly balanced lobby and party democracy based to some considerable extent on the distrust of the demo in democracy.(4)   By the mid-sixties a new generation of West
Germans had grown up who had not themselves experienced
pre-1945 Germany.   This new generation began to question
the very essence of West Germany's democratic system.
The appearance of drop-outs (Gammler), critical writers
whom Chancellor Erhard called pipsqueaks (Pinscher), the
turmoil of the 1968 student rebellion, urban terrorism,
and more recently the large-scale ecological movement are
the symptoms of a steady crisis of West German democracy.
The extra-parliamentary opposition (APO) of the late

sixties and early seventies and the more recent "green movement" are attempts to realize democracy beyond the well-defined lobby and party democracy establishment. This "democracy crisis" has resulted directly in a "police crisis".

The peril of internal de-stabilisation is compounded by the potential danger of external attempts at de-stabilisation. The Federal Republic is a front-line state. It shares a border with the German Democratic Republic, the eastern front-line state. The potential of mutual de-stabilisation is enhanced infinitely by the existence of a common language, relatives etc. Clearly, such a front-line bulwark situation will be reflected in the "maintenance of public security and order".

Although the Federal Republic of Germany is a new creation both constitutionally and as a state, this does not however mean that 1945 or 1949 constituted absolute zero positions. Despite the fact that before 1949 all major parties agreed that Germany's socio-economic structure had to be changed away from monopoly capitalism to a planned economy with a considerable degree of nationalisation (cf. Article 15 Basic Law), the socio-economic structures eventually remained unchanged. This also applies to the people within these structures. Little change of personnel took place for example in the judiciary, the civil service, and the police. During the Third Reich the police had become an integral and integrated part of the SS terror and surveillance mechanism. In fact, at the 1938 Greater German Party Congress the police marched in the ranks of the SS. Police power had become SS rule and enjoyed unlimited discretionary powers. It could take 'preventive' action against persons who were at most suspected of possible opposition or infraction.(5) The police had become highly compromised between 1933 and 1945.(6) The western allies were most certainly cognizant of this state of affairs, and in line with the denazification remit of Potsdam the police was to be purged. On 16th October 1945 the Control Commission's Standing Committee on Denazification reported to London: "Denazification has been carried out particularly thoroughly in the legal and education branches of the administration ... (and) particularly good progress has been made in purging the police." Tom Bower calls this "an outright lie". The police was teeming with former SS men. As evidence Bower cites the situation in Hanover, Dusseldorf, Giessen, Kiel, Hamburg, Cologne, and Munich.(7) This situation was to give rise to ever-increasing angry questions in the years to come. Not only has the police force been under criticism for personnel continuity with the resultant attacks on its "fascist mentality" and "Gestapo methods", but, because of the very existence of SS and police rule in Hitler Germany, any aspect of police behaviour will always be measured against the yardstick of a Nazi past. This fact alone means that the West German police and their new generation of policemen is faced with a particularly difficult inheritance.

History

Constitutionally, 1945 was a zero position which was only superseded with the acceptance of the Basic Law by the West Germans in 1949. At the same time, however, the old Criminal Code and the Administrative Law which included the Police Law had not yet been abolished and then substituted. These had survived since the latter part of the 18th and 19th centuries. New police laws had to be formulated to take account of the new constitutional situation. Police laws in particular always reflect the changing functions and role of the police in a changing concept of the state and the state's relationship with the citizens. Concomitantly, the means by which law is enforced has always been inseparable from the existing societal structure, and furthermore the police are not merely a means for the state to maintain order and enforce norms, but they are equally important as one of the ways in which the state attempts to legitimize itself. To put it more bluntly: any police force is as good or as bad as the government, or vice versa. Although it must be said that to this very day one cannot talk of the historical development of "the German police", because there has never been a unified policing system in German history (with the one exception of the Third Reich), certain major trends can nevertheless be observed. Originally, until the late middle ages, the concept "police" (from the Latin politia = administration, government) referred to the whole governmental administration. It described a state of affairs rather than a function. "Police" existed where citizens and subjects conducted themselves and their affairs in an orderly, civilized, and respectable manner. "Police" was order. It was the duty of all subjects to achieve what was termed "good police". The year 1530 saw the first legal attempt to define the areas of police duties binding on the whole of the Holy Roman Empire of the German Nation. Police rules for the Empire and for the individual states covered regulations concerning issues of morality, clothing, the conduct of business, weights and measures, etc. Since the 17th century the administration of the armed forces, finance and justice began to be excluded from the remit of the "police".

It was with the advent of absolutism, at the beginning of the 18th century, largely due to French influence, that the concept of the police became a functional one. The influential philosopher of German absolutism, Christian Wolff (1679-1754), argued that the limited power of reasoning prevents the ordinary subject from realizing natural law and his own happiness. The absolute ruler therefore has the absolute power of legislature, executive, and judiciary. It is the task of the state's administration to provide for public welfare including the welfare and happiness of the individual citizen. The execution of the absolute ruler's power is delegated to the police which assume an instrumental function. The power of the police represents the unconfined power of the ruler. The police are active without legal confinement, their activity is based on the use of absolute power and princely rules and regulations. The state of the subject is characterised by a lack of rights. The age of absolutism gave birth to the concept of the police state. The latter part of the 18th century saw a modification of this situation. With the advent of "enlightened absolutism" embodied in the figures of Emperor Joseph II and King Friedrich II (the Great) of Prussia, a new concept of the police emerged, based on the individualistic interpretation of natural law propagated by philosophers of the enlightenment. The subject's lack of rights vis-à-vis the omnipotence of the absolute ruler was not acceptable to these philosophers. They argued that everybody had to subject themselves to the legislative power of the state, which included the legal curtailment of the rights of the individual. Yet the executive power must not interfere with the individual's freedom of action and right of ownership on the basis of legally unconfined discretionary decisions. A clear-cut difference must be made between the state's positive activity concerning the provision of public and private welfare, and a negative activity with the purpose of averting danger both to the commonwealth as a whole and the individual. For the purposes of preemptive policing the police were to retain their absolute powers, yet for the purpose of ensuring public and private welfare the police can only become active if a law exists which explicitly allows interference with the individual's rights. The Göttingen constitutional lawyer Johann Stephan Pütter (1725-1807) defines the function of the police along these lines: "politiae est cura avertendi mala futura; promovendae salutis cura non est propie politiae" (Institutionis iuris publici Germanici 1770, Para. 331).(8) (The task of the police is to avert dan-

ger; to promote welfare is not its task.) These considerations were reflected in one of Prussia's great legal
achievements, the Allgemeines Landrecht für die preus-
sischen Staaten (abbr. ALR), which was the first modern
legal code in German. It had been initiated on Friedrich
II's orders, but appeared only after his death in 1794.
This legal code made the law independent of the ruler and
placed the ruler himself under the law in the same way as
the subject. This uniform code of law proved a strong
cementing factor in Prussian state consciousness.(9)
Para. 10 II 17 ALR defines the function of the police:
"The task of the police is to take the necessary measures
for the maintenance of public peace, security, and order
for averting impending dangers to the public on the whole
or to its individual members."

The 19th century, in the wake of the great Napoleonic
scare and the revolutionary turmoil of the thirties and
late forties, saw a resurrection of absolutist attitudes
and the worst kind of a police-state, although the picture
of the whole of Germany with its large number of individual states was rather diverse in detail. Generally speaking it can be said that during the period of Restoration
(1815-1848) the police did their utmost to implement the
principle that fear and acquiescence were the citizen's
first duty. The police were instrumental in the cementing of despotic rule. The police once more supervised
matters of religion, morality, clothing, the shape of
headwear, hairstyle, the style of beards, smoking in
public, etc. Even after 1850, with the introduction of a
constitutional monarchy in Prussia and a new police law,
matters did not change in practice. Prussia and other
states remained authoritarian police states - "peace being
the first duty of the citizen". This maxim has its origin in the 19th century. After the Prussian armies had
been defeated by Napoleon in 1806 (battle of Jena), the
then governor and police president of Berlin, von der
Schulenburg, issued a declaration calling for "Jetzt ist
Ruhe die erste Bürgerpflicht" (Now peace is the citizen's
first duty), which has retained its proverbial character
ever since and can be heard to this very day in Germany.
Although the picture in the 19th century was a rather
bleak one for civil liberties, some long-lasting reforms
were nevertheless introduced. The 1808 reforms in
Prussia defined the police authority (the government, and
administratively, the Minister of the Interior) and introduced a clearer structure of the police apparatus. But
the most important event in terms of civil liberties was
the resurrection of Para. 10 II 17 (ALR) by the Prussian
Administrative High Court in 1882. The High Court de-

fined the function of the police as the maintenance of public order. The concepts of security and peace are only secondary to public order and originate from it. Furthermore, the Court emphasized that the police can only act pre-emptively in averting a danger if that danger does in fact exist. In the opinion of the court, matters of welfare, morals and morality, religion, commerce, and aesthetics, are not police matters. This definition of the function of the police has remained the guiding principle in Germany (after 1945 West Germany) to this day. It was reflected during the Weimar Republic in the 1931 Preussisches Polizeiverwaltungsgesetz (Prussian Police Administrative Law) which defined the police authority (the State), the supervisory authorities, a general (or blanket) clause for all police action, the subject of police action, etc. President Hindenburg after his appointment of Hitler as Chancellor of Germany, changed all this with his decree of 28th February 1933, suspending practically all civil and political liberties. This once more turned the police into a mere instrument of despotic power. Germany became an SS police state.

Before 1933, the SS had inter alia functioned as the internal police organisation within the National Socialist Party. Indeed, the SS had created its own inner-party intelligence service under Heydrich in 1931, the Security Service of the Reichsführer SS, abbreviated as SD. When the Nazis came to power they did in fact inherit an existing central political police. After abortive attempts immediately after World War I to abolish the political police there eventually emerged the "Centrale Staatspolizei" of the Weimar Republic which was historically the first German central police department. This department was taken over by the Nazis and, mainly due to Göring's efforts, turned into the Gestapo. With the abolition of the individual lands (Länder) in 1934 the whole of the hitherto decentralized German police came under the nominal control of the Minister of the Interior, Frick. De facto, however, it was personally responsible to Hitler's Fouché, Heinrich Himmler, who as Reichsführer SS and Chief of Police acquired cabinet rank. It was Himmler's efforts which resulted in the total fusion of the SS and the police. Himmler in fact commanded the SS Ordinance Troops (Verfügungstruppen), the SD, the Gestapo, the SS Death Head battalions (the concentration camp guards), the Criminal Police (the German CID), the Order Police, the Border Security Service, the Fire Brigades, and the general SS. In this process of absorption the Criminal Police and the Order Police became entirely militarized. At the same time Himmler placed himself and the police above and beyond the law. He accounted for this process in his address to the German Law Academy in 1936 when he pointed out that in the reorganisation of the police "we National Socialists ... went to work not without right (Recht) which we carried within us, yet, however, without laws". The police acted not on the basis of laws but on the basis of directives from Hitler, Himmler, and other ministers. The constitutional position of the police before 1933 had been left behind. This absorption into the SS and the simultaneous delegalisation of the police resulted ultimately in the use of the Order Police in the occupied territories for the maintenance of safety and security, but also for combat purposes in the guerilla warfare, and most compromisingly, for the genocidal policies of the Nazis. The gradual depletion of the Criminal and Order Police inside Germany due to military expansion meant that the SA and the Hitler Youth with its patrols took over routine police duties such as traffic control or patrolling young people, acting like a special constabulary. The inheritance of the integration of the police into the SS and the atrocities committed by the SS and the police both inside and outside the Reich have contributed largely to the police's own legitimacy and identity crisis since 1945, compounded by personnel continuity and public antipathy after 1968 in particular.

Developments since 1945

Within the remit of the Potsdam agreement of 1945 it was incumbent upon the victorious allies to decentralize, democratize, and demilitarise areas of public life in their respective zones of occupation, such as education, the judiciary, and also the police. The allies embarked on different paths of operational implementation of this remit and thereby generated different structures and police concepts within their zones. These differing approaches have left their mark to this very day and can be detected by comparing the police in North Germany, South Germany, and South-West Germany, since the individual Länder of the Federal Republic continued their reorganisation on the basis of the respective allied measures. In the British Zone the police forces were organised under central government control as opposed to local control. Their functions were limited to the maintenance of law and order on the streets and detection of crime, they were defined as "the standing army for the suppression of crime and the apprehension of offenders". The police's administrative functions were abolished, including responsibilities and tasks such as the registration of all residents, environ-

mental health, building permits and regulations, road
supervision, and other civil matters. Although the
Americans retained central police control as an organisational principle in their zone of occupation, this applied
only to communities with less than 5000 inhabitants.
Communities in excess of this figure had their locally
controlled communal police. In the French Zone the
police's administrative functions were retained, resulting
in a "general system of police".(10) Also retained was
central police control as the organisational principle,
but certain police functions in small communities were
given to the mayors who thus acted along similar lines to
the maire in France. These differences have been largely
assimilated by now, although each Land still has its own
police law despite a recent attempt to implement a common
police law nationwide. The evidence for the differing
allied approaches displays itself most clearly on the
issue of a "general system of police" which does not separate police and other agencies of the administration as in
Baden-Württemberg, the Rhineland Palatinate, and the Saarland. Certain basic German police traditions, however,
were not affected by allied influence, such as the concept
that the state is the agent of prosecution, whereas the
police is the agent of detection. This is more akin to
the Scottish tradition than the English, where the police
can both investigate and prosecute.(11) As early as 1945,
the German police were issued with weapons again, resulting in the pistol carrying policeman so unfamiliar to the
British visitor. Also the police were given, very soon
after the war, the status of Beamte, i.e., German civil
service status with all its benefits. Until 1949, the
German police in the various Länder of the occupying zones
worked in relatively close cooperation with the military
police of the Allied troops, technically in an auxiliary
and subordinate capacity but in practice increasingly independently. In these years until the foundation of the
two German states in 1949, the German police and the military police had to face two major problems arising from
the socio-economic circumstances of the time, the mushrooming black market situation, and the roaming gangs of
criminals, youngsters, and displaced people. The foundation of the Federal Republic of Germany on the territory
of the French, British and American zones of occupation
provided the political and constitutional framework for a
social, economic, political, and ideological stabilisation
process which had already seen the end of the Allied dis-
mantling programme in the western zones, the influx of
American monies on the basis of the Marshall Aid Plan, and
the currency reform. This process was to culminate in

the Paris Treaties, the admission to Nato and the EEC, and the advent of the West German economic miracle in the fifties. The fifties were experienced by the West Germans as a period of comparative calm and peace, rarely disturbed internally, hardly disturbed externally. In fact, the involvement of her new western allies in Korea and Vietnam and her own non-involvement contributed significantly to the growth of the economic miracle. Events nearer home, such as the Berlin rebellion of 1953, and the Hungarian uprising of 1956, confirmed the position of the existing ideology in West Germany with its propagation of a capitalist free market economy, a virulent anti-communism, and the institutional structure of a western parliamentary democracy. Indeed, the majority of West Germans saw themselves as living in a heile Welt (a world of harmony), and the most popular electioneering slogan of the Adenauer era was that of his own party, the ruling CDU/CSU: Keine Experimente (no experiments). In this context the fifties signified for the police and the maintenance of public order almost a golden age, as one police historian has put it.(12)

The sixties by stark contrast heralded the beginning of a new era in the West German polity. A new generation of Germans left school to enter universities, or other tertiary educational institutions. This generation did not carry the ballast of the Nazi past and a conscience fraught with guilt, but rather had fallen victim to the propaganda of the fifties and early sixties which had inculcated in their minds Leibnitzian notions as to the state of the world and West German democracy in particular. The Western World was the best of all possible worlds, and West German democracy was the best of all possible democracies. As Leibniz had pleased the queen of Prussia in his day, so he was popular with the civics teachers in Germany in the fifties and sixties. When these young people left their schools, they encountered a university and apprenticeship system little different from that of the 19th century, untinged by anything democratic, at best evincing forms of authoritarian paternalism. These young people also became witnesses to the formation of the "Grand Coalition" which virtually resulted in a parliament without an opposition. West Germany showed itself to be a party and lobby democracy. Even the end of the CDU or Adenauer era and the advent of the SPD or Brandt era, although promising at first, did not realize the dreams and aspirations of this generation of Germans. They saw themselves forced to think in terms of extra-parliamentary opposition. In fact, this extra-parliamentary opposition took concrete shape in the formation of

a loose organisation with the actual name Ausserparla-
mentarische Opposition (APO) (Extra-parliamentary Opposition). A further specifically German dimension was added
to this rebellion of students, apprentices, and intellectuals by the rather belated trials of Nazi criminals during the sixties, which divulged the widespread involvement
of the older generation in the Nazi genocidal terror.
This applied equally to individuals and also to well-
respected industrial firms such as I.G. Farben (known today as BASF) and Hoechst. Horror and shock were experienced because of the manner in which these trials were
conducted and of the light sentences passed and the number
of acquittals. The best known example of these trials
during the sixties was the Auschwitz trial, which was
dramatized in the form of a documentary play by Peter
Weiss (Die Ermittlung, 1965). The American war in Vietnam and dictatorial terror regimes such as the Shah of
Iran's were experienced with the same horror and shock.
When the Shah of Iran was invited to the Federal Republic
for an official state visit, the bloody demonstrations
against the Shah's visit marked the true beginning of the
West German student rebellion of 1968. It also marked a
new era for the police and public order in West Germany.
From now onwards the police were in the public limelight
on an almost daily basis through the media coverage of
battles between demonstrators and police. This reached
its horrific climax with the killing of a student demonstrator, Benno Ohnesorg, by a West Berlin policeman.

But the sixties marked a new era for the police and
public order for a further reason. With the sixties the
West German economic miracle reached its peak despite a
minor slump in the late sixties. This era brought with
it the usual crime statistics commonly associated with
affluence. Whereas in 1963 1.6 million crimes were committed, this number rose to 2.4 million in 1972, by which
time nine people were murdered or badly injured per day, a
robbery or blackmail occurred every 39 minutes, a burglary
every nine minutes, and a thief was active every twenty
seconds. This increase in crime has continued right
through the seventies and into the eighties. Furthermore, although the student rebels admitted failure in
their attempt to democratize West Germany in the early
seventies, which manifested itself in the self-disbandment
of the student organisation, the Sozialistischer Deutscher
Studentenbund (SDS) and the APO, the legitimacy crisis of
West Germany as a democracy and as a state has continued.
It manifests itself most drastically through urban terrorism, anti-nuclear demonstrations on a vast scale, demonstrations for environmental causes, the occupation of

properties by squatters, and the emergence of the Green Movement as a strong political protest force. This meant that the police and questions of public order have remained in the public limelight to date, through regular and persistent media coverage. This public exposure and criticism has in itself resulted in a police identity crisis, both inside and outside the institution.

Organization

In terms of organization, the development of the West German police since 1945 has seen what is termed a de-policing process (Entpolizeilichung). It is no longer true to say that an administrative police (Verwaltungs-polizei) is still characteristic of West Germany, i.e. one which performs administrative functions for the mainten-ance of public order such as the issuing of passports and identity cards or the enforcing of regulations concerning prices, trade, commerce, building permits, hunting, fish-ing, health and veterinary matters, roads and other civil matters. These duties have in most Länder been given to civil departments in the localities and are no longer as-sociated with the concept of police, nor is the term ad-ministrative police in use any longer. On the other hand, it is also the case that with the exception of Bavaria and Northrhine-Westphalia, the particular munici-pal departments execute their special measures for the maintenance of public order on the basis of the same legal code as the police themselves. In that sense it could and has indeed been argued that "depolicing" has not really taken place since. In terms of the material content of the activity involved, there has been no more than a change in name of the agencies involved in respect of the administrative police.(13)

However that may be, today's police are held to be the executive police (Vollzugspolizei) of the various lands with their three branches, the constabulary (termed Schutzpolizei or Schupo in most lands), which on most oc-casions wear uniform, the CID (Kriminalpolizei or Kripo), which are not uniformed, and the para-military Bereit-schaftspolizei ("stand-by" police). The Bereitschafts-polizei, unlike the other two branches are quartered in barracks; their members never act individually but only in units. Their traditional function is the training of young policemen, but their other – more public – function is to support individual police operations when large bodies of police are deemed necessary. In that sense they operate like a riot police. At present the federal strength of this force is over 18,000. On the basis of an agreement between the various lands, its units are uniformly supplied by the Bonn central government with motor vehicles, telecommunications equipment, and weapons. An inspecting officer of this force is permanently attached to the Federal Ministry of the Interior to monitor the operational readiness of the stand-by police, since the training and equipment are standardized across the lands according to federal specifications.

Although this basic tripartite organisational principle can be said to be valid for all the lands of the Federal Republic, a multifarious picture presents itself when one considers other aspects of police organisation in each land in terms of police authorities, local and district control, police committees, police codes, police functions, police force hierarchies, etc. Basically one can speak of a South German and a North German grouping, where the lands in the north still evidence the influence of the Prussian past and more recently of the British occupation, whereas the lands in the south show American and French influence. For example, in Schleswig-Holstein according to the Polizeiorganisationsgesetz of December 1968, the police is a land institution. The chief police authority is the minister of the interior of Schleswig-Holstein. Among the various departments of the ministry of the interior, Department IV deals with the police. Within Department IV there exist the department for the constabulary (Schutzpolizeiamt) and the CID (Kriminalpolizeiamt). Both these departments are headed by a policeman and are non-political appointments, i.e., the Chief Police Director of the Schutzpolizeiamt and the Chief Police Director of the Kriminalpolizeiamt. Within the department for the constabulary there are a number of administrative units which coordinate certain subject matters on a land basis, such as personnel, organisation, vehicles, equipment, weapons, etc. Directly responsible to the department for the constabulary are sections with specific functions such as (1) the section "stand-by" police (Bereitschaftspolizeiabteilung or BPA), which is headed by a Chief Police Director, whose salary is equivalent to that of a university professor. The "stand-by" police is actually billeted in the picturesque town of Eutin, south of Kiel. The force is organized in groups of one hundred (centuries) for either training purposes or as task forces. Each century is headed by a chief inspector. He receives the equivalent salary of a junior lecturer in a university or secondary school teacher. A 2nd section directly responsible to the department for the constabulary is a traffic unit based in Neumünster, which monitors the motorways with its police stations and a "stand-by" traffic unit.

Also directly responsible to the Chief Police Director of the constabulary (comparable to the chief constable) are the four divisions of North (Flensburg), South (Lübeck), West (Itzehoe), and Centre (Kiel). These divisions themselves are the actual true superior police authorities for the various police stations. Each division is headed by a Chief Police Director (comparable to assistant chief constables or chief superintendents). The four divisions are then further subdivided. For example North (Polizeidirektion Schleswig-Holstein Nord), with its headquarters in Flensburg, has administrative units for such aspects as administration, personnel, operations, public relations, communications, support services, training, etc. Directly responsible to division North is the river and harbour police north with its three stations of Flensburg, Wyk and Husum. Division North itself is subdivided into three areas (Inspektionen), Flensburg, Husum, and Schleswig, each headed by a Police Director or Police Chief Counsellor (comparable to a superintendent) who would earn the salary equivalent of a headmaster of a large secondary school. Flensburg itself is a pure city area. Its area headquarters contain the same administrative departments as division North with the exception of public relations. It is itself subdivided into three sub-areas (Reviere) and the traffic service. Each is headed by a chief inspector. These sub-areas deal with traffic, accidents, traffic offences, minor criminal offences, and also provide round-the-clock patrolling. Husum on the other hand, is a typical rural area. Apart from its administrative units it contains the sub-areas of Westerland, Niebüll, and Husum. These sub-areas contain a number of police stations. Niebüll for example consists of twelve police stations, the biggest, Leck, employs ten officers, six of the stations employ only one officer. The person in charge of Leck police station would be a police inspector. The CID, although totally separate, is organized along almost exactly parallel hierarchical and organizational structures with, of course, different administrative units at the various levels such as criminal investigation, intelligence, fraud, drugs, etc. It might be noted in this context that in other lands such as Hamburg there is no strict separation between the constabulary (Schutzpolizei) and the CID. There it is much simpler for example to be in uniform one day and out of uniform the next.

In terms of the control of the police, there exists provision according to paras. 10-12 of the Schleswig-Holstein Polizeiorganisationsgesetz, whereby municipal or district authorities act as police committees. There are furthermore police committees for the four divisions. These are elected by the districts and towns. The function of these committees is to foster a relationship of trust between local government and the police, and to support the police in the fulfilment of their tasks. In other lands the head of a division (Polizeidirektion) can be a civil, i.e. political appointment. In southern Germany in particular, it is not only the land which operates as the police authority but also the districts or even the mayors (Baden-Württemberg).(14)

The police pay scale is the same as that of the rest of the West German civil service (Beamtentum) which virtually covers the whole of the public services sector. The pay scale reflects in its incremental nature the promotional aspects and with its "bars" the tripartite nature of the promotional hierarchy. This tripartite allocation of the individual within the hierarchy is primarily, certainly initially, based on academic qualifications and reflects the traditional tripartite nature of the West German school system. The differentiation is between the mittlerer Dienst (middle echelon), the gehobener Dienst (higher echelon, the inspector grade), and the höherer Dienst (upper echelon). Around 90% of the police force are within the mittlerer Dienst, around 10% within the gehobener Dienst, and less than one per cent within the höherer Dienst. This distribution over the various echelons does not compare favourably with other sectors of the civil service, and this has in fact been recognized. In order to overcome police disaffection, attempts are being made to adjust this distribution. In Schleswig-Holstein for example, the percentage of those in the higher echelon was increased from 8.3% to 10.3% for the constabulary (Schupo) between 1979 and 1982, and for those in the CID (Kripo) from 38.9% to 43.75%. For 1983 an increase up to 11.2% and 45.9% respectively is being planned. The discrepancy between the CID and the constabulary is further compounded by the fact that roughly three quarters of the land police forces belong to the constabulary (Schupo). A further very concrete reason for general police dissatisfaction has been the demand on the police force in terms of overtime. In 1981 overtime amounted to approximately ten million hours, for which the individual policeman received roughly £ 4 per hour overtime pay. This considerable overtime figure is in itself indicative of increased police activity in West Germany, beyond the manpower situation of the force. This increased police activity has to be seen in the context of an increase in the actual police forces of around thirty per cent between

1969 and 1980, from 128,900 to 191,400. This increase has resulted in a higher police density of at present 1 : 351 (1969: 1 : 400; the figures for England are 1 : 420 at the moment and for Scotland 1 : 395). Clearly there are regional, urban, and rural differences, West Berlin for example has a police density of 1 : 134, Schleswig-Holstein 1 : 386. West Berlin's population density per square kilometre is 4,446, Schleswig-Holstein's 163. Schleswig-Holstein spent DM 316.5 Mill. on her police force in 1979, which increased to 360 Mill. in 1982; in other words this amounts to a per capita spending of DM 139 per year (= £37). This shows an almost one hundred per cent increase during the last twelve years, and is a nationwide phenomenon.

Trade Union Organisation

In terms of trade union organisation, the Gewerkschaft der Polizei boasted a membership of 162,000 in 1980, which is a considerably higher percentage membership than in the other trade unions in the Federal Republic. Historically, the first police officer associations originated at a local level in the latter part of the 19th century. The beginning of the twentieth century saw organisations at regional and state level such as in Prussia Die Kameradschaft, Bund der Kommunalen Polizeibeamten Preu ens. After World War I, in 1919, there arose police associations like the Vereinigung deutscher Kriminalbeamten, and more significantly the Reichsverband der Polizeibeamten Deutschlands which declared itself a trade union officially in 1920. After considerable reorganisation there emerged in 1931 the Reichsgewerkschaft Deutscher Polizeibeamten, which in its very name denoted itself as a trade union (Gewerkschaft). 1933 marked the end of the German trade union movement. The officials of the Reichsgewerkschaft Deutscher Polizeibeamten were among the first to be arrested and tortured to death in concentration camps. Emil Winkler, secretary of the union, was arrested in September 1933, and died the same year in a concentration camp. Ernst Schrader, president of the union, died in a concentration camp in 1936, the summer of the Olympic Games in Berlin. After 1945, the allies obstructed the formation of a police trade union. The French and the British in particular were most adamant about their dictum which denied police officers the right of association. The Americans did not go as far as that but did not allow the formation of a police trade union. This issue was not solved until the Federal Republic had been founded. In these circumstances one of the biggest West German unions, the ÖTV (Public Services, Transport and Communications), exploited the situation by creating a section in its own organisation for police officers. When in 1950 the Gewerkschaft der Polizei (GdP) was founded, this created a situation of vehement rivalry between the two organisations. Although the GdP went from strength to strength and was in fact internationally recognized by becoming a member of the Union Internationale des Syndicats de Police (UISP), the ÖTV was successful in blocking GdP membership of the DGB (the West German equivalent of the TUC) until 1978.

Due to its gradual recognition by the various governmental authorities, the GdP has been involved constructively and successfully in the "normal" union business of wage and salary settlements and the improvement of working conditions. For example, in 1972 the GdP was successful in achieving overtime pay for members of the police force. Since 1978 the GdP has intensified its campaign against the tripartite career structure and in favour of a single tier structure. But apart from these "normal" union matters the GdP has been most outspoken against the "militarisation" of the police. Since the fifties the GdP has been campaigning against existing elements of "militarisation" and attempts at further "militarisation". The GdP has continuously presented the case against the existing internal hierarchical authoritarian command structures and has pleaded for a less "military" democratisation of the command structure. When in 1963 the ministers of the interior of the various lands of the Federal Republic decided to award combatant status to the police, this was successfully resisted by the GdP. It was argued that the police should not be seen as an instrument of power of the state but as providing a public service, thereby providing a contribution to democratic life. In terms of the arming of the police with mortars, machine guns and hand grenades which is the case in most lands, the GdP has continuously reiterated its view that such arms are anathema to a democratic police force, which should strive hard to foster mutual trust and cooperation between police and public. This then means implementing an alternative policing policy on the basis of the concept of community policing, whereby the police become part of the community again and are organized to watch on behalf of, rather than to watch over the community.

Special police forces

Apart from the land police forces there are federal authorities with policing functions.

1. The Federal Border Police (Bundesgrenz-schutz or BGS), whose police authority is the federal ministry of the interior, is organized along paramilitary lines and has combatant status, very much to the disapproval of the police trade union. The BGS's principal function is to safeguard the Federal Republic against unlawful disturbances which might jeopardize border security up to a depth of 30 kilometres. Within this remit the BGS act as passport control officers, i.e. immigration officers. But additional functions have been assigned to the BGS under the emergency legislation. The BGS may be employed as a task force throughout the territory of the Federal Republic in the event of natural disasters and grave accidents but also if there is a threat to the free democratic order of the Federal Republic or an individual land, or in the event of war. The BGS is legally defined as a police force. At present the strength of the BGS is over 20,000 with 1,000 members acting as immigration officers.

2. Apart from the BGS there is a further institution for the maintenance of public order which is not a land affair but laid down constitutionally in the Basic Law as a federal matter. Article 73 of the Basic Law reads: "The Federation shall have exclusive power to legislate in the following matters: ... 10. co-operation of the Federation and the Lands in matters of criminal police and of protection of the constitution, establishment of a Federal Criminal Police Office, as well as international control of crime." The Bundeskriminalamt (BKA) at Wiesbaden is now manned by 3,000 officers, a three-fold increase during the last ten years. Its main task is the gathering of criminal intelligence, for which it depends on the specially established Land Criminal Police Offices. Furthermore, it is particularly engaged in criminal research, both scientifically and technologically. Its most highly advanced data processing equipment

stores and provides information on known criminals and also suspected persons. The figures for 1977 published by the Federal Ministry of the Interior itself make astonishing reading. The BKA was administering 2.3 million criminal files, finger prints of 2.2 million people, and photos of 1.8 million people. The number of fingerprints was growing by 14,000 per month. It seems rather extraordinary that West Germany should boast such a high number of known or suspected criminals, i.e. 3% of the total population, children included. The extent and the sophistication of the gathering of intelligence is becoming a growing concern in the interest of civil liberties. The BKA, however, is not merely a criminal records office – it can engage in its own executive policing in terms of investigation, search, and arrest. This is the case when its assistance is required by a competent land authority or the Federal General Attorney, or when a particular case covers more than one land (the "travelling criminals" for example). It also executes policing functions in cases involving arms and ammunition, explosives, drugs, counterfeit money, and most spectacularly in recent years, acts of terrorism. The BKA also acts as the central German agency of INTERPOL. Finally, the BKA discharges the functions of protecting the Federal President, the government, members of parliament, foreign diplomats, official guests of the Federal Republic, West German diplomatic missions abroad, and also members of the West German Special Branch (the Bundesverfassungsschutz or BfV).

3.   According to Article 40 of the Basic Law the Federal President acts as police authority inside the Bonn houses of parliament. Furthermore, the federation is also the police authority for the Railway Police and the Air Police with their specific functions of primarily safeguarding installations and public safety along railway lines, stations, airports etc.

4.   On the basis of article 73 X. the Federal Republic established the Bundesamt für

Verfassungsschutz (BfV) for the purpose of
the "protection of the constitution", i.e.
a federal special branch. In 1950 the
West German parliament (Bundestag) passed a
"Law on Collaboration between the Federal
Government and the Lands in Matters relating to the Protection of the Constitution", which established the BfV in Cologne
and the various land bureaus for the protection of the constitution. The law
specified the objects as collection and
evaluation of information, reports and
other material about movements hostile to
the state. The BfV has as its purpose the
detection of espionage, treason and sedi-
tion against the state. It acts as the
official federal surveillance agency in
terms of subversive organisations, political activities, but also ideas. It acts
as an agency of surveillance of people who
process official secrets or who are in contact with those who do, etc. It is also
the main agency for the prevention of acts
of terrorism. The 1950 law made it quite
explicit that the Bundesamt für Verfassungsschutz should have no police powers
such as the right to confiscate or to arrest, and the right to use force. The
federal law for police officers makes it
quite clear that the members of the BfV,
the military intelligence service (MAD),
and the Federal Bureau of Intelligence
(BND), are not regarded as police officers
and therefore cannot use police powers.
The Federal Republic adheres officially to
this notion of a clear legal separation
between the police forces and the intelligence services. This separation resulted from the memory of the unlimited
power and methods of the GESTAPO (the state
secret police during the Third Reich).
The western Allies were particularly concerned about any possible revival of a
centralized and powerful state security
service. It is for this reason that the
1950 Law does not even mention the right or
grant the right to the BfV to use secret
service methods to procure information,
although this has been rectified.(17)   A

more recent specific function given to the BfV is the surveillance of foreign citizens in the Federal Republic, which includes 4.6 million "guest workers" and their families. Evidence of espionage, sabotage and other "activities inimical to the constitution" is then passed on the judicial authorities competent to prosecute.

The Law

Article 20 of the Basic Law states that "all state authority emanates from the people. It shall be exercised by the people by means of elections and voting and by specific legislative, executive, and judicial organs." For the average citizen, the police constitutes the daily manifestation of state authority more than any other institution. The task of the police is understood to be the protection of the citizens from danger, but thereby the police will also impinge on the rights of other citizens. The potential conflict between the maintenance of public security and the use of police powers is traditionally seen as the locus of police laws. The police are also the organ of the state responsible for the maintenance and administration of public order. The police laws are therefore a facet of administrative law and more generally, public law. Within this framework of the administration of public security, the police are responsible for the protection of the rights of the individual, the averting of danger to the individual and the state, and the maintenance of law and public security. In some lands of the Federal Republic there exist specific and separate police laws, whereas in others the laws governing police functions and conduct are part of the administrative law, which provides for all agencies responsible for the administration of public order. Despite these differences between the various lands, it has, however, been traditionally accepted that the police, unlike the other agencies, deal with matters of urgency in cases of danger. They also act in the prevention of infringements of the law and other public order regulations. Furthermore, they conduct the prosecution and detection of infringements of the law. In order to assess "urgency" the police have to make "dutiful" discretionary decisions ("pflichtgemässes Ermessen"). Once the decision has been made that a danger exists requiring urgent action, a discretionary decision has to be taken as to the nature of the action required in terms of the principles of appropriateness and proportionality or balance of the means.

However, the police are also required to make "reasonable" discretionary decisions when danger is "suspected" and act according to the same principles of "urgency", appropriateness and balance. The police are duty-bound to inform the appropriate administrative agency responsible (for parks, roads, public buildings, etc.) of the danger and infringement; in the case of violations of the law the police must inform the public prosecutor, for whom according to police law, the police merely act as an executive arm. It is in this sense that the police have been called "executive" police ("Vollzugspolizei"). In pursuit of police action the police are entitled to certain measures as part of preliminary proceedings. These police powers include the identification of individuals, arrest, search, confiscation, but also raids. In the case of resistance the police are empowered to use force including weapons, according once more to the principles of appropriateness and balance of means.(18) These definitions of police functions and powers common to all lands of the Federal Republic are known as the "polizeiliche Generalklausel" (police general clause) which originates from the 1794 ALR (Para. 10 II 17 ALR), reaffirmed by the Prussian Police Administrative Law ("Preussisches Polizeiverwaltungsgesetz") of 1931, which included as a new element the term "dutiful discretionary decision" (Para. 14 PrPVG). The police laws also, of course, deal with the actual organisation of the police and the police authorities. A more recent addition to the police laws has been the extension of police duties and powers in respect of the fight against terrorism. This fight is now the function of the police, but the new powers (especially re/identification) are not only directed against actual terrorists but also against sympathisers, which includes those who provide terrorists with weapons, identity papers, accommodation, etc., and also those who support them or are deemed to support them or are suspected of supporting them by what they say or write. Under these anti-terrorist laws the police have become connected with policing political activity and political ideas on the basis of pre-emption.

The present legal debate

This particular anti-terrorist involvement, coupled with the almost continuous public appearance of the police at ecological demonstrations and evictions of squatters, has meant that the traditional picture of the police as a force responsible for the prevention and detection of crime and other public order matters such as traffic has changed. It is no longer readily accepted that police law is merely part of administrative law, ostensibly concerned with the administration of public order. Apart from its obvious nexus with the penal code, recent discussion of police law has increasingly focussed on its nexus with constitutional law, since the police operate de facto as one of the judicial organs mentioned in the Basic Law, and police law deals with the maintenance of public security and the appropriate necessary organisational forms. Police law and police action itself in execution of constitutional remits and governmental orders are the manifestation par excellence of public authority, which in turn demands that a police action appears transparent in its constitutional purpose, otherwise this manifestation of public authority will lose its legitimation. This in turn means that any deployment of public authority is not just a legal matter (including police law) but always also a political problem. It is this issue which has been highlighted by the continued public appearance of the police at demonstrations etc., and which has led to a shift in the role-expectancy of the police on behalf of the public and politicians in particular, and also a shift in the role self-expectation of the police themselves. This shift from the traditional readily accepted picture of the police has led to a state of uncertainty on the part of the police and the public, compounded by accusations of autocratic arbitrariness which the media and demonstrators and their sympathisers have levelled against the police. This factor, plus the existence of an ever-increasing crime rate, prompted the ministers of the interior to consider the possibility of a unified police law for the whole of the Federal Republic in order to establish an improved legal basis for police action as compared with the Generalklausel with its rather too loosely defined police powers. The Conference of the Ministers of the Interior of the various lands finally issued the so-called model draft of a unified police law (Musterentwurf eines einheitlichen Polizeigesetzes des Bundes und der Länder) in November 1977. This draft defines the functions of the police, its powers, its use of force, and in particular the use of weapons.(19) So far, however, only Bavaria (Polizeiaufgabengesetz of August 1978) and North-rhine-Westphalia (March 1981) have issued new police laws on the basis of the model draft (known as Musterentwurf or ME). On the other hand the model draft has generated a comprehensive debate, mainly conducted by academics, on issues of police law. For example, a group of academics presented an alternative draft in 1978, which attacks the Musterentwurf on the basis that it goes too far in terms of police powers which would place the police outwith the constitution. Rather than specifying police functions and powers, it was argued, the _Musterentwurf_ enlarges police powers beyond constitutional tolerance. But the argument is not so much a quantitative one but rather a qualitative one, as this extension of police powers would result in ultra-preemptive policing violating beyond any reasonableness the notion of "presumption of innocence".

Whereas on the one hand it has often been argued that the _Generalklausel_ does not meet the necessary legally defined criteria of constitutionality, the Bavarian 1978 police law has been criticized on the other hand because of a large number of specifically defined functions, tasks, and powers, which makes it too unwieldy for the average police officer and ultimately results in less police efficiency. It has also been noted that the Bavarian law with its specifications benefits the citizen as police actions are more transparent to him and appear less arbitrary. Discussion has, however, also focussed on a number of traditionally acceptable terms. Para. 14 PrPVG (the model _Generalklausel_) reads: "Die Polizeibehörden haben im Rahmen der geltenden Gesetze die nach pflichtnässigen Ermessen notwendigen Massnahmen zu treffen, um vor der Allgemeinheit oder dem einzelnen Gefahren abzuwehren, durch die die öffentliche Sicherheit oder Ordnung bedroht ist." Thus the task of the police is to prevent dangers which threaten public security or order (_öffentliche Sicherheit oder Ordnung_). Both these terms are vague legal terms. The classic and authoritative definition of public security is provided by a judgement of the Bavarian Constitutional Court of 1951, whereby public security comprises the inviolateness of the citizen's life, health, honour, dignity, freedom and property, and also the inviolateness of the legal order and the institutions of the state. The violations are specified in the penal code (Paras. 211ff and Paras. 223ff StGB in respect of the citizen, and Paras. 80ff,84ff 92ff,105ff StGB as regards the state). In terms of public security the police and the Federal Border Guard also protect public buildings. The accepted definition of public order is provided by Para. 14 PrPVG, whereby public order is seen as the sum total of all those unwritten laws determining the behaviour of the individual in public, laws whose observance is regarded as a necessary precondition for an ordered life by existing common sense. Equally, although to a lesser degree, discussion has also focussed on the term "danger".(20) Of these three concepts, public order is the most problematic one from the police point of view. Historically, "good police" or public order can be demonstrated to be a function of particular social and politi-

cal circumstances. The concept of public order embodies
the maintenance of the status quo by its insistence on
consensus, i.e. the majority view of ethics, manners,
behaviour, values, aesthetic and political views, etc.
It has been argued that the notion of public order is a
historical relic from the days of constitutional monarchy
and before, and that it is an anachronism in a democratic
society, where democracy is taken seriously as an active
democracy. In the first instance, public order protects
the majority; constitutionally the minority must also be
protected; but when is a minority a minority? More substantially, however, public order, and thereby the police,
views anything with deep suspicion which threatens "ordered life", which, certainly since 1968, includes meetings,
demonstrations, leafleting, petitions, etc. The Basic
Law, on the other hand, stipulates in its first section
"Basic Rights": Article 5: (1) Everyone shall have the
right freely to inform himself from generally accessible
sources. ... (2) These rights are limited by the provision of the general laws, the provisions of law for the
protection of youth, and by the right to inviolability of
personal honour. Article 8: (1) All Germans shall have
the right to assemble peaceably and unarmed without prior
notification or permission. (2) With regard to open-air
meetings this right may be restricted by a pursuant to a
law." - In terms of an active democracy which is not
merely restricted to the houses of parliament, and where
citizens make use of their constitutional rights through
extra-parliamentary activities, the retention of the
notion of public order may be seen to constitute a threat
to democracy in the sense that governmental agencies and
the police can and do abuse this particular legal provision of the Generalklausel. In order to tackle issues of
violence, indecency, etc. existing laws such as the penal
code and other codes such as the one concerning meetings
(Versammlungsgesetz) and similar bye-laws are perfectly
adequate from a public security point of view. The danger to the inviolateness of the legal order and the institutions of the state are covered by public security
anyway. The application of the notion of public order
rather than the legally much more specific notion of public security to ecological, political fringe demonstrations, etc. could and has to some extent already resulted
in the following situation: When, in the context of the
1981 demonstrations in Berlin, Brokdorf and Nuremberg the
question was raised as to where the limits of public (i.e.
governmental) authority were vis-à-vis political protest,
the then Federal Minister of Justice proclaimed that the
issue at stake was "our political culture". In the in-

terest of the public (öffentliches Interesse) the police were ordered to jump into the breach between the adherents of the status quo ("our political culture") and the protesters.(21) In this context it might be appropriate to note the lesson which the eminent German historian Karl Dietrich Bracher draws from his account of the Nazi reign of terror in his The German Dictatorship. "Instead of revising the constitution to achieve greater efficiency at the expense of parliamentary democracy, instead of extending political command centres, as Carl Schmitt's disciples, who confuse politics with administration and authority, are demanding, the democratic-parliamentary process should be improved."(22) In such a context of an improved democracy the notion of public order would seem to be anathema. It was after all during the Third Reich that "public order" was one of the legal mainstays of the police and SS reign of terror.

There have been a number of critical voices in West Germany since 1968 who have argued that the police forces have served as an instrument for the reduction of (legitimate and constitutional) political conflict to problems of law and order. Probably the most vehement has been Sebastian Cobler, particularly with his book Law, Order and Politics in West Germany (A Penguin Special, Harmondsworth 1978, first published in West Germany in 1976). One of the features of political criminal law is its ragbag of vague terms such as "support", "advocate", "induce", "give approval to", "subvert", "undermine", "disturb", and also "public peace", "security", etc. Cobler criticizes "liberals" who have deplored this state of affairs for having missed the real point of political criminal law. According to Cobler "its raison d'être is to have definitions flexible enough to allow every new set of 'enemies of the state' to be labelled and fought at any time, or, more accurately, as the occasion demands." In this context Cobler quotes the former Federal Attorney-General Wagner who claimed that state security law had to deal with "events and phenomena which by their nature cannot have a constant shape or structure, but are like viruses. For this reason it is very hard to reduce them to the normal, clearly defined formulas of legal language."(23) This quotation with its use of "viruses" is not only reminiscent of the language used by Nazis for enemies of the regime and Jews, but also in terms of substance it conjures up the Third Reich. One of today's leading constitutional lawyers, Theodor Maunz, wrote in 1943:

> "The concepts of security, order and danger
> showed themselves so flexible that they could be

used to justify more or less any action by the
police protecting v̈lkisch values, strengthening
the community, and supporting social order.
This gives them a tactical superiority over
their attackers. Hardly a new case appears but
the previous rulings ... are abandoned and the
defence against danger is extended to include
the new case."(24)

In fact, the Federal Constitutional Court has ruled that
"if such flexible terms were not used, the legislators
would be unable to control the complexity of life".(25)
    The inadequacy of legal terminology is, however, not
the only instance of obfuscation as regards police actions
and public order issues. Since 1968 in particular, the
public at large has witnessed how the methods and equipment employed in police operations especially against
squatters, anti-nuclear demonstrators, students etc. have
blurred the line between police and paramilitary operations. Furthermore, since 1968, the traditional, constitutional, and legalistic division of powers between the
executive, i.e. the government, the judiciary, and the
police has de facto shown itself to be threatened. Conflicts which cry out for political solutions are increasingly tackled by the police at the behest of the executive
or the judiciary with paramilitary operations. In more
recent years this applies particularly to questions
concerning the environment, nuclear power, and nuclear
weapons. The police, however, are also increasingly taking over in their own way the work falling into the political domain. Obfuscating concepts like "public security", "public interest", "threat" coupled with the notion
of pre-emptive policing concerning itself with those whom
the police believes will commit offences at some future
point, have pointed the police in a direction where they
have exchanged their merely instrumental strong-arm role
for an individual role in societal and particularly political conflict management, where they define what constitutes public security and whoever threatens to disrupt it.
This function of conflict management is not provided for
in the constitution. It must be emphasized that this is
not merely a development recognized and criticized by defenders of civil liberties, but one which is actively encouraged by such people as the head of the Federal Criminal Police Office who stated:

Of all the organs of the state, the one most immediately and forcibly confronted with reality,
the police force, has uniquely privileged access

169

to knowledge which enables it to understand a
multiplicity and diversity of socially deviant
and antisocial forms of behaviour, structural
defects in society and laws governing social
mass behaviour.

Herold proceeds to argue that therefore the police are in
a position to recognize "subliminal changes" at a very
early stage. Because of this privileged position the
police should leave behind its position as a subordinate
object with merely executive functions and take on an
active role as initiators of social change, i.e. turn
itself into "a sort of institution of social hygiene".(26)
    This function of conflict management is not provided
for in the Basic Law, an addition was, however, made in
1968 which has encouraged what Cobler calls the "perfect-
ing of surveillance". Until 1968 Article 10 read: "Secrecy of mail, post and telecommunication shall be inviol-
able. This right may be restricted only pursuant to a
law." The addition reads: "Such law may lay down that
the person affected shall not be informed of any such restriction if it serves to protect the free democratic
basic order or the existence or security of the Federal
Republic or a Land, and that recourse to the courts shall
be replaced by a review of the case by bodies and auxiliary bodies appointed by Parliament." Coupled with amendments to the Code of Criminal Procedure, surveillance
covers people also who are suspected of offences or "pre-
paratory acts" or "advocacy" etc. These provisions have
legalized the use of surveillance techniques such as telephone tapping, opening of mail, police cameras at demonstrations, storing of personal details in police computers, etc., which seem to be operated on a vast scale and
often indiscriminately.(27)

The Kohl government and law and order

The late autumn of 1982 saw the end of the second era of
post war West Germany, which was confirmed by the elections of 6th March 1983. It is possible to advance more
than an informed guess as to the attitude of the new Kohl
government towards the police and public order. In 1980
the then leader of the CDU/CSU opposition, Helmut Kohl,
deplored the systematic press campaign against the police,
the intolerable situation in respect of squatters, and
spoke of universities as legal vacua. He demanded a
stronger law for demonstrations and the reintroduction of
the law against "breach of the peace of the land", which
would punish participation in a public assembly where

violence was used against persons or things. Kohl furthermore demanded adequate arms for the police on the
grounds that pistols are not sufficient for instances of
kidnapping and violent mass demonstrations. In the same
1980 publication the strong man of the CSU and right wing
policies, Franz Josef Strauss, went further by discarding
the concept of the police as "social referee" or "social
engineer" as mere fancy. The task of the police is the
ruthless implementation of the law and the prevention of
crime. The police is the agency for the execution of
state authority and not an agency of arbitration. Specifically, Strauss demanded a law against the carrying of
"passive weapons" and the use of disguises by demonstrators. And finally, he stipulated that a special police
task would be the elimination of the ideas giving rise to
terrorism. This, together with his emphasis of pre-
emptive policing, sounds extremely ominous in terms of
civil liberties.(28)

In the meantime, some aspects of the Kohl administration's programme concerning public order have emerged.
The old Para. 125 of the Penal Code will be reintroduced
fully, which will mean prosecution for participation in
violent demonstrations. Demonstrators will not be allowed to carry "passive weapons" or use disguises. Furthermore, it is envisaged that the police and the law courts
can as a rule present demonstrators with a bill covering
the cost of policing the demonstration which would seem to
conflict with the basic right to assemble (Article 8 of
the Basic Law).

However, the immediate future will also see the passing of a new police law in the Land of Bremen, one of the
few Länder still governed by the Social Democrats. This
law will relieve the police of its function to maintain
public order and will establish as their domain "dangers
to public security". This means that the police will no
longer have to deal with public order issues where there
is no element of illegality in terms of actually specified
laws. For example, the police will not have to deal with
topless waitresses in bars or lounging punks in public
places anymore. According to the new Bremen police law,
machine guns and handgrenades are no longer permitted as
police weapons as they are for example in Baden-
Württemberg and in Bavaria. The Bremen police will not
be allowed to shoot with the intent of killing ("gezielter
Todesschuss"), which is permissible in Bavaria, the
Rhineland-Palatinate, and Lower Saxony. The use of guns
aimed at persons in a crowd is no longer permitted if
there is a danger to innocent persons. The powers of identification are also to be restricted, especially in the

case of demonstrations. Also severely restricted are the powers in terms of information gathering and the storing of information about persons. The police will also not be allowed to charge the costs of police time on the occasion of football games and demonstrations. This contrast between Bremen and the new Federal government is a good illustration of the parameter of federalism, when one deals with the "West German" police and public order.

Police weapons and their use

On the 16th of January 1983, two days after a group of CID men shot and almost fatally wounded a young man in Kensington, whom they took for an escaped criminal, The Sunday Times carried an editorial which expressed the writer's outrage at what had happened. He likened it to scenes in New York or Paris, and deplored its occurrence in Great Britain. The editorial concluded: "Anyone who values the role and reputation of the police must feel bitterly critical of what occurred: and anxious that both the commissioner, Sir Kenneth Newman, and the Home Secretary, Mr Whitelaw, move with the utmost speed to curb and control the use of guns." The writer pointed out in particular that the police itself has always opposed the arming of the force, and that the incident showed one very good reason why. Police guns, if widely possessed, are capable of turning city streets into shooting galleries. Such an editorial is unlikely to have occurred in the West German Sunday press, as there are few voices in the Federal Republic who would argue against "wide possession" of guns.

It is by and large an accepted fact that every police officer carries a gun. Whereas in Great Britain about one in ten police officers are trained to use guns, and the use of guns and rifles is usually restricted to specialist squads, this is not the case in West Germany. Nor is it the case that the carrying of guns is a public relations issue for the police, as Martin Kettle pointed out in his article in the same Sunday Times issue(p. 3) in respect of the British police forces: "But there are strong public relations incentives too. The British bobby's enviable image of reassurance might take a knock if the full extent of the commitment to firearms were widely known." One rather suspects that the situation is the reverse in West Germany, where the gun is seen as the symbol of reassurance. The debate focusses not so much on the restricted possession of guns, but rather on the type of guns and other fire-arms, the use of grenades, when exactly the police is allowed to open fire, and on

the question of whether and when exactly a police officer
can shoot in order to deliberately kill the other person.(29)
     Police weapons are the truncheon, the pistol, the
rifle, the submachine gun, and chemical irritants.   Of
these, the firearms are the most extreme instance of state
authority because of their potential and intentional fatal
design purpose.   This has become publicly apparent since
the killing of a student in Berlin in 1968 by a policeman,
and since then by the use of firearms in the fight against
terrorism.   This most extreme use of force involves a
considerable number of legal and ethical problems.   For
example, is the use of firearms compatible with the
principle of a democratic state which must only violate
basic human rights as little as possible and only if
totally unavoidable?   Furthermore the question has been
raised as to whether weapons should be used which endanger
life when it is not the judiciary which decides upon the
use but the police.   Also, since the death penalty is unconstitutional in West Germany, it could and it has been
argued that "the death penalty has in practice been reintroduced through the back door in the face of the constitution and the law, decided now individually and on the
spot, and carried out by police officers."(30)   This would
seem to be the case especially where the "shot aimed to
kill" is permitted – which is the case practically everywhere in the Federal Republic.   Apart from such more fundamental questions, there are also serious problems in
terms of the legal considerations which are to guide the
individual police officer.   The use of weapons is subject
to the guidance provided by the Generalklausel with its
referential terms of dutiful discretionary decisions,
urgency or necessity of the means, appropriateness of the
means, and balance or proportionality of the means.
There are, however, some specific provisions.   Weapons
can be used for the prevention of crimes which involve
weapons or explosives or are presumed to involve them.
Weapons can also be used in instances of stop and search,
where a suspect attempts to escape and where a crime involved the use of weapons or explosives.   The problems of
this provision are highlighted by the killing of a young
Scot, Ian McLeod, in Stuttgart in 1972.   He was woken up
by a knocking at his door, and after having opened it (in
the nude) was confronted by a number of men, in plain
clothes and heavily armed.   McLeod slammed the door shut
and was shot dead through the door.   His "mistake" had
been that he lived in a flat the police suspected of having been used by terrorists.   The police were deemed to
have acted correctly.

Police weapons, and in particular guns, can also be used in order to facilitate the re-arrest of runaway prisoners. Also, but far more problematically, the police can use weapons against crowds or members of a crowd who are committing acts of violence or are about to commit acts of violence. In this context, the question has been raised as to what constitutes an act of violence, whether such an act also includes damage against property, and what constitutes a "violent demonstration". Furthermore, the police can use weapons on property such as locks, doors, or car tyres, when for instance a criminal is being pursued. Finally, and again this has given rise to much heated debate, the police can use weapons in cases of self-defence, or in cases specifically of so-called putative self-defence. In all cases, however, of the use of weapons against persons, the police must issue a warning, either in the form of a verbal warning or a warning shot.

It has been notoriously difficult to obtain statistics in this area. Rainer Buchert in his 1975 study provides the following selective data: In the land of Northrhine-Westphalia, between 1963 and 1973, shots were fired in 1,767 instances; 781 of these were warning shots, 272 were aimed at animals. In 58 instances, guns were used against attacks or in order to prevent crimes; in a further 643 instances shots were fired to prevent a criminal from avoiding arrest; in 127 cases shots were directed against runaways from prisons or police stations. During these ten years 251 people were shot, including six innocent bystanders. Of these 34 were shot dead. During the same span of time 23 people were shot dead by the police in Baden-Württemberg, and a further three in Schleswig-Holstein.(31) These figures would most probably represent under one third of the total figure for the Federal Republic. It is very difficult to assess the number of unrecorded shots fired. Also, these statistics do not of course provide any information about the exact circumstances of when firearms have been used. These include cases such as the one quoted by Cobler: "In the spring of 1975 the High Court quashed the conviction of a policeman who had shot in the back a seventeen year old youth who was in local authority care. According to the court, the 'use of firearms for the purpose of recapturing a criminal in flight' was justified if the criminal constituted 'a not inconsiderable danger to the public'. This condition had been satisfied: the youth who was shot had repeatedly "stolen groceries and delicacies, portable radios, record-players and cash. In four cases he also stole bicycles. When caught in the act, he had broken away violently and escaped ... Public safety therefore required his immediate recapture ... in view of the danger to the community presented by this young criminal ... The fact that a risk of killing was present did not make the firing of a careful shot at the fugitive's leg wrong."(32)

Furthermore, these statistics and the statistics about the number of police officers shot dead which in comparison is infinitely smaller,(33) do not provide an answer to the question of how effective the comprehensive arming of the police force is in combating dangerous criminals or in protecting the police. What, however, would seem to be quite clear is the fact that firearms are military equipment and not specific police equipment – something which becomes evident from the type of weaponry used by the police. Such firearms are designed to kill. It is in this context that the inadequate training provided both in qualitative and quantitative terms becomes especially disconcerting.

In its issue of 30th March 1983 the German illustrated weekly stern carried an article entitled "Who protects us from the police?". This article referred to four killings by the police during March 1983. In Hamburg a police officer put his gun to the back of the head of a suspected car burglar and inadvertently killed the eighteen year old school pupil. In Augsburg twenty-two shots were fired at a car driven by a nineteen year old bank trainee who had driven through a one-way street in the wrong direction and had attempted to get away from the police. The young man was killed. No shots hit the tyres of his car. In Übersee in Bavaria police killed a publican who had just killed his girl-friend. And in Gauting in Bavaria a Special Patrol group killed a fourteen year old in a youth centre who it would seem had only intended to spend the night there because he could not get into his home. The article draws attention to the fact that during the last twenty years only a tenth of those police officers who had killed were tried for manslaughter through culpable negligence. No police officer had to give up his career after killing somebody. The stern deplored a situation where special treatment is given by the courts to the police. This results in turn in a situation where police officers are encouraged to be trigger-happy as they have no consequences to fear. The article

175

also argues that this special protection of the police by the law courts cannot be justified in terms of the dangerous tasks the police face. The article points out that in respect of fatal accidents at work the police is about average compared to other jobs. Furthermore, most police officers are not shot dead by criminals, but two thirds of the fatal accidents can be accounted for by road accidents. What the article finally pleads for is the proper prosecution of police officers who use firearms improperly. It is symptomatic that the idea of the gun carrying police officer itself is not under attack, which stands in strong contrast to the Sunday Times editorial of 10th April 1983. The editorial referred to the Kensington incident and the announcement by the Chief Constable of Greater Manchester that there would now be armed police patrols in the streets. The editorial indicated that policemen should be law enforcers, not law makers. It furthermore warned that the "short-term advantage of firepower puts at risk something far more precious to our way of life". And it demands that instances when an officer needs a gun be kept to a minimum "to those times when police face a known and specific threat of being fired at". These two press instances from the stern and the Sunday Times highlight the differences between the two countries in this area of the maintenance of public security.

Daily practice and problems

The actions and behaviour, views and sentiments of the police officer are, however, not only determined by the legal framework within which he has to operate. There are many other factors such as his own personality, his socio-economic background, his colleagues, daily routine and practice, etc. The vast majority of police recruits comes from a farming or working class background. Most of them have completed the minimum amount of schooling, i.e., gone through the last year of the West German High School (Hauptschule), which is the least respected of the three secondary schools. Most recruits have learnt a trade. Having been accepted by the police the recruit spends three years in the training school of the Bereitschaftspolizei with its heavy emphasis on paramilitary and physical training. However the true socialisation of the "green" police officer will take place at his first police stations where the master-apprentice structure determines future behavioural patterns and police officer practice. The young officer will observe, discover and learn what is normal police practice. He

176

will discover that the police station sub-culture is hostile towards writing and paperwork, and yet he will learn that promotion also depends on his efforts in terms of reports and other administrative work. Another socialisation problem is one of role expectation, where on the one hand the police officer is to be "friend and helper" (Freund und Helfer) and on the other the preserver of law and order. At the same time, his colleagues talk a lot about threats of violence and also of meting out violence.(34) The young officer will learn to ignore a considerable number of public order violations partly because the eventual paperwork involved seems to bear no relationship to the gravity of the offence. The young officer is also being influenced here by public opinion which demands that the police concentrate on "real" crime. In the inner city situation petty offences are treated with far more disregard than in rural areas due to the different crime distribution. In this context of an "ethnography of police sanctions" the young officer will, however, also learn that certain areas of a city or town receive considerably more police attention, which is not only the case with red-light districts but also with those parts inhabited by the poorer sections from the unskilled worker downwards. He will furthermore observe that when the police are called upon to solve situations of conflict such as fights, a social class bias is obvious.(35) In actual fact, a 1973 survey found that 83 per cent of police officers questioned stated that "rich people" received better treatment from the police.(36) But not only does the young police officer suffer from an inordinate amount of paperwork, overtime demands, and the problem of having to establish his authority all the time, more than anything else he suffers from the monotonous routine aspects of his work (70 per cent of police time is spent on traffic duties, which has given rise to the argument to "de-police" this area). The young recruit also realizes that in the towns and cities the uniform police in their panda cars devote most of their time to petty crime and offences, whereas special patrol groups in plain clothes (but not CID) deal with major crimes and offences where much time is spent in panda cars not in order to prevent crime, but to catch the criminal in flagrante delicto.(37) Finally, the more "glamorous" crime detection work is of course undertaken by the CID (Kripo) which amounts to less than 15 per cent of the police force depending on land and area and is a strictly separate force in most Länder. In view of police dissatisfaction and what seems to be a growing gap between the police and the public, voices are growing louder demanding a return to community policing and improved relationships between the police and the public, based on the idea that policing requires consent if the police is to police on behalf of, rather than to watch the community. Ever increasing crime figures, especially the disproportionately growing number of thefts, are in no way matched by the number of cases solved despite an extraordinary increase in manpower and finance. In Schleswig-Holstein the number of reported crimes increased by 63 per cent between 1960 and 1981, with a 75 per cent increase in thefts. The number of cases solved decreased from 66 per cent in 1960 to 42 per cent in 1981, although of course the absolute figure of cases solved increased by almost 80 per cent.(38) This increasing crime figure has further contributed to the West German police crisis, both in terms of the public image of the police and the police's own self-image.

The media

As the 1931 Adalen incident marked a turning point in Swedish police history, so the anti-Shah demonstrations in West Berlin, and in particular the killing of the student Benno Ohnesorg, must be seen as the start of a new era in the history of the police in West Germany. Since then issues of police and public order matters have received unprecedented media coverage, reflecting very much a continuing law and order and police crisis. The media have of course enhanced the public awareness but might also have had a share in propelling the crisis. Clearly, an analysis of the media coverage has to be undertaken very cautiously, especially in a situation where the West German press baron Axel Caesar Springer owns over two thirds of the West German press which propagates a right wing editorial policy. On the other hand, weeklies like Der Spiegel, Die Zeit, and stern have been quite vociferous in their criticism of the police over the years. A further point to be considered is the fact that, often, media criticism addresses the wrong "culprit", of which the police are painfully aware. As far back as 1962 the media seemed to blame the police for the police raid on the Spiegel offices rather than the persons who gave the instructions. More recently the media tended to criticize the police for the fact that they were to be armed with machine guns and hand grenades, when in actual fact this is being done on behalf of or by other agencies. Such misdirected criticism has over the years contributed greatly to the "police crisis" both in terms of the public image of the police and also the police's own self-confidence.(39)

During 1981 the three weeklies mentioned above carried a number of articles postulating an identity crisis
of the West German police.   This marked the beginning of
the latest phase in the history of the West German police.
Whereas the public image of the police suffered greatly
during the years of the student rebellion, when the forces
of law and order were often seen to be the state's instruments against the extra-parliamentary opposition (APO),
which formed itself in the face of the Grand Coalition,
police activities seemed more acceptable in the aftermath
of the student rebellion when terrorist groupings became
active such as the Baader-Meinhof group and the Red Army
Faction (RAF).   By the beginning of the eighties, however, an increasing number of critics had begun to appreciate what Sebastian Cobler had propagated as early as 1976
in the German edition of his book Law, Order and Politics
in West Germany.   West Germany was seen to undergo a
crisis in democracy based on a growing loss of social and
societal consensus, and the forces of law and order were
used to counteract this loss of consensus.   This loss of
societal consensus manifested itself most publicly in the
case of squatters and demonstrations by their supporters,
and in demonstrations concerning matters ecological, such
as the demonstrations against the extension of Frankfurt
airport, or against the building of nuclear power stations, to name but a few instances of demonstrations on a
truly massive scale, often exceeding 100,000 participants.
Massive police forces were sent in to combat the demonstrators.   At best the police saw themselves as some sort
of social mediator, at worst as the politicians' truncheon.   In fact, the president of the Police Trade Union
(GdP), Günter Schröder stated: "We are the politicians'
truncheon.   And we are fed up with it."(40)   The position
of the police between the crisis in democracy with its
ensuing growth of the "them and us" symptom and the state
apparatus will not be improved by laws enabling the forces
of law and order to charge for the costs of demonstrations.   Such laws which are also envisaged for the
U.K.(41) raise the whole issue of legitimate political behaviour in a democracy in relation to public order.   Certainly it would not seem at all obvious that direct action
protests and democracy are in conflict.(42)
     An increasing number of articles in the press over
the last two years have dealt with police corruption scandals, the victimisation of colleagues, neofascist tendenc-
ies in the police force, gruesome police misconduct, and
the abuse of overtime.(43) Again, this has not helped the
public image of the police on the one hand, and it has
strengthened the feeling within the police as the "whip-

ping boys" of the nation on the other hand. Frustration and aggression would seem inevitable results. The most recent spate of articles in the press have dealt with two issues in particular - fatal shots fired by the police and the "Big Brother State". Die Zeit in an article of the 8th April 1983 predicts a "record year" of fatal shootings for 1983, where nine such incidents had occurred in the first quarter of that year already.(44) Der Spiegel carried articles on the technical aspects of a "Surveillance State" which has already become reality. The articles refer in particular to the advanced state of bugging devices, personal data storage, and the exploitation of video cameras.(45) These well-documented articles make the demands for a return to increased community policing look extremely unreal.

Finally, it is interesting to note that in West Germany issues of public order and the police have been taken up in quarters which might seem unusual to a British reader. For example, a paperback published by Goldmann publishers entitled The police and public prosecutor: what are my rights? has by now run into five editions. (Meine Rechte gegenüber Polizei und Staatsanwaltschaft by Hermann Messmer, first published in 1966, 5th edition (60,000 copies) 1979). Or: Heinrich Böll's novel Die verlorene Ehre der Katharina Blum which appeared in 1974. It dramatizes the societal pressures on the individual, and deals specifically with agencies which are traditionally seen to protect the individual's rights but which seem to interfere most with these rights such as the police and the public media. The novel and the film version of 1975 met with considerable success, public acclaim, discussion, and criticism. Most recently Günter Grass took up the issue of the "Surveillance State" in a speech entitled "Vom Recht auf Widerstand" (Of the right to resist).(46) Discussions of civil liberties, public order, and the police have always been accorded a high standing by intellectuals and writers in particular, who play a significant role in shaping public opinion in West Germany. In common with their European counterparts, the West German police has had the difficult challenge of rapidly changing social and political conditions and public attitudes which have made enormous demands on the police's resources, strategies and effectiveness. Public order has been the major challenge on all three counts and there is little likelihood that the future will bring much change. There is indeed every indication that public order will become an even more dominant and intractable task confronting the West German police. How it meets that challenge will have profound repercussions on German society.

FOOTNOTES

1. Cf. Jürgen K.A. Thomaneck, "The Relationship between the GDR and the FRD: the Origins", GDR Monitor 2 (Winter 1979/80), 7-14.

2. Cf. Karl Dietrich Bracher, The German Dictatorship, Penguin University Books, Harmondsworth 1973, p.573.

3. Cf. Gebhard Schweigler, "Whatever happened to Germany?", in E. Krippendorff and V. Rittberger, eds., The Foreign Policy of West Germany, Sage Publications, London and Beverly Hills 1980, 101-121.

4. Peter H. Merkl, The Origin of the West German Republic, OUP, New York 1963.

5. Cf. Bracher, loc.cit., p.442.

6. For details cf. Heinz Höhne, Der Orden unter dem Totenkopf, Wilhelm Goldmann Verlag, München 1978.

7. Tom Bower, Blind Eye to Murder, Andre Deutsch, London 1981, pp. 184, 186, 395.

8. A. Dietel and K. Gintzel, "Die Polizei - Ausdruck staatlicher Macht", in: Gewerkschaft der Polizei, Die deutsche Polizei, Verlaganstalt DEUTSCHE POLIZEI, Hilden 1980, 61-103, p.61.

9. Cf. H. Conrad, "Das Allgemeine Landrecht von 1794 als Grundgesetz des friderizianischen Staates", in: O. Büsch and W. Neugebauer, eds., Moderne Preussische Geschichte, Walter de Gruyter, New York and Berlin 1981, vol. 2, 598-621.

10. For a definition of the term cf. Paul Gordon, Policing Scotland, Scottish Council for Civil Liberties, Glasgow 1980, p. 19.

11. Ib., p. 124.

12. T.M. Wilhelm, 200 Jahre Deutsche Polizei, Verlag Polizei intern, Lübeck s.d., p. 98.

13. Cf. H. Scholler, S. Bross, Grundzüge des Polizei- und Ordnungsrechts in der Bundesrepublik Deutschland, 3rd ed., C.F. Müller Juristischer Verlag, Heidelberg 1981, p. 18, and O. Model, C. Creifelds, Staatsbürger-Taschenbuch, C.H. Beck'sche Verlagsbuchhandlung, Munich 1982, p. 295f.

14. Model, Creifelds, loc.cit., pp. 311-318.

15. P. Gordon, loc.cit., p.36.

16. Dietel and Gintzel, loc.cit., p.94.

17. Cf. Hans-Ulrich Evers, "Verfassungsschutz und Polizei", in: Bundesministerium des Innern, ed., Verfassungsschutz und Rechtsstaat, C. Heymanns Verlag, Köln/Berlin/Bonn/Munich 1981, 65-86, p.69.

18. For a traditional account cf. D. Schipper and F. Hainka, Allgemeines Verwaltungsrecht und Polizeirecht, Richard Boorberg Verlag, Stuttgart/Munich/Hanover 1978.

19. For the full text cf. Scholler/Bross, loc.cit., pp. 267-294.

20. Cf. a recent dissertation, Frauke Hansen-Dix, Die Gefahr im Polizeirecht, im Ordnungsrecht und im technischen Sicherheitsrecht, C. Heymanns Verlag, Berlin/Bonn/ Munich 1982.

21. Joachim Wagner, "Knüppeln oder kneifen?", Die Zeit 8.5.1981, p 9f.

22. Loc.cit., p.613.

23. p. 119.

24. E. Denninger and K. Lüderssen, Polizei und Strafprozess im demokratischen Rechtsstaat, suhrkamp taschenbuch wissenschaft, Frankfurt 1978, p. 106.

25. Cobler, loc.cit., p.119.

26. Ib., p. 148.

27. Cf. the lead article of Der Spiegel 3.1.1983, "Die neue Welt von 1984", pp. 19-30.

28. F.J. Strauss, "Unsere Polizei in der rechtsstaatlichen Demokratie", in: Gewerkschaft der Polizei, Die deutsche Polizei, loc.cit., pp. 141-150.

29. For a discussion of the legal aspects cf. Scholler/Bross, loc.cit., pp. 238-247.

30. Cobler, loc.cit., p. 137.

31. R. Buchert, Zum polizeilichen Schusswaffengebrauch, Verlag Max Schmidt-Römhild, Lübeck 1975.

32. Cobler, loc.cit., p. 138f.

33. For the most recent figures cf. Michael Schwelien and Jay Tuck, "Vorsicht Schusswaffen!", Die Zeit 8.4.1983, 9ff., p.11.

34. Johannes Feest and Erhard Blankenburg, Die Definitionsmacht der Polizei, Bertelsmann Universitätsverlag, Düsseldorf 1972, p.31f.

35. Ib., p. 109.

36. Rudolf Wasserman, "Wer arm ist, bekommt weniger Recht", Die Zeit 2.11.1973, p. 65.

37. Feest/Blankenburg, loc.cit., pp. 80-86.

38. "Das Kriminalpolizeiamt", Polizei Schleswig-Holstein 2 VI (1.11.1982), 5-17, p.8.

39. Dietel and Gintzel, loc.cit., pp. 80-86.

40. G. Barth and R. Müller, "Wir haben die Schnauze voll", stern 23.11.1981, 20-32, 207, incl. interview with Günter Schröder, p. 32; "Die Polizei hat die Schnauze voll", Der Spiegel 23.11.1981, 26-32.

41. Cf. "Pay as you demo", The Scotsman 22.4.1983, p.4.

42. Cf. W.L. Miller, "The people, protest and a modern democracy", The Scotsman 10.2.1983, p. 9.

43. Cf. "Beispielloses Treiben", Der Spiegel 19.4.1982, p. 103; "Vater verbrennen" and "Freund und Hehler", Der Spiegel 27.12.82, p. 55 and p. 58; Wolfgang Metzner, "Drogen nach Dienstschluss", stern 20.1.1983, p. 136f; Joachim Gründer, "Polizisten schweigen", Die Zeit 4.2.1983, p. 12; "Ausgeschlafene Jungs", Der Spiegel 14.2.1983, p. 66-68.

44. M. Schwelien and Jay Tuck, loc.cit., cf. also Rupp Doinet, "Wer schützt uns vor der Polizei", stern 30.3.1983, 21-31.

45. "Die neue Welt von 1984", Der Spiegel 3.1.1983, 19-30; Hans-Wolfgang Sternsdorff, "Auf dem Weg zum Überwachungsstaat", Der Spiegel 10.1.1983, 46-67.

46. Die Zeit 4.2.1983, p. 39.

Further Reading

Cobler, S., Geulen, R., Narr, W.-D. (Eds.), Das Demonstrationsrecht, Rowohlt, Reinbek 1983.

Denninger, E., Lüderssen, K., Polizei und Strafprozess im demokratischen Rechtsstaat, Suhrkamp, Frankfurt 1978.

Feest, J., Blankenburg, E., Die Definitionsmacht der Polizei, Bertelsmann, Düsseldorf 1972.

Gewerkschaft der Polizei, Die deutsche Polizei, Verlagsanstalt Deutsche Polizei, Hilden 1980.

Gössner, R., Herzog, U., Der Apparat, Kiepenheuer und Witsch, Cologne 1982.

Scholler, H., Bross, S., Grundzüge des Polizei- und Ordnungsrechts in der Bundesrepublik Deutschland, C.F. Müller Juristischer Verlag Heidelberg 1981.

Glossary

APO - extra-parliamentary opposition, a loose organisation at the end of the sixties.

Bereitschaftspolizei - "stand-by" police, responsible for training and special police operations.

Bereitschaftspolizeiabteilung - sub-department within ministry of the interior.

BfV - Bundesverfassungsschutz, the West German Special Branch.

BKA - Bundeskriminalamt, Federal Criminal Office, the centralized police records office.

Bundesgrenzschutz - Federal Border Police

Gastarbeiter - foreign workers in the Federal Republic.

Generalklausel - police general clause, defining police functions and powers.

Gestapo – the secret police of the Hitler era.

Gewerkschaft – trade union.

Inspektion – second largest administrative unit of police organisation within a Land.

Kripo – the West German equivalent of the CID.

Kripoamt – sub-department within the ministry of the interior.

Land/Länder pl. – the federal states of the Federal Republic.

Musterentwurf – model draft of a unified police law

Öffentliche Sicherheit – public security.

Öffentliche Ordnung – public order.

Polizeidirektion – largest administrative unit of police organisation within a Land.

Revier – third largest administrative unit, a police station.

SDS – Socialist Student League, the most influential student organisation in the late sixties.

Chapter 7

THE BLUNT INSTRUMENTS: ITALY AND THE POLICE

Richard O. Collin

When Carabiniere General Carlo Dalla Chiesa and his young wife were gunned down on the streets of Palermo on 5 September 1982, there was something bleakly symbolic about the barbarous murder of Italy's most famous policeman, another casualty in a long war. General Dalla Chiesa had spent his entire life in the Carabinieri, one of the oldest police forces in the world, and had led Italy's successful battle against the most efficient political terrorists in Europe, the Red Brigades. He was perhaps the first popular policeman in Italian history, already being mentioned as a candidate for the presidency of the Republic, despite his well-known dislike for the country's leading political party. When he arrived in Palermo to deal with the Mafia, criminal circles in Sicily decided that he could not be bought off, or subjected to political pressures, or frightened away, and therefore resorted to the timehonoured Mafia option of violence, having him killed, quickly and ruthlessly. For the foreign press, it was a standard cops-and-robbers story, but Italians immediately saw the murder in a much deeper historical context. To comprehend who Dalla Chiesa was, and why he had to die, we need to understand more fully the world in which he lived.(1)

The structural duality of the Italian police

The law enforcement establishment which stood behind General Dalla Chiesa is one of the most complicated in Europe and like most nations with a Napoleonic heritage, Italy faces terrorists and gun-men with a dual police structure. To a large extent, the story of law enforcement in Italy is the history of an ancient conflict between the nation's two principal corps of police and we must begin with a discussion of this fact.

The Italian Constitution assigns to the Interior Ministry the basic responsibility for the keeping of domestic peace and the enforcement of the law, but the structure of the Interior Minister's law enforcement apparatus is convoluted. Government in Italy is still firmly based upon the Napoleonic prefectural system, and police-work within each of the country's ninety-two provinces is the specific responsibility of the local prefect, who is directly answerable to the Minister himself. When trouble occurs, the Interior Minister issues general guidance and emergency instructions to the provincial prefect, who is theoretically empowered to direct the activities of all police forces within his province.

Within the Interior Ministry, however, the central figure is the Chief of Police, who gives more detailed instructions to the senior police official in each province, the questor, who corresponds roughly to a British chief constable. Serving under the questor, there is a hierarchy of high-ranking civilian officials and each major city will be supervised by a commissario (or chief superintendent) with more junior officials for other less important population centres. For the actual work on the streets, the Interior Ministry has at its disposal a lower-ranking corps of uniformed patrolmen who are called Public Security Guards. To avoid confusion, we will refer to this entire apparatus as the Interior Ministry Police.(2)

Complicating the lives of prefects and questors is the largely autonomous role played by their great rivals, the Carabinieri. Constitutionally, Carabiniere units within a given province are supposed to follow Interior Ministry instructions, but unfortunately, there has always been institutional rivalry, competition, and a relatively high degree of animosity between the two corps of police, and the Carabinieri have always been more responsive to orders from their own headquarters in Rome than directives from the Interior Ministry. The Commanding General of the Carabinieri is always a three-star general on temporary assignment from the regular army, an appointment which is frequently given to top officers who are headed for further promotion within the Ministry of Defence. Carabiniere officers and enlisted men are recruited after service with the regular army.

The Carabinieri have expanded into an impressive range of activities: standard police work and crime detection, anti-drug and narcotics investigations, rescue operations with ski and scuba teams, disarmament of bombs, accuracy control of weights, measures and advertisements, investigations into food and drink adulteration, inspection of industrial establishments for worker safety, services to the judiciary for assorted tasks, protection of the President of the Republic, supply of trained personnel for intelligence and counter-espionage services and numerous other duties. In addition, the Carabinieri maintain their own miniature army, a mechanized brigade, a model air force with helicopters and fixed-wing aircraft, and an efficient navy of coastal patrol vessels for distress work and anti-smuggling operations.(3)

To the eternal confusion of foreigners in Italy, there is a wide area of overlap between the two forces; while there are some areas of exclusive competence, in actual practice, these two police forces tend to behave as competitors when it comes to normal criminal work and anti-terrorist operations. Small villages will normally have only Carabinieri, but in a larger town or city, a distressed citizen may call either group, and an incident of any kind will normally be handled by whoever arrives first on the scene, with real competition to solve crimes involving substantial public interest or publicity.

By and large, Carabiniere officers come from the ranks of the older bourgeoisie and sometimes even the aristocracy, tending to be stylish and well-dressed, while the Interior Ministry men are more frequently recruited from the new and generally urban middle class, and can sometimes seem drab and colourless in contrast. For their enlisted ranks, both groups recruit widely among the southern peasantry, but the Carabinieri are able to enforce higher physical, mental and moral standards in their selection procedure. Furthermore, the Carabiniere organization takes better care of its men, both during their years of active service and in retirement, with the consequent development of a greater sense of institutional self-identification. Rates of corruption among both corps of police are comparatively low.

Politically, the Carabinieri have always tended to see themselves as a national institution which belongs at the absolute centre of Italian life, sensitive to the formal and material continuity of the "state" and the eternal and unchanging nature of the law. In contrast, the Interior Ministry establishment has always been seen as being more immediately responsive to the demands of the transient political leadership, more pragmatic, and less concerned with its own dignity.

To complete this portrait of organizational confusion, a number of smaller independent police forces arose in the nineteenth century and survived into the present era. Presently numbering about 40,000 men, the Guardia di Finanza assists the Ministry of Finance in enforcing

tax, excise customs and tariff legislation. The Capitanneria del Porto, subordinate to the Ministry of Merchant
Marine, boasts about 2,500 men and looks after ports and
harbours. The Corpo Forestale began as an element of the
fascist militia and survived the fall of Mussolini as a
6,000-man enforcement agency for the Ministry of Agricult-
ure and Forests. Even Italy's prison guards are regarded
as policemen; subordinate to the Justice Ministry, they
number around 12,000 men at the present time. In addition, both the post office and the state railways have
small police forces of their own. Furthermore, the
mayors of most towns and villages have some form of local
police. These local police forces, said to number about
60,000 men at the present, have historically been troubled
by inefficiency and corruption and have always been marginal as far as law enforcement is concerned.(4)

The Police in the Nineteenth Century

In the immediate aftermath of the Napoleonic conquest of
the Italian peninsula, the king of Piedmont imitated the
departing French by creating his own version of their Gendarmerie Nationale, re-organising pre-existing police forces into the Corps of Carabinieri described above, and
making it the senior branch of the Italian army. At the
beginning of the period of Italian unification (1848), the
Piedmontese government took its first steps towards constitutional government by developing a modern cabinet system of government, assigning law enforcement to the Interior Ministry and creating the dualistic police structure
described previously.(5)
    Disliked by the general public, suspicious of one an-
other, disinclined to cooperate, and jealous of their respective prerogatives, the two groups of police found
themselves for the remaining third of the nineteenth century charged with the administration of an extremely un-
ruly country. While common criminality was rampant in
the new nation, the major threat to the national government came from revolutionaries of various types, and the
police quite naturally concentrated their energies on internal security rather than the suppression of criminality, a tendency which was to remain standard for the following century.(6) In the 1860's and 1870's, the police
fretted over a lengthy series of real, threatened, and
sometimes imaginary insurrections planned or executed by
disgruntled Garibaldians and Mazzinians, Bakuninist
anarcho-socialists, a few early Marxists, and a variety of
others not susceptible to precise political identification. When suitably menacing plots against the national

government failed to emerge, the police occasionally invented conspiracies where none existed.(7)

The basic operational philosophy for both police forces in the nineteenth century was a deeply-rooted notion that perfection in police work consisted in preventing crime from happening rather than merely arresting criminals after a breach of the law had taken place. Preventing crime from happening, however, involved some basic departures from liberalism: intensive police espionage against the general public, the surreptitious reading of mail and telegrams, the building of dossiers and the development of massive nets of informants. In addition to these dubious measures, the new Italian state had provided its police with a variety of legal ways of preventing lawlessness. When the police suspected that an individual was likely to commit crimes, the sospetto was subjected to an ammonizione, or warning, after which he was forbidden to go to restaurants, carry weapons, or keep irregular hours; if unemployed, he was given five days to find a position or face a prison sentence. The next step was the so-called vigilanza speciale, which included all of the measures associated with the ammonizione, plus the requirement that the vigilato had to report to police authorities several times a week. In more extreme cases, the domicilio coatto (or internal exile) was imposed, obliging an individual to reside in an isolated village or on an island.(8)

Despite the intensive use of repressive policing, the law enforcement community entered into a protracted period of crisis during the last decade of the nineteenth century. The hated phenomenon of trade unionism was growing and the rhythm of violent strikes rising rapidly. A collection of old enemies were finding their way into the Italian Socialist Party (PSI) which emerged to give a focus to social discontent and the country was rocked by a series of violent insurrections. To make matters worse, international anarchist organisations were assassinating one national leader every eighteen months, and taking potshots at Italian royals and prime ministers. In the midst of all this political unrest, the police had even less time to dedicate to the problem of common criminality, and ordinary crime began to boom as the century drew to a close.(9)

The result was an authentic crisis of confidence. Given the magnitude of the tasks facing them, the police found themselves to be massively understaffed, having only about 7,000 Interior Ministry Police and 18,000 Carabinieri to police all of Italy; by comparison, Britain and France each had about four times as many police per capita during the same period as well as substantially lower crime rates. While police forces are never very popular in any society, the Italian police came to feel by the end of the century that they were now genuinely hated, not only by an increasingly politicized working class, but also by large segments of the bourgeoisie, who regarded them as hopelessly inefficient. A great deal of this inefficiency stemmed from the utter inability of the two major police forces to work together, a fact recognized by many senior officials.(10)

The final blows to the pride and self-confidence of the Italian police, however, came at the end of the century, when civil disorders became so violent that the police were frequently impelled to shoot their way out of difficulties, leaving large numbers of dying people behind them. In 1898, a long series of rural and urban insurrections culminated in an explosion of popular fury in the turbulent city of Milan, where the police lost control of the situation so completely that the Italian army had to be called in to drop artillery shells on a tumultuous city. Just over a year later, an anarchist slipped through the protective net which the police had organized around King Umberto I, and murdered him. A police force incapable of controlling the citizenry and protecting the life of the sovereign could rightly be said to have failed across the board, and as Italy crossed uneasily into the twentieth century, a sense of desperation took hold of the law enforcement community.(11)

The Police from Giolitti to Mussolini

From 1901 to the March on Rome in 1922, political life in Italy was dominated by the democratic liberal Giovanni Giolitti, who reacted to the 1890's crisis in law enforcement by developing an entirely new approach to the question of internal security. Giolitti began by attempting to convince the PSI and the working class generally that the government and its police were genuinely interested in their welfare and would remain truly neutral in labour disputes and class conflict, demanding in return moderation from the socialist leadership.

Conversely, Giolitti sought to avoid the danger of political reaction by persuading wealthy conservatives that the police would continue to protect their vital interests, keeping both common and political criminality within manageable limits. Finally, Giolitti had to control the police themselves, making them obey his orders, cooperate with one another, refrain from harassing the left, learn to control crowds without violence and generally accustom themselves to the idea that they were no longer the instruments of class warfare, but the keepers of the peace among the social classes.(12)

Opposition to these ideas was considerable, and Giolitti found that changing police behaviour was not easy, since his new policy called for a radical revision of deeply-felt attitudes towards socialists and strikers. To enforce obedience, Giolitti supervised his police closely, issuing severe reprimands when his instructions were not followed. The Prime Minister was politically powerful enough to force even the doubting Carabinieri to obey orders and the top ranks of the Interior Ministry Police became converts, accepting the system as the only option left to them.(13)

The police grew more confident as Giolitti's policies were tested under fire. There was a flurry of strikes in 1901, followed by riots in Tuscany in 1902 and a general strike in 1904; the years between 1906 and 1908 saw a rise in anarcho-syndicalist activity and a number of politically-inspired strikes. Seeing that the war against common criminality was going well, that shooting matches between police and people were becoming less common, and that rioting was starting to be less dangerous, even the stubborn Carabinieri began to change some of their thinking.(14)

Under Giolitti, the police had to live with the assumption that the government's enemies would always be too moderate or too disunited to make a serious insurrectionary effort against an understaffed police. The Italian seizure of Libya in 1911, however, seriously radicalized the Socialist Party and the young socialist Mussolini delivered a hint of what could happen to the entire country as he made the province of Forli ungovernable for nearly a month.(15) In 1914, Giolitti took one of his occasional holidays from office, and Antonio Salandra was Prime Minister in June when the police foolishly fired on a crown of protesters in Ancona, propelling the nation into "Red Week", a spontaneous expression of popular discontent which was so violent that some (working) policemen began to wonder if Giolitti had not been wrong in believing that a potentially violent nation could be gently controlled by a comparatively tiny group of non-violent policemen.(16)

The explosion of general European war a few weeks later posed another problem in law enforcement as neutralists and interventionists mounted violent demonstrations to oppose or demand Italian entry into the war. While the top men in the Interior Ministry followed Giolitti in doubting the wisdom of entering the conflict, the Carabinieri and most of the lower-ranking Interior Ministry pol-

ice became ardent interventionists, allowing interventionist mobs to run wild during the "Radiant Days" of May 1915
as the nation slid into war.(17)

During the actual conflict, both police forces took
on a host of new responsibilities, dealing with a restive
nation behind the front lines and expanding their intelligence and counter-intelligence capabilities, but relations
between the two forces declined to a record low and the
police emerged from the war in worse shape than at any
time since the original crisis of the 1890's.(18)   Police
morale and police popularity with the public were so dis-
asterously low that it was becoming impossible to recruit
new personnel. Furthermore, the tasks facing them had been
made more difficult by the post-war economic and political
crisis, as the country staggered through a two-year wave
of strikes, riots and demonstrations, with much of the
violence being directed specifically against the police.(19)

In the years after 1919, the government's ancient
enemies on the left were joined by a new menace from the
right, as early fascists, nationalists like D'Annunzio,
and some senior military men plotted coups and revolu-
tions.(20)   Becoming Prime Minister in June of 1919,
Francesco Savario Nitti moved energetically to deal with
the crisis in the police, doubling the size of the Carabinieri and re-building the Interior Ministry police.
The violence continued, however, and by the time Nitti was
replaced by Giolitti in June of 1920 revolutionary socialists had become bolder in their defiance of authority, and
the fascist movement was slowly building its strength.(21)

Ironically, it was during Giolitti's last government
that his own police system broke down finally and completely.   The moderate wing of the PSI was now almost
completely without power; the bourgeoisie began looking
to fascism to protect its interests and many policemen had
simply stopped obeying the government's orders.   By September 1920, most Carabinieri and some low-ranking Interior Ministry police began covertly making common cause
with Mussolini's blackshirts, despite the opposition of
senior policemen.   Replacing the aged Giolitti in the
summer of 1921, first Ivanoe Bonomi and then Luigi Facta
attempted to stop the rot, but the blackshirts continued
their triumphant rampage against the faltering socialist
and communist parties with the help of policemen at the
working level.(22)

By the summer of 1922, the Carabinieri had passed
almost completely to the fascist camp, and within the
Interior Ministry, only senior officials were still opposing the inevitable, albeit weakly.   Knowing that they

could expect little backing from either police or military, the remaining democratic liberals in the government were reluctant to try to stop Mussolini's march on Rome with force. In many important respects the success of the October 1922 march was a consequence of the breakdown of Giolitti's internal security system and what amounted to a coup d'état engineered by the Italian army, the Carabinieri, and many of the Interior Ministry Police.(23)

The Police Under Fascism

Mussolini had no permanent loyalties to any single institution, but in the immediate aftermath of the march on Rome, he decided to punish the top men in the Interior Ministry for their opposition and to placate the powerful Carabinieri. Knowing that the Carabinieri still desired to regain their supremacy in the law enforcement field and that a gesture in their favour would be welcomed by the King and the military, he detached most of the Interior Ministry's police and placed them under Carabiniere command. The Carabinieri were predictably delighted, but the new prime minister soon offended them unintentionally by collecting his riotous blackshirts into the Militia (Milizia Volontaria Sicurezza Nazionale or MVSN), which the Carabinieri saw as a possible rival.(24)

Not satisfied with depriving Interior Ministry police of their manpower, Mussolini moved quickly to bring them under his control, keeping the Interior Ministry portfolio himself and appointing the loyal General De Bono as his Chief of Police. Radical changes, however, ended here, and most of the prefects and senior Interior Ministry officials remained in their posts, including some who had been active in opposing fascism. Despite their rough treatment at his hands, the Interior Ministry saw no immediate alternative to Mussolini, since the top police officers feared both the Communist Party (PCI) on the left and the assortment of "intransigent" fascist wild-men like Farinacci, who threatened to launch a "second wave" of fascist violence which would destroy the last remnants of the liberal state. While most Ministry policemen had been "Giolittiani" before October of 1922, they became "Mussoliniani" rather than fascists.(25)

During the first two years of fascist government, these senior Interior Ministry police worked with skill and patience to convince Mussolini that they could be more useful to him than rival institutions like the Carabinieri and the Militia. The Ministry quickly demonstrated its skill with a general clean-up of the regime's enemies to the left, but it was several years before they could get any real backing against the fascist hard-liners, who continued to commit illegalities.(26)

On 10 June 1924, a prominent opposition deputy named Giacomo Matteotti was murdered by a gang of fascists thugs and Mussolini's legitimacy as leader of Italy was quickly called into question. As the scandal gathered, Mussolini brought in the highly respected Luigi Federzoni to lead the Interior Ministry and substituted the hapless General De Bono as Chief of Police in favour of a career policeman. While remaining roughly within the law, the Interior Ministry police worked loyally under their own leaders to contain the scandal while the Carabinieri misread the situation and began sending out clear signals that they were prepared to stand against the Prime Minister.(27)

Mussolini's triumphant counter-attack on 3 January 1925 marked not only the effective beginning of his personal dictatorship, but also the victory of the Interior Ministry over both Militia and Carabinieri. In the early months of 1925, the Ministry was rewarded with new authority and increased manpower while the Carabinieri were relegated to a secondary role for the remainder of the dictatorship. Furthermore, a series of assassination attempts, running from November 1925 to October 1926, seems to have concentrated Mussolini's mind wonderfully on the advantages of an efficient police and once again the Interior Ministry seized the opportunity to prove its loyalty and ability, as an experienced policeman named Arturo Bocchini became the new Chief of Police.(28)

Bocchini was never more than a pro forma fascist, and while he quickly became one of Mussolini's most trusted advisors, he carefully maintained the essential political independence of the police from the Fascist Party, enforcing fascist laws but without the terrible violence which the German police later felt obliged to employ.(29) The attacks on Mussolini's life provided an excuse for "Special Legislation" against subversion, laws which gave the police a range of new powers at the end of 1926, including a Special Tribunal for political offences and the reintroduction of the death penalty.(30)

Mussolini is frequently blamed for having turned Italy into a police state, but in fact, he did little more than allow Bocchini to re-organize the pre-existing Interior Ministry political police into a new secret police group with the meaningless title of OVRA. The Communist Party and several other groups continued to conspire actively against the government, but Bocchini's men were able to contain the opposition without much difficulty, neutralizing the fascist intransigents at the same time. For the remainder of the dictatorship, Bocchini's position as the "Shield of the Duce" was never seriously questioned, and under him, the Interior Ministry police became one of the basic tools of government at Mussolini's disposal.(31)

The jovial Bocchini quickly established superficially good relations with the Germans after 1936, but he and his deputy Carmine Senise privately disliked them, a feeling shared by most policemen, who further regarded the 1938 anti-semitic laws as nonsense. By 1940, Bocchini was desperately trying to show the dictator that the Italian people were profoundly opposed to war but he died suddenly that year, leaving police power to Carmine Senise, an honest Neapolitan Catholic and a liberal policeman of the old Giolittian school who had never bothered hiding his dislike for the Germans or his contempt for the vulgarities of fascism. With the war going badly for Italy by 1943, the Interior Ministry and the Carabinieri began to cooperate temporarily, making plans for Mussolini's removal, which they accomplished at the King's instructions after the Grand Council Meeting of 24 July 1943.(32)

Unfortunately, there was a price to be paid for acting twenty-two years too late, and the police began paying it as the Germans swept into Rome, despite courageous Carabiniere efforts to defend the city. Senise and large numbers of Carabiniere officers were arrested and placed in concentration camps while civil war divided the country. Both police forces redeemed themselves somewhat by participating in the Resistance movement, and consequently both institutions managed to survive the war despite severe casualties. Even OVRA remained in existence, losing only its ominous title and a few of its senior officials; men who had been anti-Marxists under Mussolini survived, in large measure, to be anti-Marxists in the new democratic state.(33)

The Police in the Post-war World

Fascism had flowered after World War One because a badly frightened bourgeoisie had come to believe that traditional law enforcement agencies could no longer defend its interests against the dangers of revolution. With the fall of fascism in 1945, political leadership in Italy passed to an equally fearful class of bourgeois Catholics (the Christian Democratic Party or CD) who viewed with great concern the surprising vigour of the Communist Party (PCI). After twenty years of clandestine existence, PCI had emerged with solid roots in the industrial north and victorious partisan units were appointing their own left-wing prefects and questors, openly proposing themselves as the future leadership elite.(34)

The two principal forces of police had ended the war with their prestige diminished and their organizations in tatters; still viscerally anti-Marxist, they now found themselves required to serve a government which contained both socialists and communists, and even to accept substantial numbers of leftist ex-partisans into their ranks. Having been marginal since the beginning of fascism, the Carabinieri were in a very bad shape, having lost some of their best men in the war against the Germans. Indeed, by virtue of having been somewhat less heroic when it came to fighting the enemy, the Interior Ministry police had survived more or less intact, and were skilfully exploiting the bourgeoisie's fears of a communist-led uprising to win political approval for rapid increases in their numbers.(35)

Anxious to establish its police power over the country, the government of Alcide De Gasperi began to substitute left-wing partisan appointees with career Interior Ministry personnel in December of 1945, enrolling into the two police forces a large number of ex-military officers with pro-fascist pasts, reliable anti-Marxist sentiments and no observable interest in criminology.(36) The terrible social misery of the post-war period produced widespread civil disturbances and an increasingly right-wing police found itself opening fire with great regularity against angry crowds rioting in the streets, peasants occupying land and workers once again staging violent strikes.(37)

The forced resignation of the King in the summer of 1946 upset many monarchist Carabinieri, but the police were re-assured when De Gasperi expelled his communist ministers in 1947. Still operating under Mussolini's 1926 penal legislation, the new Interior Minister, Mario Scelba, strengthened the government's anti-communist defences by recruiting even more men, many with undisguised fascist sympathies, for a new interior Ministry unit, the Celere. These new policemen were given virtually no police training, but Scelba quickly formed them into rapid-response units which attacked popular unrest with unusual brutality.(38) Post-war political tension was highest in 1948, thanks to bitterly contested elections and the attempted assassination of PCI leader Togliatti. Politically, most Carabinieri and many Interior Ministry employees in the post-war years were apolitical rightists and while a few allowed their fear of communism to push them into neo-fascism, the average policemen yielded to the intense propaganda directed against serving officers and voted for the CD.(39)

Inevitably, power struggles between the two police forces broke out again with the Carabinieri insisting upon their traditional operational autonomy, and the early post-war years saw a number of scandals in which Carabinieri and Interior Ministry Police sabotaged one another's operations. At the end of the 1950's, the Carabinieri were given the chance to assert themselves once again thanks to their role in repressing a pro-Austrian terrorist campaign in Alto Adige among members of the German-speaking populaion.(40)   In 1960, political violence exploded again as an ex-MVSN officer named Fernando Tambroni became prime minister and attempted to consolidate his position by recruiting support from among the Interior Ministry police as well as from the Movimento Sociale Italiano (the MSI or neo-fascist party).   With talk of a rightist coup in the air, the Carabinieri adopted a carefully constitutional position, helping to suppress the street violence but doing their work even-handedly and without the violent brutality of the Interior Ministry police.(41)

Shaken by the Tambroni experience, CD Secretary Aldo Moro began exploring the possibility of bringing the PSI into the governing majority in the hopes of relaxing tensions and creating a wider political base for government. Alarmed at this idea, General Giovanni De Lorenzo, an army intelligence officer who had become Commanding General of the Carabinieri, used his control over both police and intelligence organizations to plot the overthrow of the constitutional government.   As Moro successfully negotiated the first centre-left government, bringing the PSI into the governing majority, De Lorenzo put men loyal to himself into key positions, re-built the strength of the Carabinieri, and recruited irregular forces with secret service funds, plotting feverishly for the establishment of concentration camps and the seizure of communications centres.

The terminal difficulty with De Lorenzo's plan, however, was the opposition it provoked among the very men who were meant to carry it out.   When the senior Carabinieri learned the details in the spring of 1964, they dug in their heels and stalled desperately until the autumn, when Aldo Moro and PSI leader Pietro Nenni were able to consolidate the centre-left experiment.   Disloyalty to the Italian government within the Carabinieri was restricted to the immediate circle around De Lorenzo himself, but the scandal reverberated through to the end of the decade, and it was difficult to convince the public that the   Carabinieri had not   contemplated a coup d'état.(42)

The end of the 1960's also produced a wave of student unrest and civil disorders; mistaking youthful restlessness as the beginning of insurrectionary violence, both Interior Ministry and Carabiniere forces slipped back into cold war, hard-line policing, attacking crowds of students viciously, sometimes deliberately turning peaceful demonstrations into riots through the use of agents and provocateurs and frequently using terrible brutality against those arrested. As the events of the following decade were to reveal, this was an error, and a costly one.

Terrorism, Red and Black

It is an over-simplication, but perhaps a useful one, to say that terrorism in the 1970s was to some extent the continuation of the 1943-45 civil war between the fascist 'Republic of Salo' and the left-wing partisan resistance movement. Unfortunately, the Cold War of the 1950s had left many policemen with harsh right-wing sympathies; when the wave of terrorism began, it was difficult for them to free themselves from neo-fascist influences in order to deal with gun-men and bombers of both right and left as the representatives of a democratic and libertarian nation.(43)

The continuance of neo-fascism in Italy was assured by the electoral survival of the MSI, and as early as the 1950s, a number of frankly right-wing terrorist groups emerged, pursuing a so-called "strategy of tension" in which bombing incidents were used to persuade the general public that an ungovernable country could only be controlled by an undemocratic right-wing government. It is now clear that this strategy was to some extent aided and abetted by forces within the police and intelligence communities.(44)

Hence, when neo-fascist elements carried out their first large-scale atrocity, the Piazza della Fontana bombing in Milan in December of 1969, the police ignored evidence leading to the right and arrested a harmless group of anarchists; when one of them mysteriously fell to his death from the window of a Milanese police station, public confidence in the even-handedness of the police plummeted with him. The "strategy of tension" in the late sixties and early seventies included the MSI's provocatin of mindless rioting in Reggio Calabria, a number of abortive coup scares and a long series of bombing attacks, in which the police were generally unsuccessful (in some cases deliberately so) in coming to grips with the real culprits.(45)

Terrorism on the left is related to the abandonment by the PCI of its revolutionary tradition, and the increasingly reformist and bourgeois character of the party. More specifically, the left-wing terrorist groups of the 1970's evolved from the failure of the 1960's student movement to achieve real reforms, as well as the brutal police reaction to that movement, the general hopelessness of the political situation and an atmosphere of mounting economic troubles. While many political dissidents came from the ranks of Communist youth organizations, others made their way to terrorism after disillusionment with the Roman Catholic Church, a phenomenon which has been called "Cathocommunism".(46)

By 1969, a group of dissident Catholics and Communists had joined forces in Milan under the leadership of Renato Curcio and Margherita Cagol. Eventually styling themselves <u>Brigate Rosse</u> (or BR), they began their revolutionary careers by infiltrating northern factories, committing relatively harmless acts of sabotage, and pamphleteering. After a series of early strategy meetings in the autumn of 1969, the BR issued their first public statements in early 1970 and conducted a sabotage attack against the Pirelli Company in 1971. The following year, they staged their first kidnapping, but their victim was released unharmed after a "proletarian trial".(47)

Not immediately sensing a serious menace, both government and police were slow to react and many Italians shared the PCI's early belief that left-wing terrorism was manipulated by the right or by foreign governments as part of the "strategy of tension". In an effort to get the police to attack the problem with some degree of unity, the government invented a General Inspectorate for Action Against Terrorism in 1974, but the two corps of police continued resolutely playing separate hands.(48)

By 1974, it was clear that the "historic phase" of terrorism, both red and black, was coming to an end. On the right, intense adverse publicity had at last forced the government to break links between senior police and military figures and neo-fascist bombers. While the crazies on the right felt strong enough to plant a series of very lethal bombs in May and August 1974, the future was clearly going to belong to the violent left. In June of 1974 the BR claimed responsibility for the killing of .two MSI militants and in September, General Dalla Chiesa's Carabinieri managed to arrest Curcio; Margherita Cagol was killed some months later in a gun-fight with police. In October 1974, a BR leader tried to shoot his way out of an arrest, and killed a Carabiniere. The "phoney" war was over.(49)

With a second generation of terrorists now in charge, the Brigades moved into a more violent phase with a major increase in woundings and killings after 1974, joined in the field by the Naples-based Nuclei Armati Proletari (NAP) and Torino's Prima Linea as well as several other groups, most of them ephemeral.(50) Financing themselves by bank robberies and kidnappings, the BR established regular working "columns" in most northern cities, and the police found significant penetration of their ranks difficult because the groups were linked only by the meetings of their respective leaders in what was called the Direzione Strategica. Discipline was good, and morale was high, so that arrested brigatisti tended to remain uncommunicative under police questioning.

By 1977, the violence was approaching the early stages of a civil war as the Brigades rampaged through Italy, apparently unstoppable. (51) Since the 1976 elections, Aldo Moro had been negotiating for a government of national unity which would include the PCI, the so-called Historical Compromise, but on 16 March 1978, Moro was abducted by the BR. After 54 brutalizing days of captivity, the body of the former prime minister was found dumped symbolically half-way between the headquarters of the DC and the PCI. If the Red Brigages had hoped to sabotage the Historic Compromise, demoralize the security forces, and traumatize the Italian people, they can only be said to have succeeded brilliantly. If they were trying to win for themselves the legitimacy which would come with a set of negotiations between themselves and the government, they failed, since the government had adamantly refused to budge. (52)

The murder of Aldo Moro stunned Italy's security forces into a desperate reaction, although the early stages of this recovery were characterized by uncertainty and incompetence. Responding to police demands for stronger legislation, the government had already passed the first of a group of new laws in 1975, tightening sanctions against terrorism, restricting the rights of the accused, allowing the police to search for weapons with warrants. In 1976, the government broke up the old fascist-infested Servizio Informazioni Difesa (SID), replacing it with a "Democratic Security Information Service" (SISDE) for internal security, and a "Military Security Information Service" (SISME) for foreign intelligence and counter-espionage. In the meantime, the Interior Ministry re-organised its Political Office (Mussolini's old OVRA) into a new anti-terrorist task force called the Direzione per le investigazioni generali e per le operazioni speciali (DIGOS). (53)

In June of 1978, however, the government turned in desperation to the Carabinieri, asking Carlo Dalla Chiesa to take over-all command of the war against terrorism. The general began to produce results almost immediately, raiding BR base apartments in Rome and Milan, arresting some important brigatisti and capturing crucial documents. Despite some well-founded criticisms that he was careless where civil rights were concerned, Dalla Chiesa was re-appointed in the summer of 1979 with unanimous backing from all the political parties.   In the meanwhile, the Interior Ministry's DIGOS pursued its own clues and sus-pects, sometimes arresting real terrorists and sometimes catching Carabiniere secret agents. (54)

The terrorists were not immediately intimidated, fighting back throughout 1979 and 1980 with a fierce counter-attack against the government.   Casting his net widely, Dalla Chiesa arrested prominent members of the anti-parliamentary left, guessing that they could be in-duced to reveal solid information, a policy which forced the "legal supporters" of the BR to choose between aband-oning their intellectual positions and joining their he-roes in prison. On a more subtle level, Dalla Chiesa suc-cessfully induced a few captured terrorists to "repent", informing on their colleagues in exchange for reduced sen-tences.   Once important leaders began to talk, the Cara-binieri began rolling up some of the major "columns". (55)

In the early spring of 1980, another captured BR chieftain "repented" in Dalla Chiesa's presence, leading to the collapse of the potent terrorist organisation in Turin.   While the notion of making special deals for re-pentant terrorists was politically controversial, BR loss-es began to be more significant after the summer of 1980 as an increasing number of terrorists chose to give evid-ence rather than face harsh prison sentences.   In 1981 and 1982, a number of top BR leaders were captured, and in what many have seen as the final turning point, the NATO general James Dozier was liberated without loss of life from BR captivity.   During the same period, black terror-ism continued to claim occasional victims, perhaps profit-ing from a certain amount of neglect by the police forces, but by the end of 1982, there was a consensus among ob-servers that both left-wing and right-wing terrorism were under control. (56)

The effects and implications of the war against ter-rorism will be debated for many years.   Certainly a new professionalism and sense of competence is now observable among the police in both forces.   In terms of public es-teem, the greatest gains have gone to the Carabinieri, who seem to be losing their ancient image as the instruments of right-wing repression, a process doubtless helped by Dalla Chiesa's status as an ex-partisan.   This is not to say that the Carabinieri have become philo-communists, or that the left is uncritical in its admiration, but merely that they are now trusted by people within the constitutional left who had never been guilty of trusting a policeman of any kind. (57)

The Police and the Mafia

Despite the fact that the Mafia now engages in "high-technology" crime on several continents and earns enormous profits from the trans-Atlantic heroin trade, it began as a humble instrument for the maintenance of control over mediocre land in central Sicily. Agricultural property around Palermo was traditionally held in the form of large latifundi and owned by Sicilian aristocrats who relied upon campieri, or private guards, to defend this property from a land-hungry peasantry. The conquest of Sicily by the Piedmontese in 1860 accelerated the slow erosion of classical feudalism there, and by the second half of the nineteenth century, the aristocrats had largely become absentee landlords, surrendering day-to-day control of their estates to a class of omnipotent gabbelotti (or managers) who frequently forced the original owners to sell their estates at give-away prices, forming the basis for a landowning bourgeoisie. In the absence of a governmental system capable of enforcing their rule over the peasantry, these gabellotti employed gangs of thugs to do their dirty work, thus laying the basis for the modern Mafia.(58)

After the unification of Italy, this early Mafia resisted efforts on the part of the Italian police to impose any real control over Sicilian affairs, until the landowners realized that the new Italian government was pathologically frightened of popular unrest and was prepared to allow the use of police and army forces to protect bourgeois interests. To ensure support at this level, the Sicilian elite began to send deputies to the Rome parliament who would vote for any government as long as it did nothing to threaten the social system in Sicily.(59)

This backing from Rome meant that the landowners could dispense with some of their expensive and unreliable retainers. Knowing only violence as a profession, some of these redundant killers retreated to the mountains and formed gangs of brigands. Since these brigands no longer served a useful function, the police were encouraged to hunt them down, giving the public the impression that the forces of law and order were striking at the Mafia. Quite separate from the bandits, however, there remained an interlinking system of patronage and social control, reinforced by the use of violence, increasingly centred on

Palermo and frequently called the "High Mafia". The notion that this Mafia was ever one monolithic centrally-controlled organization is, of course, nonsense; power has always been divided among rival cosche (clans) originally based on parentage.(60)

The weakness of Italian governments after World War One and demands for the re-distribution of the land advanced by the PSI and PCI forced the "notables" of Sicily to rely more upon their own resources, increasing the power of the mafiosi. When Mussolini offered them the genuine possibility of social control in exchange for political support, however, another whole generation of low-level mafiosi was made redundant, and the famous war against the Mafia waged after 1925 by the "Iron Prefect" Cesare Mori can be seen as a successful operation to clean up criminal elements who were now superfluous. When Mori got too close to the "High Mafia", however, and began arresting men who had made themselves important to fascism, his crusade was quickly brought to a close.(61)

A new chapter was opened by the Allied invasion of Sicily in July 1943, however, when the US government deployed convicted American mafiosi as agents, and relied upon the criminal infrastructure of the island to provide a securely anti-communist governing class once the island had been conquered. During the post-war period, the landowners of Sicily found that the threat to their position was once again serious since the PCI and PSI were now demanding access to land on behalf of peasant organizations. In the context of terrible confusion and increased social misery, the Sicilian crime-rate soared as the island's elite turned once again to a re-invigorated Mafia it could now only partially control. After a few turbulent years, the entrepreneurial classes on the island once again found that their interests would be best served by an alliance with the ruling power in Rome, and threw their weight behind the CD. This left the reactionary police forces of the period and the Mafia working essentially in tandem against the parties of the left, and the police stood carefully aside when mafiosi shot up public meetings, assassinated prominent leftists, and burned down party headquarters.(62)

In the years since this immediate post-war period, Mafia criminality has changed substantially, penetrating the mainland and developing a trans-Atlantic dimension. This "New Mafia" is less concerned with maintaining control over farm land and more involved in pure criminality with heroin smuggling, prostitution, protection rackets and kidnapping becoming the hallmarks of a serious crime wave which has continued since the 1950's. For most of the post-war period, efforts to deal with the Mafia have been hampered by the formidable level of institutional rivalry between the two forces of police. Limited by their provincial organization and to some extent penetrated and corrupted by mafiosi, the Interior Ministry police have only sporadically been capable of effective work against Sicilian criminality. The Carabiniere policy of transferring officers away from their native provinces, as well as a substantially higher esprit de corps, has kept them relatively free from contagion, but their success has still been uneven.(63)

As policemen from the mainland, the Carabinieri are seen as foreigners by most Sicilians, and they are effectively isolated in their dealings with the locals. When crimes are committed, the Carabinieri duly render reports, although the famous Sicilian omerta normally denies them the cooperation even of the Mafia's victims and local courts often set the guilty free after intimidated witnesses refuse to testify. The sheer complexity of modern Mafia crime is a staggering problem; with millions of dollars flowing in and out of Palermo, the police forces need teams of lawyers and accountants as much as detectives and investigators, but given traditionally low police salaries, it is difficult to attract this kind of expertise.(64)

In the past, there have been periods when the police and the Mafia managed to achieve a delicate truce in which they avoided killing one another. During these truces, the Mafia accepted that the police must occasionally arrest someone, and a few minor figures or the losers in gangland conflicts would be delivered - normally dead - into the hands of the police, who were then able to claim the credit. When the police did arrest prominent Mafia, the truce broke down and policemen would be killed in revenge. The murder of a very major policeman like Dalla Chiesa means that the truce is currently shattered, probably beyond repair.(65)

In 1962, a parliamentary commission, the so-called Antimafia, was instituted to study the problem and its final report, issued in 1976, showed clearly that the multi-level contacts between the High Mafia and the Christian Democratic Party were the primary obstacles to police operations against criminality. While this revelation was hardly news to the law enforcement community, the report has deepened the antagonism felt by many policemen against the nation's leading political party, and to some extent, the Antimafia report has reinforced feelings of helplessness among many otherwise energetic officers. At the present writing, however, there are signs of a serious

commitment on the part of many senior Carabiniere officers to the development of effective styles of policing for
Sicily and those parts of the mainland infested by Mafia
criminality, a change which is closely related to the internal desire of the Carabinieri to move themselves back
to the centre of the law enforcement stage.(66)

Among senior Carabinieri, however, this enthusiasm is
tempered by practical thinking, especially after the killing of Dalla Chiesa and a number of other top men in recent years. There is a general belief that one of Dalla
Chiesa's errors was to suggest that he meant to return to
Cesare Mori's draconian methods of the 1920's and proposed
to wage an all-out war. Instead, Carabinieri "mafiolog-
ists" speak of tackling the problem in stages, moving
against one criminal power group while offering at least
temporary guarantees to other groups that they will be
left alone. Most senior Carabinieri do not believe, however, that a final victory over Sicilian criminality is
possible until they receive serious political backing from
the Christian Democratic Party. Indeed, some have expressed private fears that the CD itself is too corrupt
ever to deliver this backing, and that serious action
against the Mafia might have to await a change in government.

The Police and Society

Urban Italy today looks like a concentration camp. The
streets are dotted by young men wearing badly tailored
uniforms and carrying sub-machineguns they barely know how
to handle. The war against terrorism seems to be winding
down, and although gunmen from the right and left can and
will continue to carry out their deadly missions, the days
when they could threaten the future of the Italian state
seem to be ending. However, the phenomenon of common
(and increasingly violent) criminality remains at epidemic
proportions.

While the Interior Ministry police have gained some
self-esteem, new skills and professional abilities during
the war against terrorism, they are restless and discon-
tented. Since the mid-seventies, there have been increasing demands for a civilianization and unionization of
the corps, demands which have largely been met. The government has even signalled its desire to make fundamental
alterations in the Interior Ministry police by changing
the name of the uniformed patrolmen who do most of the
hard work on the street from Corpo degli Agenti della Pubblica Sicurezza to the more euphonic Polizia di Stato; it
remains to be seen, however, whether the Ministry can re-

store morale and efficiency to this unit, whatever the name.(67)

Thanks to the outbreak of the so-called P-2 scandal, public confidence in the financial honesty of some top policemen has been shaken. Led by an ex-fascist named Lucio Gelli, P-2 was the name of a maverick masonic lodge which brought together important men in various branches of the public administration and in at least some important cases, P-2 members engaged in criminal conspiracies. While several Carabiniere and Interior Ministry figures have been implicated, the worst damage was done to the Guardia di Finanza when its commanding officer was arrested in 1980 for involvement in an excise-tax evasion scheme which cost the Italian tax-payer hundreds of millions of pounds.(68)

As a consequence of their decisive leadership in the face of the terrorist threat, the Carabinieri have achieved a new prominence in Italian life, and while Interior Ministry enrolments are sagging, the Carabinieri are in a position to turn away applicants. The bulk of the new Carabiniere officers are for the first time being trained through the university level, in belated recognition of the fact that well-educated terrorists and computer criminals require highly trained police personnel. Today, the number of neo-fascists in police ranks is declining; political loyalties in both departments run in an arc from the Liberals on the right to the Socialists on the left, although many Carabinieri have nothing but harsh words for the Christian Democratic Party and many enlisted Interior Ministry policemen are members of the PCI.(69)

Unfortunately, the two police departments have continued their timeless vendetta against one another. Occasional calls for a unification of the two police departments have been howled down by representatives of both sides, and many believe that a unified police would not work, and would constitute a danger to democracy if it did. From the far left, the notion of locally controlled police departments (on the British model) is still occasionally raised, but there is no visible political movement in this direction.

Despite some of their achievements in recent years, none of the country's several police forces can be described as popular, and the average patrolman is seen as ignorant, blindly obedient to orders, potentially vicious and authoritarian, images often reflected in the enormously popular plays of Dario Fo.(70) The Carabinieri are substantially more respected than any other police force, but they must live with the knowledge that jokes directed against the Irish in Britain and against the Polish in

America are told about the Carabinieri in Italy.

As a result of the terrorists and the Mafia, the work of the police has become a popular media issue in the Italian press. While left-wing newspapers once tended to criticize the police furiously while the right automatically defended them as bastions of law and order, there has been a tendency since the era of terrorism to report police matters somewhat more even-handedly. Most commentators have stressed that the basic tasks of the police in Italy for the coming decade will be the following: to continue the process of de-politicization, freeing themselves from dependence upon one political party, and making themselves trusted by citizens of all constitutional political views; to evolve strategies for mutual co-existence and cooperation with one another; and lastly to mount a determined assault upon criminality. A police force, however, does not exist in a political vacuum; the Italian police will need the backing and assistance of a political elite which shares these ambitions, and - at the present writing - no such political elite exists.

FOOTNOTES

1. See Pino Arlacchi et al, Morte di un generale (Milano, 1982).
2. See Robert Fried, The Italian Prefects (New Haven 1963); Angelo D'Orsi, La Polizia: le forze dell'ordine italiano (Milano, 1972); Romano Canosa, La polizia in Italia dal 1945 a oggi, (Bologna, 1976) and Fabio Isman, I forzati dell'ordine (Venise, 1877).
3. See Enrico d'Alessandro, Arma dei Carabinieri (Rome, 1972) and Giovanni Artieri, I Carabinieri (Rome, 1964); Richard Collin, The De Lorenzo Gambit: the Italian Coup Manqué' of 1964 (London, 1976).
4. See Gino Bellavita's Il paese delle cinque polizie (Milano, 1962) and Guido Corso's L'Ordine Pubblico (Milano, 1979).
5. Artieri, op.cit., pp. 2-3; Brian Chapman, Police State (London, 1970); John Coatman, Police (London, 1959); James Cramer, The World's Police (London, 1964).
6. Giovanni Bolis, La polizia e le classi pericolose della società (Bologna, 1879); Federico Giorio, Ricordi di questura (Milano, 1882); Giuseppe Alongi, "Polizia e criminalita in Italia", Nuova Antologia, Vol. 68, 1 Jan 1897; Emilio Saracini, Crepuscoli della Polizia (Napoli, 1922).
7. See Richard Hostetter, The Italian Socialist Movement, Vol. I (Princeton, 1958); Maurice Neufield,

Italy: A School for Awakening Countries (Ithaca, 1961), pp. 14, 172-3.

8. cf. Christopher Seton-Watson, Italy from Liberalism to Fascism (London, 1967), p. 76; e.g. Giorio, op. cit., p. 55; S. Merlino, Questo e l'Italia (Milano, 1890), p. 101; A. Coletti, Anarchici e questori (Padova, 1977) pp. 7-20.

9. See Augusteo Bondi, Memorie di un questore, (Milano, 1910), p. 185; Gaetano Arfe', Storia del socialismo italiano (Torino, 1965), pp. 9-11; A. Borghi, Mezzo secolo di anarchia (Naples, 1956).

10. Giusepe Sensales, "L'Anagrafe di polizia", Nuova Antologia, 16 May 1901; Istituto Centrale di Statistica, Sommario di statistiche storiche (Rome, 1958), pp. 39 ff; cf. Alongi, op. cit., p. 121; Saracini, op. cit., p. 65; d'Alessandro, op. cit., p. 43; Ex-Ministro dell'Interno, "La Polizia", Nuova Antologia, 16 Feb. 1890; Giuseppe Codronchi, "Sul riordinamento della Pubblica Sicurezza", Nuova Antologia, Vol 59, 15 Sept. 1895; Amadeo Nasalli Rocca, Memorie di un prefetto (Rome, 1946), p. 31.

11. Napoleone Colajanni, L'Italia nel 1898(Palermo, 1901).

12. Giovanni Giolitti (1842-1928) had previously been Prime Minister in 1892/3, and returned to power in 1901 as Interior Minister under Giusepe Zanardelli, emerging as both Prime Minister and Interior Minister in his own right after 1903; for basic statements of his police policy, see Giovanni Giolitti, Discorsi Parlamentari, Vol. I (Rome, 1953-6), p. 566 and ibid, Vol. II, pp. 569 ff, 626 ff. and pp. 638 ff; cf. Carlo Ghisalberti's "Governo, parlamento e burocrazia", in Emilio Gentile (ed.) L'Italia Giolittiana (Bari, 1977), pp. 121-132.

13. See Nino Valeri's introduction to Giolitti's Discorse Extraparlamentari (Torino, 1952) pp. 33-36; Roberto Chiarini, "La svolta liberale del governo Zanardelli-Giolitti" in Aldo Mola (ed.) Istituzioni e metodi politici dell'eta giolittiana (Torino, 1979); Saracini, op.cit., p. 159. cf. Bondi, op. cit., pp. 123-4.

14. See G. Natale, Giolitti e gli italiani (Milano, 1949) p. 447; Giolitti, Quarant'anni, II, p. 63; G. Procacci, "Lo sciopero generale del 1904", Rivista Storica del Socialismo, 1962, pp. 451 ff. and F. Fiorentino, Ordine pubblico nell'Italia giolittiana (Rome, 1978).

15. cf. Renzo De Felice, Mussolini il revoluzionario (Torino, 1965) pp. 103-9.

16. Luigi Lotti, La settimana rossa (Firenze, 1965).

17. See Brunello Vigezzi, L'Italia di fronte alla prima guerra mondiale, Vol. I. L'Italia neutrale (Milano, 1966); Brunello Vigezzi, "Le radiose giornate del maggio

1915 nei rapporti dei prefetti", Nuova Rivista Storica, 1959, pp. 313-344, and 1960, pp. 54-111.

18. A. Salandra, Italy and the Great War (London, 1932), p. 68; Natalia De Stefano, "Moti poplari in Emilia-Romagna e Toscana; 1915-1917", Rivista Storica del Socialismo, 1968, pp. 191-216; Renzo De Felice, "Ordine Pubblico e orientamenti delle massi popolari italiane", Rivista Storica di Socialismo, 1963.

19. See P. Spriano, Storia del Partito Comunista, Vol I, (Torino, 1967) p. 89; Roberto Vivarelli, Dopoguerra in Italia e l'avvento del fascismo (Napoli, 1967), pp. 309-312; P. Corner, Fascism in Ferrara (London, 1975), pp. 83-84; 104-5; B. Maione, Il biennio rosso, (Bologna, 1975).

20. De Felice, Mussolini il rivoluzionario, pp. 527 ff.

21. L. Donati, "La Guardia Regia", Storia Contemporanea, Sept. 1977; V. Nitti, L'Opera di Nitti (Torino, 1924); Paolo Alatri, Nitti, D'Annunzio e la questione Adriatico (Milano, 1959); Michael Ledeen, The First Duce (Baltimore, 1977).

22. Seton-Watson, op.cit., pp. 505-629; A. Tasca, Nascita e Avvento di fascismo (Firenze, 1950).

23. A. Repaci, La Marcia su Roma, (Rome, 1963); A. Lyttelton, The Seizure of Power: Fascism in Italy 1919-1929 (London, 1973) pp. 15-120; G. Salvemini, The Origins of Fascism (New York, 1973).

24. Corso, op. cit. pp. 51-3; Salvatore Foderaro, La Milizia Volontaria e le sue specialita (Padova, 1939); D'Orsi, op.cit., p. 33; Canosa, op. cit., p. 98; De Felice, Mussolini Il Fascista, I (Torino, 1966) pp. 437 ff; Guido Leto, OVRA, Fascismo e antifascismo (Bologna, 1951).

25. B. Mussolini, My Autobiography (London, 1928) pp. 195 ff; C. Rossi, Personaggi di ieri e di oggi (Milano, 1960) p. 217.

26. De Felice, Fascista I, pp. 388-96, 431-440; Fried, op.cit., p. 182 ff.

27. Leto, op. cit., p. 16; A. Dumini, 17 Colpi (Milano, 1958); Giuseppe Rossini, Il Delitto Matteotti (Bologna, 1966); Cesare Rossi, Il Delitto Matteotti (Milan, 1956); Carlo Silvestri, Matteotti, Mussolini e il dramma italiano (Rome, 1947).

28. See D'Orsi, op. cit., p. 34; Corso, op. cit., p. 28; Giovanni Artieri, Tre ritratti politici e quattro attentati (Rome, 1953) pp. 171 ff.

29. Leto, op. cit., p. 38; R. De Felice, Mussolini Il Fascista, II (Torino, 1968) pp. 213 ff.

30. Canosa, op. cit., pp. 70, 117 ff; E. Rossi, Pupilla del Duce (Parma, 1956) p. 47; Leto, op. cit., p. 57.

31. Charles Delzell, Mussolini's Enemies (Princton, 1961); E. Rossi, Pupilla del Duce (Parma, 1956), Clara Conti, Servizio Segreto: Sronache e documenti dei delitti di stato (Roma, 1946); E. Rossi, Una Spia del regime, Milano, 1955).

32. C. Senise, Quando ero capo della polizia (Rome, 1946); Meir Michaelis, Mussolini and the Jews, (Oxford, 1978).

33. Arnaldo Ferrara (ed.) I Carabinieri nella Resistenze e nella guerra di liberazione (Rome, 1978); Canosa, op. cit., pp. 103 ff.

34. See Norman Kogan, A Political History of Postwar Italy (London, 1966), pp. 9-35; D'Orsi, op. cit. p. 40.

35. Giancarlo Lehner, Dalla parte dei poliziotti (Milano, 1978), p. 27; D'Orsi, op. cit., p. 39; cf. Giorgio Boatti, L'Arma: i Carabinieri da De Lorenzo a Mino: 1962-1977 (Milano, 1978) pp. 28-29; Silvio Bertocci, "Indagine sull'Arma dei Carabinieri" Il Ponte, July 1969, pp. 1060 ff.

36. See D'Orsi, op. cit., p. 40; cf. "La recostruzione delle forze di polizia del dopoguerra", Documenti di vita italiana, 1952, p. 763; Sandro Medici, Vite di poliziotti (Torino, 1979) pp. 20, 28-30.

37. G. Viola and M. Pizzola in Polizia: controinchiesta su abusi ed eccidi delle forze dell'ordine in Italia dal 1943 al 1976 (Roma, 1976).

38. Koogan, op. cit., p. 38, 188-9; Boatti, op. cit., pp. 26-7; cf. Medici, op. cit., pp. 1, 35.

39. Medici, op. cit., p. v, 29; D'Orsi, op.cit., pp. 47-49; Lehner, op. cit., pp. 33, 59.

40. Boatti, op. cit., pp. 30, 39-40; Lehner, op. cit., p. 27; Bertocci, op. cit., pp. 1073 ff; E. Vollini and P. Alatri, La questione dell'Alto Adige (Milano 1961).

41. K. Robert Nilsson, Italy's Opening to the Right: The Tambroni Experiment of 1960, Ph.D. dissertation, Columbia University, 1964.

42. Pietro Nenni, "Where the Italian Socialists Stand", Foreign Affairs, Jan 1962; Collin, op. cit., R. Trionfera, Sifar Affair (Rome, 1968); R. Zangrandi, Inchiesta sul Sifar (Rome, 1970); Senato della Repubblica. Commissione Parlamentare D'Inchiesta sugli eventi del Giugno-Luglio 1964 (Rome, 1971, two volumes).

43. cf. Alberto Ronchey, "Terrorism in Italy", Foreign Affairs, Spring 1979, p. 923; G. Bocca, Storia della Repubblica Italiana dalla caduta del fascismo a oggi (Milano, 1982), pp. 201, 244; cf. Paul Furlong, "Political Terrorism in Italy: Responses, Reactions and Immobilism", in Juliet Lodge (ed.) Terrorism: A Challenge to the State (Oxford, 1981), p. 61.

44. Ronchey, op. cit., p. 924-8; Bocca, _Storia_, pp. 212 ff.

45. Bocca, op. cit., pp. 195 ff; See M. Fini and A. Barberi, _Valpreda: Processo al processo_ (Milano, 1972); Stephen Hellman, "The Longest Campaign: Communist Party Strategy and the Elections of 1976" in Howard R. Penniman (Ed.) _Italy at the Polls_ (Washington, 1977) pp. 155 ff; Furlong, op. cit., pp. 69-70; 78-79.

46. A. Silj, _Mai piu senza fucile: alle origini dei NAP e delle BR_ (Firenze, 1977), pp. 79-93; V. Tessandori, _Brigate Rosse, imputazione banda armata_ (Milano, 1977); G. Mazini, _Indagini su un brigatista rosso: La storia di Walter Alasia_ (Torino, 1978)

47. Renato Curcio born in Trento 1941, now in prison; his wife, Margherita Cagol (1945-1975) freed Curcio temporarily from Casale Monferrato prison in 1975 but was killed later that year in a gun fight with police; cf. Bocca, Storia, p. 199 ff; cf. Ronchey, op. cit., pp. 929-31; Clair Sterling, _The Terror Network_ (London, 1981) pp. 31 ff; Furlong, op. cit., p. 72; Ronchey, op. cit., p. 931.

48. It is clear that the Red Brigades have enjoyed contacts with the Palestinians and the German Red Army Faction, but the notion that they were pawns manipulated by the Soviet Union or the CIA, is doubtful despite Clare Sterling's strong advocacy of this view and my own use of this theme in a novel, _Imbroglio_ (London, 1981); cf. Giorgio Bocca, _Moro, una tragedia italiana_ (Milano, 1978) pp. 24 ff.

49. "Il nero non paga", _Panorama,_ 18 August 1980; Bocca, _Storia_, pp. 214-5; Furlong, op.cit., p. 73-4; in Arlacci, op.cit., see both Giorgio Bocca "I Dalla Chiesa", pp. 8-9; and Ferrari, "Carriera di un militare", p. 33.

50. Bocca, _Storia,_ pp. 209-20; _Bratach Dubh, Armed Struggle in Italy: A Chronology_, Anarchist Pamphlets, No. 4, (Catania, 1979).

51. Bocca, _Storia_, p. 209; Furlong, op.cit., p. 58.

52. Furlong, op.cit., p. 75; Bocca, _Storia_, p. 201; Ferrari, "Carriera di un militare", op.cit., p. 35; Hellman, op.cit., pp. 162 ff; Bocca, _Storia_, pp. 233 ff; Ronchey, op cit., pp. 926-7.

53. See F. Coisson, "Quanto costa la vittoria?", _Panorama_, 7 January 1980; Furlong, op. cit., p. 83; P. Buongiorno, "Un servizio troppo militare", _Panorama_, 16 November 1981; Corrado Augias, "Questo documento e tre volte importante", _La Repubblica,_ 13 February 1979.

54. Bocca "I Dalla Chiesa", op.cit., p. 11; Furlong, op.cit., p. 81; Ronchey, op.cit., p. 939.

55. At the same time, Carabiniere General Grassini was Chief of SISDE and Carabiniere General Arnaldo Ferrara was special advisor to the President for anti-terrorism, while several other Carabiniere officers had been appointed prefects, giving the Corps a complete coverage of the scene at the top; cf. Augias, op.cit.; Ferrari, "Carriera di un militare", op.cit., p. 37.

56. M. Bussoletti and A. Carlucci, "L'infiltrato", Panorama, 6 April 1981; M. Ventura, "I nazi-brigatisti", Panorama, 7 July 1980.

57. Tana de Zuluetta's conclusions in The Sunday Times of 31 January 1982 are confirmed by my own interviews among senior Carabiniere officers.

58. Anton Blok, The Mafia of a Sicilian Village: 1860-1960 (Oxford, 1974); Filippo Gaja, L'esercito della lupara (Milano, 1962) and Carlo Levi, Le parole sono pietre (Torino, 1960).

59. Michele Pantaleone, The Mafia and Politics (London, 1966) pp. 25-27; Norman Lewis, The Honoured Society (London, 1967) pp. 25 ff; Napoleone Colajanni, Nel regno della Mafia (Rome, 1900); L. Franchetti, La Sicilia nel 1876 (Firenze, 1877).

60. cf. Blok, op.cit., p. 106; Jeremy Boissevain, Friends of Friends: Networks, Manipulators and Coalitions (Oxford, 1973).

61. See C. Mori, The Last Struggle with the Mafia (London, 1933); Arrigo Petacco, Il prefetto di Ferro (Milano, 1975).

62. cf. Danilo Dolci, Waste (London, 1963) pp. 69-85; Pantaleone, op.cit., pp. 133 ff.

63. Pino Arlacchi, "La mafia nel sistema mondiale della droga", in Arlacchi, op.cit., pp. 56-79.

64. M. Sorgi, "Mafia e impreditori" in Arlacchi, op. cit., pp. 96-114; see L. Sciascia's Il giorno della civetta (Torino, 1961) for a moving fictional portrait of a young Carabiniere officer in a Sicilian town; R. Candida, Questa Mafia (Rome, 1960); S. Romano, Storia della Mafia (Verona, 1966).

65. This information comes from my interviews with senior Carabiniere officials who have served in Sicily.

66. See M. Pantaleone's L'antimafia: occasione mancata (Torino, 1969); M. Cimino, "L'antimafia" in Arlacchi, op.cit., pp. 135-151.

67. See G. Deriu, "Le due anime della PS", La Repubblica, 27 March 1977.

68. See C. Sottocorona, "Tutti ai vostri posti", Panorama, 21 September 1981; T. Oldami, "La rapina del secolo", ibid., 10 November 1980.

69. Personal conversation with senior Carabiniere officials; cf. F. Ceccarelli and P. Buongiorno, "Stellette rosse", Panorama, 27 July 1981.

70. Fo's plays, Accidental Death of an Anarchist and Can't Pay Won't Pay, have run successfully in London's West End theatres.

Further Reading

Arlacchi, Pino, et al, Morte di un generale, Milano, 1982.

Artieri, Giovanni, I Carabinieri, Rome, 1964.

Bellavita, Gino, Il paese delle cinque polizie, Milano, 1962.

Bondi, Augusto, Memorie di un questore, Milano, 1910.

Canosa, Romano, La Polizia in Italia dal 1945 a oggi, Bologna, 1976.

Collin, Richard Oliver, The De Lorenzo Gambit: the Italian Coup Manqué of 1964, London, 1976.

Corso, Guido, L'ordine pubblico, Milano, 1979.

D'Alessandro, Enrico, L'Arma dei Carabinieri dalla fondazione ai nostri giorni, Rome, 1972.

Donati, Lorenzo, "La Guardia Regia", Storia Contemporania, VIII, n.3., September 1977, pp. 441-489.

D'Orsi, Angelo, La polizia: le forze dell'ordine italiano, Milano, 1972.

Fried, Robert, The Italian Prefects: A Study in Administrative Politics, New Haven, 1963.

Furlong, Paul, "Political Terrorism in Italy: Responses, Reactions and Immobilism", in J. Lodge (ed.) Terrorism: A Challenge to the State, Oxford, 1981.

Isman, Fabio, I forzati dell'ordine, Venise, 1977

Lehner, Giancarlo, Dalle parte dei poliziotti, Milano, 1978.

Medici, Sandro, Vite di poliziotti, Torino, 1979.

Mori, Cesare, The Last Struggle with the Mafia, London, 1933.

Pantaleone, Michele, The Mafia and Politics, London, 1966.

Rocca, Amadeo Nasalli, Memorie di un prefetto, Rome, 1946.

Ronchey, Alberto, "Terrorism in Italy", Foreign Affairs, Spring, 1979, p. 923.

Saracini, Emilio, I crepuscoli della polizia, Napoli, 1922.

Senise, Carmine, Quando ero Capo della Polizia: 1940-1943, Rome, 2nd ed., 1946.

Glossary

BR - Red Brigades
brigatisti - Members of Red Brigades
Capitanneria del Porto - harbour police
Commissario - chief superintendent in major city
Corpo Forestale - forest police
Direzione per le investigazioni generali e per le operazioni speciali (DIGOS) - anti-terrorist police
Guardia di Finanza - fiscal police
Milizia Volontaria Sicurezza Nazionale (MVSN) - Mussolini's militia police force
Movimento Sociale Italiano (MSI) - neo-fascist party
PCI - Italian Communist Party
PSI - Italian Socialist Party
Questor - senior police official in a province
SISDE - Post-1976 Intelligence Service
SISME - Military Security Intelligence Service
Servizio Informazioni (SID) - Pre-1976 Intelligence Service

Chapter 8

THE POLICE SYSTEM OF SPAIN

Ian R Macdonald

Foreign images of the Spanish police are not flattering.
Memories of their treatment of political dissent in the
days of the dictator Franco, the poet García Lorca's pre-
Civil-War vision of the 'patent-leather souls' of the
Guardia Civil (a police force whose shiny tricorn hats are
to the Spanish image what the bobby's helmet is to the
British), the worldwide television pictures of the Guardia
Civil Colonel Tejero brandishing his pistol in the Spanish
Parliament in 1981, all these mingle with visitors' memories of men publicly and routinely armed with rifles and
sub-machine-guns. But the Spanish Civil War ended over
forty years ago, Franco is dead, and Tejero has been given
thirty years. This chapter will look behind the images
and assess the nature and extent of change - and continuity - in the Spanish police forces.

Spain has changed since General Franco's death in
1975, but Spain also changed radically under Franco. In
1936 he and fellow-officers rose against the elected
government of the Second Spanish Republic and defeated it
in a horrifying civil war that lasted almost three years.
From 1939 to 1975 he ruled Spain as dictator. When he
came to power Spain was still predominantly an agricultural economy with industrialised areas in the Basque country
and Catalonia. His backers, apart from the Church and the
military, were essentially what Spaniards call the 'oligarchy', the owners of the large landed estates. But at a
constantly accelerating pace, especially in the 1960's and
early 1970's, the Spanish economy grew and was transformed. By 1975 Spain had become, in economic terms, a developed industrial country, and leadership had passed from
the landowners to the industrialists. The swift transition from the authoritarian Franco system to a system of
parliamentary democracy was simply a catching-up operation
in terms of political institutions that reflected the new
shape of economic power.

215

In 1940 52% of the Spanish working population lived from the land. By 1975 only 22% did and they were producing only 9% of the Gross National Product. The rural population had dwindled and what was left had, relatively speaking, not shared in the new prosperity. This massive and rapid shift in the economic shape of Spain had its obvious outward signs. First, there was a dramatic movement of people to the big cities. By 1970, 37% lived in cities of over 100,000 inhabitants, compared with 19% in 1940. Migrants from rural areas poured into the industrial regions of Catalonia, Madrid, and the Basque country, settling in hastily-built cheap apartments, facing totally unfamiliar environments, and in the cases of Catalonia and the Basque country, unfamiliar languages.

This rapid economic growth was underpinned by three sources of foreign exchange: tourism, the Spanish emigrants who had left to find jobs in Western Europe, and the rapid growth of foreign investment. All of these brought Spaniards into touch with a neighbouring world from which they had been traditionally isolated. Spain became, little by little, socially, politically, and economically, more like the rest of Western Europe. Even the Catholic Church, originally a bulwark of the Franco régime, had changed in response to outside trends and distanced itself somewhat from Franco, though it had simultaneously lost its rigid grip on the nation's moral life. Spain was becoming urban, industrial, European, and its problems moved nearer to those familiar to the policemen of other European countries. The provinces of Madrid and Barcelona, for instance, with 25% of Spain's population, now account for 60% of all bank robberies and 40% of all crime reported to the Policía.

But the pattern of continuous rapid economic growth was ended by the oil price crises of 1973 and 1979. The European economies no longer needed foreign workers, and Spanish emigrants returned home to find growing inflation and unemployment, which, with all their associated social tensions, remain high. Youth unemployment has become especially serious: by 1983 43% of those under 25 were out of work. And of all the unemployed, only a quarter receive unemployment benefit.

Meanwhile Franco's death in 1975 opened a process of rapid political change. Juan Carlos was crowned King in November 1975, a year later the Cortes, the Spanish Parliament, approved the Law of Political Reform, and in June 1977 the first democratic elections since 1936 were held, returning a centre-right government. By the end of 1978 Spain had an entirely new constitution. Fresh elections confirmed the centre-right in power, and then in October

1982 the election of a parliament with an overall majority for the Socialist Party under Felipe González brought a new stage in the development of parliamentary democracy. Not only were the institutions in place, but a peaceful transfer of power to a party, however moderate, opposed to the traditional oligarchy had become possible.

The political institutions of post-Franco Spain are dramatically different from those under the dictator. The new 1978 Constitution sets out to establish an 'advanced democratic society'. Parliament is elected by all those over 18. Political parties and trade unions, illegal under Franco, have been given constitutional status, with guaranteed freedoms of operation. The Constitution abolishes the death penalty and prohibits torture and inhuman or degrading treatment. It guarantees freedom of expression, and proscribes advance censorship. It gives the right to meet peacefully and unarmed without prior authorization, though meetings in public thoroughfares and demonstrations must be notified in advance. The right of association is recognized, though, with a backward glance at Spain's history, secret and paramilitary associations are banned. There is a right to strike, though the law may make provision for the maintenance of essential services, and may limit the right to join unions in the case of bodies under military discipline. And constitutionally the armed forces have as their commander-in-chief the King.

If post-Franco Spain has rejected the dictator's institutions, it has also, and this too is embodied in the 1978 Constitution, rejected one of his most important political aims, the rigidly centralized unity of the Spanish state. This unity has been a traditional aim of the armed forces for more than a century, and one of the functions of the Guardia Civil, created in 1844, has always been the strengthening and preservation of a centrally united state. But the forces of regionalism and nationalism within Spain, rooted in profound geographical, economic, and linguistic differences, have remained strong. Franco failed to impose his uniformity and in consequence governments from 1976 on have espoused a policy of granting autonomy to areas that requested it, to the extent that all of Spain is now divided into seventeen 'Autonomous Communities'.

Nevertheless the dramatic social and economic changes in Spain over the period since 1960 and the political changes since 1975 are not a straightforward break with the past. The political changes themselves were carried out by a 'negotiated break', that is to say, Franco's unelected parliament voted itself out of existence and created its successor, which in turn created the Constitution. The latter abrogates all previous laws that are in conflict with it, but those not abrogated remain. Another important kind of continuity lies in the fact that changes, if they are to be more than verbal, have to be implemented and enforced by the civil service, the judiciary, and the forces of law and order, staffed essentially by the same people who had operated the old system, obviously conditioning the results of reform.

The judicial system, for instance, is of long standing and typically continental, with an inquisitorial style of criminal proceeding in which an examining magistrate, assisted by the police, investigates a case in full before the trial proper. There are no juries (though the 1978 Constitution opens up this possibility it has not yet been implemented). The basic structure was inherited by Franco and survives him, but in his hands it had lost all independence since the principle of the separation of executive and judicial powers had no place in his system. He had also created a series of special courts to deal with political cases, the most notorious and hated being the Tribunal de Orden Público, the Public Order Court, instituted to deal with activities 'undermining the foundations of the state'. Military courts, too, were used routinely to deal with political and public order charges against civilians, a long-standing Spanish practice intensified under Franco.

The Tribunal de Orden Público was abolished in 1977, and military courts limited to strictly military affairs in 1980, but it takes time for a fully independent judicial system to develop. While there have been remarkable changes, public confidence in the courts is still not high, in part due to suspicion that old practices and men still linger, in part due to the gross inadequacy of the unmodernized and underfunded court system to cope with current crime rates. The judicial system is thus a reminder of the importance of the historical context, a context that, in a broader sense, is the constant backdrop to the process of change. The breakdown of law and order followed by civil war and brutal repression is the remembered threat that hangs over Spanish political life.

The Spanish Police: a brief history

The development of the police system is closely bound up with Spain's long, halting journey from absolutism to parliamentary democracy. The Guardia Civil, for instance, was created in 1844, the precise moment at which 'moderate' (that is, conservative) liberalism established itself in power. The functions of the Guardia Civil of protecting property and order, especially rural property and order, of guarding the roads, and of reinforcing the authority of central, as opposed to local, government, derive from this moment of creation, as does its military character, reflecting the reality of Spanish political life that the Army was not an arm of the state, but its spinal column. This military character gave the Guardia Civil not only efficiency and a sense of tradition, but also techniques and an autonomy that made civil authorities and city police chiefs in the later nineteenth century be unable or hesitate to use it in the growing urban centres, and a distinct urban police system slowly and hesitantly evolved, comprising the plain-clothes Vigilancia in the rôle of judicial police, and the uniformed Seguridad concerned with public order and law enforcement. The Guardia Civil came to specialise in rural policing. Beyond these national corps there was a patchwork of forces, often traditional, with local or specific functions. Only one of these, the Carabineros, needs mention. Founded in 1829 they were created to 'make war on contraband'.

By 1936 the Guardia Civil had some 31,150 men and the Seguridad 17,660, while the Carabineros numbered 15,306. It was on this basic structure that Franco, after the Civil War, built his police system, for in 1940 the Carabineros were absorbed into the Guardia Civil who took over their anti-smuggling duties. In 1941 the Policía Armada y de Tráfico was created out of the Seguridad, while Vigilancia became the Cuerpo General de Policía. Later, in 1959, traffic control on the main roads was transferred from the Policía Armada to a newly-created section of the Guardia Civil, the Agrupación de Tráfico. The strength of the Guardia Civil by 1960 was 60,366, while the Policía Armada numbered 18,799.

These structural continuities and modifications of course conceal major changes. The armed forces, or a part of them, between 1936 and 1939, had overthrown the constituted legality of Spain and even though the police system had always been dominated by the military, the police forces of Franco's subsequent régime reflected the violent change. The officers of the Policía Armada were drawn in large majority from the victorious army, while the Guardia Civil underwent a process of further militarization. To its own military traditions were added those of the Carabineros, and its senior officers and newly-created General Staff were drawn from the army. Thus Franco's military exercised total control over the bulk of the police system, and the uniformed police were both legally part of the armed forces and functionally their public face. In a

political system with an almost total unity of powers and
with the absolute domination of the executive, police and
régime were completely identified and the security forces
became the decisive element in the régime's survival for
36 years. Though the armed and police forces were poorly
paid and equipped, the identification of officers with the
régime ensured almost complete loyalty.

In the early years of the régime the tasks of the
police forces confirmed them as extensions of the armed
forces. The more than 100,000 executions after the end of
the Civil War, the imprisonment of perhaps 300,000, and
the conflicts with guerrilla forces, suggest clearly enough the major rôles of the police during the 'forties.
In such circumstances techniques and attitudes towards
those suspected of a lack of loyalty to the régime were
brutal.

Throughout Franco's period strikes remained illegal,
censorship was plentiful, party political activity was
banned, meetings were carefully controlled. To cover this
area of political offences, the Cuerpo General de Policía,
the plain-clothes branch, popularly known as the 'policía
secreta', had its élite Brigada Político-Social, quite
separate from the department concerned with ordinary
crime. The Guardia Civil dealt with the same area through
its intelligence organisation, the Servicio de Información. To opponents of the régime it was this system of
political surveillance and repression that was most characteristic of the Spanish police forces under Franco: the
Brigada Político-Social operating through the grey-uni-
formed Policía Armada (the grises or 'greys'), and the
Guardia Civil with their ficheros (files) covering the entire rural population. These functions overshadowed the
more run-of-the-mill police duties, and it was commonly
alleged that correspondingly little attention was paid to
'ordinary' and especially white-collar crime. Within the
police service itself the ethos was harshly authoritarian.
The other half of divided Spain, at least until the 'seventies, regarded the system as a necessary protection
against social revolution, and pointed to the, by European
standards, low prison population as evidence of the effectiveness of the police system as a whole.

The modern police system

It is against this background that the development of the
forces of law and order in the context of parliamentary
democracy must be seen. The 1978 Constitution carefully
separates the military from the police, and in Article 104
assigns to the 'security forces and corps' the duty of

'protecting the free exercise of rights and freedoms, and guaranteeing the safety of citizens'. But it explicitly leaves detail to a future law that has still not appeared, though legislation is promised for 1985. In current practice therefore it is the Police Law of 4 December 1978 which sets out the basic structure. The Security Corps are to consist of the Guardia Civil and the Policía, the Policía comprising the Cuerpo Superior de Policía and the Policía Nacional – the first a renamed Cuerpo General, the second a new version of the Policía Armada y de Tráfico. (In the new legislation promised for 1985 it seems that the two corps of the Policía will be amalgamated, but remain separate from the Guardia Civil.) In the 1978 Police Law all the corps are given the same basic duties as in the Constitution, but with the addition of the 'defence of constitutional order'. Three functions are set out in amplification of these basic duties: a) 'The maintenance and reestablishment of public order and of the safety of citizens, guaranteeing the exercise of their rights and liberties', b) 'The prevention of the commission of criminal acts, and, where they have been committed, their investigation, the detection and arrest of the presumed offenders, and the safekeeping of the effects, instruments, and evidence of the crime, placing these at the disposal of the competent judicial authority', c) 'The provision of assistance in case of public disasters and private accidents, collaboration with the emergency services, and assistance, at the request of the parties, with the peaceful settlement of disputes between private individuals'.

The existence of two separate national forces, the Policía and the Guardia Civil, to carry out these functions means that there must be coordination at the highest level. In theory at least this is achieved through the Director de la Seguridad del Estado (Director of State Security), a political appointee responsible to the Minister of the Interior and in charge of the Directors-General of the Policía and the Guardia Civil. However there is no symmetry about these last two relationships, for while the Director-General of the Policía is solely responsible to the Director de la Seguridad del Estado, the Director-General of the Guardia Civil is responsible to him only for the three functions set out in the previous paragraph. For military functions he is responsible to the Ministry of Defence, while the organization of the Guardia Civil is governed by its own regulations, to be agreed between the two Ministries. The Director de la Seguridad del Estado, for instance, cannot control postings or promotions within the Guardia Civil.

At the local level coordination is in the hands of the Civil Governors, one to each of the fifty provinces which are the basic administrative divisions of Spain. The Civil Governors, political appointees, are, in the 1978 Police Law, given direct command of the State Security Corps in their provinces, subject to directives from the offices of the Directors-General of the Policía and Guardia Civil.

The counterpart of coordination is demarcation and here too the 1978 Police Law makes provision. In terms of territory the Policía operate in all provincial capitals and in every municipality whose population exceeds a number to be fixed by the government. The Guardia Civil operate in the smaller municipalities though for purposes of crime prevention and detection the Cuerpo Superior de Policía may operate anywhere. Currently the dividing line is set at a population of 20,000, so that the Guardia Civil is basically a small-town and rural police, remembering that Spanish country workers tend to live in towns and villages rather than scattered in individual farmsteads.

Functionally, the Policía are given the task of issuing National Identity Documents and passports. They control entry and exit into and from the country and foreign nationals. The Guardia Civil deal with the control of arms and explosives, guard ports and airports, coasts and frontiers, the outside of prisons and public buildings, and are also responsible for civil defence, though this is also the province of the Director-General of Civil Defence at the Ministry of the Interior. The Guardia Civil also have two major traditional functions: the prevention of smuggling, deriving from the incorporation of the Carabineros in 1940, and the patrolling of main roads. All other functions, under a final provision of the Police Law, are to be assigned on a territorial basis. In practice this means that some specialities are largely the province of one or other force: gaming, for instance, is dealt with by the Cuerpo Superior de Policía, while the Guardia Civil tend to deal with matters of hunting and conservation.

The Policía

The Policía consists of two corps, the plain-clothes Cuerpo Superior de Policía and the uniformed Policía Nacional. They function together at the local level, but since they have quite different personnel and structures, it is essential to examine them separately first. The new legislation promised by 1985 will amalgamate the two bodies into a civilian one, with officers probably receiving a common training, but separate description of them here will not only show the current structure, but also reveal the serious difficulties that will have to be faced in uniting two such very different forces. In the long term there will be important gains in effectiveness, but the proposals have also revealed publicly tensions between the officers of the two forces, with some Policía Nacional officers feeling threatened by a takeover. At stake is the future self-definition of the Policía, as either 'a component of national defence' or 'protective, dissuading doves', to quote two extremes.(1)

The Cuerpo Superior de la Policía is a force of some 8,700 plain-clothes officers. The 1978 Police Law assigns to them the following functions: a) Direction and co-ordination of police services, b) Intelligence, defined as the 'acquisition, reception, and analysis of all data of interest for public order and security; study, planning, and execution of methods and techniques for the prevention of delinquency and other anti-social behaviour, all within the limits of current law and regulations and with due respect for civil rights', c) Investigation, defined as operations relating to information about and prevention of crimes, and, once they have been committed, their investigation in order to verify them, to discover and arrest the suspects, and to secure the effects, instruments or evidence of the crime, and to provide technical and expert reports, d) Documentation, that is, the issue of identity documents, and control of foreign nationals, e) Assistance to and collaboration with foreign police forces.

In common with other continental countries the Spanish criminal justice system makes the police responsible to the courts and the public prosecutor for the investigation of crime. Every member of the police forces is automatically a member of the judicial police and as such responsible to the courts. Any crime must be reported without delay to the courts or public prosecutor and from then on the investigation is formally their responsibility. In practice the work of investigation on behalf of the judicial authorities is normally carried out, within the areas of competence of the Policía, by the Cuerpo Superior, and this is reflected in the Police Law where it provides for the creation of specific units of judicial police without prejudice to the responsibility to the courts of all members of the security forces. At present this requirement is discharged by the existence of a central Comisaría General de Policía Judicial, regional judicial police squads, and judicial police groups within each police station, though in April 1984 it was announced that, to improve court efficiency, some police officers would be attached directly to the courts in major cities. The Guardia Civil of course act as judicial police where they are competent. In practice about four-fifths of all crime is investigated by the Cuerpo Superior.

Recruitment to the Cuerpo Superior is by examination from candidates, men and women, who must be in possession of university entrance qualifications. Officers are trained at the new Escuela Superior de Policía (Higher Police School) in Avila, where at present they undergo a three-year course, shortly to be developed into a five-year course which will give successful students a degree-level qualification. Up to a quarter of the places may be allocated to serving members of the Policía Nacional and of the Cuerpo Administrativo de Seguridad (senior civilian staff), provided they meet the usual entrance requirements.

The current three-year course starts with a basic year devoted to legal studies and to complementary basic studies in social science, physical education, personal defence, weapons, ethics, and languages. The student goes on to two years of specialized training, with further legal study, courses on police techniques, and continued complementary studies in the second year, and study of police practice and operations in the third year. This last year includes assignment for part of the time to operational units and the production of a dissertation. The proposed five-year course will include a three-year basic first part, success in which will give entry to the last two years of specialized study.

Graduates from the Avila school become inspectors, of which there are three classes. Promotion within the inspectorate and to the rank above, subcomisario, is by strict seniority. For promotion to comisario (of whom there are 750), officers have to return to the Escuela Superior at Avila for at least three months to complete and pass a course including further legal studies with especial emphasis on the Constitution and civil liberties, management of personnel and equipment, command practice, and police operations. Candidates qualify for this course on the basis of seniority, merit, and ability, with a substantial reliance on seniority, characteristic of Spanish civil service practice.

The Policía Nacional has a quite different style. It is a force of some 49,000 men (though the first 54 women recruits started training in 1984), which with its new title acquired a new uniform of light-brown trousers and dark-brown jackets. The 1978 Police Law defines it as a 'Corps with a military structure and organisation, not part of the Armed Forces, and responsible to the Ministry of the Interior'. This curious definition and the hybrid it creates can only be understood as an historical compromise. The Policía Nacional is an armed force that is not part of the Armed Forces. It is called a 'corps' to avoid the term 'force'. It is civilian yet its style and structure are military. It is subject to both civilian and martial law. And in spite of these paradoxes it has undergone the most successful reform of all the police forces, under a staunchly democratic general who in November 1983 went on to become Director-General of the Guardia Civil.

The 1978 Police Law sets out the functions of the Policía Nacional as follows: a) To assist the Cuerpo Superior in its duties, b) To maintain and reestablish public order, c) To protect persons and property, d) To give assistance in cases of conflict, accident, or disaster, e) To protect the buildings of the Policía. Its strength is distributed according to these functions as follows: assistance to the Cuerpo Superior - 15,800 men; public order - 20,500; assistance in accidents - 2,300; protection of buildings - 7,500. A further 800 are assigned to logistics, 600 to training, and 1,600 to administration.

No men are assigned to function c), drawing attention to a special provision in the 1978 Police Law for the creation of units of policía de barrio, community police, whose function is precisely to be c), protection of persons and property. In fact such units have not been created, although a central department was given responsibility for the policía de barrio. A recent Policía handbook discusses the idea of community policing wih great enthusiasm but admits it is an expensive development in the Spanish context, and regrets that so far funds have not been available, 'not to mention the implication of far-reaching reform of police structures'.(2) Instead, in 1984 in major cities, part of the Municipal Police were given policía de barrio duties.

The forces of the Policía Nacional have a national Inspector-General, but are for the most part organised regionally. There are mobile and reserve groups to fulfil public order functions, and an important new central group is the Grupo Especial de Operaciones, trained and equipped for special operations, in particular assaults on buildings where hostages are held. Regular Policía Nacional arms include 9 mm pistols, Star Z-70B 9 mm sub-machine-guns, Cetme and Nato 7.62 mm rifles, .38 special revolvers, and rifles for rubber bullets. All men carry at least a pistol, but sub-machine-guns are used regularly on

225

the streets, especially in protecting buildings. Riot equipment includes tear-gas, electric batons, water-cannon, and riot shields. Bomb-disposal is another of the force's responsibilities, with units in each province.

The military structure of the Policía Nacional means that there is a sharp division in terms of training and promotion between officers and other ranks. Until recent reforms the officers of the Policía Nacional were drawn largely from the Army, though a minority were promoted from among the force's non-commissioned officers. This reflected the military control of the security forces maintained under Franco, and the fact that much of the force's operational style was military. Officers remained part of the Army, seconded to police work, and receiving only brief training. The 1978 Police Law sets up for the training of officers the Academia Especial de la Policía Nacional, housed in a new building in El Escorial. Positions at officer level are to be filled by those who have completed courses or tests at the Academia Especial. A further provision allows such posts also to be filled by serving officers of the Armed Forces, selected by the Ministry of the Interior, not the Armed Forces. These should receive appropriate training and would be permanently transferred to the Policía Nacional.

The first cadets entered the new academy in 1981, after two years' initial training at the Academia General Militar, Spain's army officer training academy. They spent two years at El Escorial, so that in 1983 the Policía Nacional received its first officers especially trained for police work, even though their initial formation is still military, and the system of ranks the conventional army one. When the new scheme is fully in operation, new officers will receive two years' military, followed by three years' police training. All entrants, whether from outside or from the ranks of non-commissioned police officers, must be qualified to enter university and male.

The period of training for other ranks has been increased from three to nine months, followed by a year of practical training. Promotion to corporal, sergeant, and sergeant-major is operated by a system that includes elements of competition, further training, and seniority.

Two other corps complete the system, the Cuerpo Administrativo de Seguridad, and the Cuerpo Auxiliar de Seguridad (the Administrative and the Auxiliary Security Corps). The first has an establishment of 1,800, the second of 2,800. They carry out bureaucratic tasks and have exclusive rights to these.

Operationally the four corps function together, though inevitably with a complex command structure. The Director-General of the Policía, at the Ministry of the Interior in Madrid, is in overall command. He is appointed from the ranks of the comisarios (senior officers of the Cuerpo Superior), and with the change of party in power in December 1982 a new appointment was made. The central administration under him includes the Deputy Director-General, the Inspector-General of the Policía Nacional, and six divisions, three of them operational, known as Comisarías Generales, three of them support divisions. The Comisarías Generales correspond to the three major functions of the Cuerpo Superior laid out in the 1978 Police Law: intelligence, investigation, and documentation, while the Policía Nacional is responsible to the Director-General for seguridad ciudadana (civil security), under the co-ordination of its Inspector-General.

The Comisaría General de Información, the Intelligence Division, is concerned with gathering intelligence 'relevant to public order and security', acting 'within the limits of the law and of respect for civil rights'. It is not restricted to pure intelligence gathering, but also has operational functions, overlapping in some ways with the Policía Judicial. In practice its major task in recent years has been the central control of anti-terrorist work, through its Brigada Central de Información (a brigada is a squad).

The Comisaría General de Policía Judicial deals with criminal investigation. It acts as a centre for investigation of crime beyond the scope of the regional judicial police squads (it has been heavily involved in investigating the recent disastrous adulteration of cooking-oil), as a channel for international cooperation through Interpol, and as a supervisory and back-up service to regional and local judicial police squads. Its most important sections include the Gabinete Central de Identificación (Central Identification Laboratory), the Gabinete de Cooperación Técnica Internacional (Office for International Technical Cooperation), the Brigada Central de Estupefacientes (Central Drug Squad), the Brigada Central de Policía Judicial, and the Brigada Móvil (Mobile Squad), who police public transport. Areas of especial activity are against foreign gangs, drug traffic, especially the rapidly rising traffic in heroin (109 kg seized in Spain in 1983) and cocaine (275 kg), juvenile crime, and illegal currency movements. Major emphasis has been placed on improving technical expertise, and scientific equipment has improved markedly in recent years. These advances were claimed by 1982 to have led to a stemming of the rapid growth of crime (between 1976 and 1982 crime known to the Policía doubled, whilst violent crime grew much faster), but 1983 saw the rise gather pace again. For what crime statistics are worth, the Policía recorded in 1981 465 homicides, 21,344 robberies with violence or intimidation, 1,941 bank robberies, and 962 cases of rape within their jurisdiction which covers about 80% of recorded crime. Clear-up rates claimed for the years 1980-82 are: homicide, 85%; bank robbery, 51%; sexual offences, 68%, though in 1983 overall clear-up rates fell as crime increased.

The Comisaría General de Documentación has four sections or Servicios, one responsible for controlling and issuing the National Identity Document, another dealing with frontiers and foreign nationals (issue of passports, deportation, temporary vehicle importation, immigration control), a third dealing with the regulation and control of gambling, while a fourth regulates public spectacles, including bull-fights. It has also recently taken over the supervision of private security companies, detectives, and security guards, and generally carries out administrative tasks related to police supervisory rôles.

The title of the fourth operational area, Seguridad Ciudadana, well expresses the reforming intentions of the 1978 Police Law: seguridad means both safety and security, ciudadana means 'of citizens'. Until recently it came under a fourth Comisaría General, run by the Cuerpo Superior, but in March 1984 the central structure of the Policía was reorganized as a preliminary to unifying the Policía Nacional and the Cuerpo Superior. The Comisaría General de Seguridad Ciudadana was scrapped, and seguridad ciudadana made the province of the Policía Nacional, giving its officers a fuller rôle in the command and organization of uniformed policing, including the "091" system of UHF radio control of operations (091 is the emergency police telephone number). At the same time the Inspector-General of the Policía Nacional, previously under the Director of State Security, was made responsible to the Director-General of the Policía, in parallel with the heads of operational divisions. These changes should make for a somewhat less divisive system of command of the uniformed police.

The remaining divisions of the central offices of the Director-General of the Policía are administrative. The División de Gestión Económica e Infraestructura is responsible for finance, buildings, and equipment, including the Helicopter Section. The División de Personal manages personnel matters, including the revision of establishments, an important area of recent reform. The División de Enseñanza y Perfeccionamiento covers recruitment and the administration of training, both initial and in-service. And finally, the Deputy Director-General of the Policía is responsible for co-ordination of the different divisions, but also has specific duties of his own: statistics, records, and recently data-processing, especially the new data-processing centre at El Escorial. This is a national centre for use by the Policía (the Guardia Civil have their own), with terminals covering all regional H.Q.'s, frontier posts, and some ports and airports, and handling an average of 1,500,000 enquiries per month. At present it handles all data on personal criminal intelligence, drugs, wanted and disappeared persons, terrorism, stolen vehicles, weapons and cash, the National Security Plan, private security guards, and firearms certificates. Plans for the near future include fingerprint recognition, and command and control systems for the 091 system.

The Deputy Director-General is also in charge of central planning of security matters, including security plans for major national events and buildings. His department organises the National Security Plan, a collection of data for use in emergencies recorded in a nationally uniform manner, and publishes manuals on self-protection for personalities and on security techniques for buildings. It is also responsible for the protection of public figures.

The 1978 Police Law lays down that the 'decentralised organs' of the Policía are the Jefatura Superior (regional headquarters), the Comisaría Provincial (provincial headquarters), the Comisaría Local and the Comisaría de Distrito (local and district police stations). The links between these and the centre are inevitably complex, with control flowing from the Ministry through the Civil Governors and the Director-General of the Policía. At the broadest level, generally speaking the political level, the government controls the police system in the provinces through the Civil Governors. At the operational level, however, command passes through the Director-General of the Policía to the Regional Chiefs of Police. There are at present thirteen regions, based on Madrid, Barcelona, Seville, Valencia, Zaragoza, Bilbao, Pamplona, Oviedo, Valladolid, La Coruña, Granada, the Balearic and the Canary islands, and the Regional Chief or Jefe Superior, a member of the Cuerpo Superior, is in command of all the forces of the Policía in his region (since most regions cover more than one province he will deal with several Civil Governors). The Regional Headquarters, the Jefatura Superior, reflects in its structure that of the central administration. It includes, for instance, a brigada regional for each of the operational specialisms, Policía

Judicial, Información, and Documentación, organised into sub-groups and specialist groups (drugs, antiterrorist, juvenile delinquency, and so on) according to regional needs. The Policía Nacional organise Seguridad Ciudadana. Each Jefatura Superior has its central laboratories and administrative offices, including data processing offices, and a press office, and a department dealing with residence permits for foreign nationals, a function delegated from the Civil Governor.

Below the regional level, each province, unless it is the seat of a Jefatura Superior, has a Comisaría Provincial, commanded by a Comisario Jefe Provincial, responsible both to his Regional Chief and to the Civil Governor of the province. This Provincial Headquarters will be situated in the capital of the province (which in most cases gives its name to the province), and will have provincial squads and departments on the usual pattern. If the province is the seat of a Jefatura Superior, it has no Comisaría Provincial, police stations coming under the direct control of the Regional Headquarters. The police station, the comisaría, is the basic operational unit. In every municipality of over 20,000 inhabitants there should be at least one comisaría. If there is only one it is a comisaría local (there are about 190 of these), but in nine of the largest cities there are more (over 20 in Madrid and Barcelona), and they are known as comisarías de distrito.

Clearly police stations will vary in size but their basic structure is a standard one and it will be simplest to describe the typical organisation of a comisaría de distrito, using the numbers of officers in a typical Madrid station to add flesh to the organisational bones. The head of a district police station is the Comisario Jefe, responsible directly to the provincial or regional chief. He is in command of the Policía Nacional attached to his station as well as the Cuerpo Superior. However the Policía Nacional retain their own military-style command structure and the normal procedure is for the Comisario Jefe to give instructions to the officer in charge of the Policía Nacional who then carries them out through his own subordinates. This officer, in our Madrid example a captain, remains responsible for matters of discipline and organisation to his own senior officers within the Policía Nacional. Thus in addition to the two chains of command running via the Civil Governors and the various police chiefs, there is a third chain for the administration of the Policía Nacional as the body responsible for seguridad ciudadana. The senior officer here is the Inspector-General, an army general, who is responsible to

230

the Director-General of the Policía. (The Inspector-General has had an important rôle to play in the reform of the style and public image of the uniformed police.) Between the Inspector-General and our typical police-station captain there is the usual military-style hierarchy, with posts at each level to correspond with the areas of overall police activity, and in each case with a dual responsibility to the local police chief and to senior officers.

In addition to the commanding officer of the Policía Nacional, the Comisario Jefe has under him a deputy whose special responsibility is for the secretariat. In the Madrid police station used as an example, covering an area of 22 sq.kms. and a population of over 300,000, the secretariat consists of six members of the Cuerpos Administrativo y Auxiliar de Seguridad who deal with the paperwork and files. The officers of the Cuerpo Superior are organised in three main groups. The first is the Grupo de Policía Judicial, the criminal investigation group. They normally work day and night shifts and in our example consist of eight inspectors. They should collaborate not only with neighbouring stations, but with the regional crime squad (Brigada Regional de Policía Judicial) that operates from the Jefatura Superior, and, if necessary, with the Brigada Central. Rivalries between these groups are of course not unknown.

The second main group is the Grupo de Sectores (corresponding to Información). The district is divided into sectors (in our case seven), and an inspector assigned to each, under the command of a more senior officer. These inspectors are required to get to know their sector, but not necessarily to become well-known in it. Their tasks are to gather local intelligence, to check on applications for licences for public establishments, to keep up records of commercial and industrial premises. The nature of their work will naturally vary a great deal with the area. In the Basque country the emphasis, as with the Brigada Central de Información, is inevitably on anti-terrorist intelligence and the typical structure will be modified.

The third main group is the Inspección de Guardia, consisting here of eight inspectors working four shifts to man the public desk at the stations (reforms are planned to free inspectors for other work). They receive reports of crimes from the public, taking statements, copies of which go to the appropriate judge and to the Grupo de Policía Judicial who will carry out investigations on behalf and on the instructions of the judge. They keep records of police actions in the district and are in charge of communications and arrested persons. When an arrest has been made by the Policía Judicial (or any other officer), the suspect is brought to the comisaría, where the Inspector de Guardia has to inform him of the reasons for his arrest and of his rights: to remain silent, to appoint a lawyer to be present during police and judicial investigations (one is appointed for him if he makes no choice), to have someone informed of his detention, and to be medically examined.

In addition to these three main groups, some comisarías also have sections that issue National Identity Documents and passports, and deal with foreign nationals. This is a recent development, part of the drive to reduce the remoteness of the police bureaucracy. In our typical Madrid station four members of the Cuerpos Administrativo y Auxiliar de Seguridad cope with this work, being in part responsible to the Comisaría General de Documentación.

The thirty-odd officers of the Cuerpo Superior here are supported by a company of the Policía Nacional, around 100 men. These are divided into three sections each headed by a junior officer or N.C.O. and they work a three-shift system. Broadly their task is a public order one, but they have several specific duties, especially in backing up the Cuerpo Superior. Some, with special training, are permanently attached to the Inspección de Guardia. Others carry out foot and motorised patrols, and fixed-point duties, serve summons, transport prisoners, and provide protection for police buildings, vehicles, and detainees. By way of example the Madrid station has four unmarked cars, known as K-cars, and 11 marked patrol-cars or Z-cars though these are being increased. It is also equipped with a full range of riot-control equipment, though in addition the Policía Nacional maintain considerable reserve strength in barracks separate from the system of comisarías, and this is always available for large-scale public order requirements, or in disaster situations.

As well as the regular comisarías there are also specialised police stations, notably those with the tasks of policing major national buildings, and those with frontier duties. Here again the Cuerpo Superior are in charge, assisted by the Policía Nacional. The traveller at a Spanish airport will find his passport stamped by a Policía Nacional, responsible to the Cuerpo Superior, security checks on his luggage done by the Guardia Civil in their rôle of airport guards, and customs clearance given by the Aduana, assisted by the Guardia Civil in their anti-smuggling rôle.

The Guardia Civil

The other national police force is the Guardia Civil. The
Police Law of 1978, it will be remembered, lays down that
the Director-General of the Guardia Civil is responsible
to the Director de la Seguridad del Estado, but only for
police functions and without prejudice to his responsibility to the Ministry of Defence. The Police Law goes on to
set out the lines of demarcation between Policía and
Guardia Civil, but thereafter says no more about the
Guardia Civil while devoting a major chapter to the
Policía. The precise legal definition of the Guardia
Civil remains a matter of uncertainty, politically too
sensitive for final clarification, though the general
position is clear: the Guardia Civil is a military corps
that is at the service of the Ministry of the Interior for
police purposes, and of the Ministry of Defence for military purposes (in time of war or state of siege it comes
entirely under the Ministry of Defence). It is also responsible to the Ministry of Finance in its rôle as fiscal
police. The Ministry of the Interior largely funds the
Guardia Civil, but its internal regulations, at present
still those of 1942, are to be jointly agreed with the
Ministry of Defence, giving the Guardia Civil in practice
considerable organisational autonomy.

The most obvious characteristic of the Guardia Civil
in comparison with the other police forces is its deep
sense of its own traditions and identity. This sense of
identity is articulated in terms of honour, discipline,
and sacrifice, by constant reference to its foundation in
1844 by the Duke of Ahumada, and by identification with
military values. Almost every characteristic of the
Guardia Civil as it is now, strength, weakness, or plain
oddity, can be traced to its early origins. The first im-
pulse behind its creation was both to remove the public
order rôle from the army and to replace the National
Militia, closely identified with the overthrown Progressive government and with demands for local control. The
new force was to be entirely under the Ministry of the
Interior, hence the title Civil Guard. But before it even
came into being, the Moderate government that had proposed
it was replaced by a military-dominated government and the
new force, title unchanged, was taken over by the military
and the dual dependency created. The original idea, a
force at the disposal of the civilian authorities, controlled by police chiefs, was thus replaced by a well-
organised, highly-disciplined, but autonomous force, its
efficiency matched only by recurring conflicts as to who

233

controlled it and who could demand its services.

The long-term result was the development, from the later nineteenth century on, of urban police forces at the direct disposal of police chiefs. The Guardia Civil tended more and more to concentrate on its rural rôle, and as Spain's population moved to the cities the relative weight of Guardia Civil and urban police changed. The maturing of the process is a surprisingly recent one: in 1965 there were still 62,000 Guardia Civil to under 19,000 uniformed Policía Armada, while by 1980 the proportions were 63,000 to 49,000 (or 61,000 including plain-clothes and auxiliary branches). Social and political circumstances have changed enormously, but the traditional identity of the Guardia Civil remains. The current regulations of the Guardia Civil, revised in 1942, but still based on those of 1844, include the following excellent example of its autonomy: 'If in consequence of riot the Guardia Civil is forced, in order to regain control, to adopt a military posture, neither Civil Governors nor Mayors may order it to retreat until order is reestablished.'

As we saw, the 1978 Police Law gives the Guardia Civil general policing functions in municipalities of less than 20,000 inhabitants, together with the following national functions: arms and explosives control, protection of coasts, frontiers, ports and airports, protection of inter-urban communication routes and urban trunk roads, traffic policing, fiscal, anti-fraud, and anti-contraband policing, exterior protection of non-military prisons and public buildings, civil defence, and civil-military coordination for public order purposes. The Guardia Civil have also traditionally been responsible for the transport of prisoners, and for the control of reservists, and they specialise in the policing of hunting, fishing, and rural conservation.

Entrance to the Guardia Civil is through two colleges at Ubeda and Valdemoro or by direct entry as an officer through the Academia Especial de la Guardia Civil at Aranjuez. Recruitment is still predominantly from the poorer, mainly agricultural regions of the interior and the south. This is accentuated by heavy recruitment of sons of civil guards, but there are in any case very few recruits from the areas with the strongest nationalist movements. One of the 1982 intakes at Ubeda, for instance, included 1.6% born in the Basque country and 4% in Catalonia, two regions that contain 21% of the Spanish population. This pattern is of long standing and it is easy to see how the Guardia Civil can be viewed from these regions as an alien force. Nevertheless recruitment in general has been rising in response to unemployment and greater public acceptance: in June 1983 there were 9 applicants per vacancy.

An important characteristic of recruitment is that a high proportion is of sons of civil guards. The Colegio de Guardias Jóvenes (Young Guards' College) at Valdemoro is exclusively for them, and they make up almost half of the intake at Ubeda. Civil guards often speak of their force as 'endogamous' and the family tradition of service in the Guardia Civil is an important factor in its remarkable unity, as well as a source of its social autonomy. Young Guards enter their college at 16 or 17 and spend two years there. A proportion, who stay a further year, are guaranteed entrance to the Academia de Cabos (Corporals' Academy) at Guadarrama after four years' service. Recruits entering through the Ubeda college, usually aged 19-24, have a total training of eleven months, including three months' practical training. Guards can then follow a correspondence course to prepare for entrance to the Academia de Cabos. Promotion to sergeant is by seniority for half the candidates and by competitive examination for the other half, and a similar system holds for promotion to officer after a minimum of fourteen years.

Direct entry to a commission is also possible, and a quarter to one third of officers (about 25 per year) enter this way. Entrance requirements are as for a university course, the average age at entry is 21, and the first two years are spent at Spain's equivalent of Sandhurst, the Academia General Militar at Zaragoza, undergoing military training, including knowledge of tactics up to battalion level. A further three years are spent at the Academia Especial of the Guardia Civil before the cadet emerges as a lieutenant. Studies include the legal system and police practice, as well as languages, psychology, and religious and moral studies, but strictly military matters remain an important part of the syllabus. Once commissioned, the officer is promoted on the basis of seniority, though for promotion to major and to general a selective course has to be passed.

The Guardia Civil also runs a number of specialist training centres: the Academia de Tráfico in Madrid, the Academia del Servicio Fiscal in Sabadell, the Escuela de Automovilismo (Drivers' School) in Madrid, and other centres for radio operation, criminal investigation, police dog handling, bomb disposal, and special training. Courses in skiing, climbing, diving, and data-processing are also available.

A very recent development is the decision to supplement regular civil guards by making it possible for the eighteen months' compulsory military service to be carried out as an auxiliary civil guard. A new training centre is under construction at Baeza, with capacity for 2,000 trainees. Each will receive three months' training and in this way it is hoped to maintain a force of some 9,000 volunteer auxiliaries. The scheme has started successfully with 12,000 applications for the first 1,000 places, and it may well have a profound influence since it is planned that, of the annual intake of 2,000 regular civil guards, 1,250 will be drawn from the auxiliaries, thus raising the calibre of recruits and lessening the proportion of sons of civil guards, since only around a tenth of auxiliary guards are 'of the family'. Also under preparation are plans for a 1,000-strong Guardia Civil Femenina, women civil guards who would take on auxiliary police functions. In these ways the Guardia Civil plans to expand its numbers without going beyond the establishment that successive governments have allowed to rise little since the early 1940's.

Recent years have, however, seen remarkable increases in the levels and modernity of the force's equipment and housing. In 1980-82, for instance, almost 70 million pounds, much needed, was spent on buildings, including 93 new barracks and 3,393 new dwelling-units. Both are central to the Guardia Civil's identity in the shape of the casa-cuartel, the 'house-barracks', for it has been traditional for the families of guards to be as far as possible accommodated in the same building or group of buildings as the station from which the force operates locally. Current plans are to maintain this tradition with accommodation for 80% of men and their families in casas-cuartel, another element in the sociology of the Guardia Civil that makes it so distinct from the other police forces.

The years 1980-82 also saw the building of major new training centres, part of a drive to modernize training methods and to increase specialist training. Equipment, too, has been much improved. The force has an establishment of some 10,000 vehicles excluding those used by the Agrupación de Tráfico. Recent developments include the purchase of 585 cross-country motorcycles for rural patrols, a modern equivalent for the traditional horse in areas with poor or no roads. Land-Rovers and a special version of the Renault 4 are staple vehicles for rural work. The Helicopter Unit has also been strengthened. Another recently modernized area is that of weapons. The traditional equipment of the Guardia Civil reflected its dual rôle as army and police, and its function in the 1940's as an anti-guerrilla force. The dual rôle remains but with standardized and modernized equipment, and an emphasis on counter-terrorist work. All members of the

force carry a Star B17 9mm pistol. All units are also
equipped with CETME 7.62mm rifles, and Star Z-70B 9mm sub-
machine-guns. In 1982 26,000 of the former were held, and
31,000 of the latter, an overall increase of 28,000 in
three years, partly in replacement of older weapons. By
contrast stocks of hand-grenades were run down from 26,000
to 17,000 in the same three years. Heavier weapons are
available to special units, especially the Grupo Antiterrorista Rural, and the reserves. Riot control equipment includes a stock of a quarter of a million rubber
bullets.

The Guardia Civil has its central headquarters in
Madrid. The Director-General, an army lieutenant-general,
has a Deputy Director responsible for administrative, personnel, and social action matters. He is a major-general
of the Guardia Civil and his is the highest post a member
of the force can aspire to. Also responsible to the
Director-General are two Guardia Civil brigadiers responsible for training and logistics, and the Chief of Staff,
an army brigadier. The post of Chief of Staff was first
introduced in 1940 when the Guardia Civil was given a more
military emphasis, and the staff rapidly grew in size and
importance. Its most senior officers are largely from
outside the Guardia Civil: it is a source of resentment
that these posts are not open to officers of the force,
though reform is under way.

The Chief of Staff has under him the Jefatura de
Transmisiones (Communications HQ), the Jefatura del
Servicio Fiscal (Fiscal Service HQ), and the Grupo de
Servicios Especiales, responsible for special intelligence
and investigation tasks on a national basis. The Deputy
Chief of Staff controls planning and publications, while
the four Sections of the Staff deal with organization,
training and postings (First Section), intelligence, pro-
tocol, press relations (Second), rural and traffic services (Third), and co-ordination and use of the various
services under the heads of weaponry, health, accommodation, transport, etc. (Fourth).

From headquarters the whole force is structured both
territorially and functionally. The country is divided
into six Zones, identical to those of the army, based on
Madrid, Seville, Valencia, Barcelona, Logroño, and León,
and each commanded by a brigadier with his own Staff (recently decision-making has been somewhat decentralised).
The zones are in turn divided into comandancias, units
that coincide with the provinces in the civilian system.
Each is headed by a lieutenant-colonel, a key figure since
he takes his orders in policing matters from the Civil
Governor in the same way as the Comisario Jefe Provincial

does for the Policía, 'subject to the directives' of the
respective national headquarters. As with the Policía,
the provincial commander deals with the provincial judicial authorities, but he also has links with the Provincial Delegate of the Ministry of Finance on account of the
Guardia Civil's rôle as fiscal police.

Recent reorganization has further reinforced the importance of the Comandancia, for it has become necessary
to deploy the force more flexibly rather than rely on the
traditional system of strict territorial coverage. Traditionally the province is sub-divided into areas covered by
compañías (companies), commanded by captains, in turn divided into líneas (lines - the term arises from the original assignment of the Guardia Civil to cover stretches of
road), and then into puestos (posts), the basic unit of
territorial deployment. The new system involves some reduction in the number of puestos and the creation of
mobile patrols commanded from the Línea, the Compañía, or
the Comandancia itself. These are controlled by a new
operating system C.O.S. (Centro Operacional de Servicio)
that on the basis of radio-control allows greater efficiency and flexibility.

This co-ordinated deployment of all of a province's
forces makes the Comandancia the key element in the command structure. Each of the specialised branches of the
force also has its provincial section centred on the
Comandancia: traffic, arms control, bomb disposal, laboratories, criminal investigation, intelligence, fiscal, and
drugs.

At present the comandancias are divided into a total
of about 300 compañías, 800 líneas, and 3200 puestos. A
puesto usually consists of between six and ten men, headed
by a corporal, sergeant, or sergeant-major. Physically it
consists of offices and family quarters in one building or
group of buildings. To it may be attached a criminal investigation, or traffic, or mobile patrol unit, and, if it
coincides with the headquarters of a línea or compañía it
will of course be somewhat larger. The basic function of
the puesto is the policing of its area by means of the
classic pareja, a pair of men traditionally on foot or on
horseback, though now the horse has almost entirely given
way to the car. The pareja, in their memorable hats and,
in cold weather, capes, form what a recent writer describes as 'an almost ecological ingredient' of the rural
scene,(3) an image, for both Spaniards and foreigners,
that conveys a host of meanings from the past. This traditional image is of an ever-present force, both controlling the population and serving it at times of calamity
through its detailed local knowledge. Its iron discipline

238

has enabled it to last little changed, in spite of its scattered deployment, since 1844. Like all police forces it has defended the existing social structure, but at times with a rigidity that in a sharply divided society led it to be seen exclusively as the defender of landed property and the persecutor of all who fell outside respectable society: gypsies, vagrants, the workless. Under the Franco régime all these characteristics were drawn on to exert detailed political control. The puesto was a centre for collecting information of every sort on the bulk of the community, all recorded and collated in the ficheros (files) of the puesto, the grassroots information for the intelligence service.

It is this traditional function that is being modified by a shift of emphasis from static supervision to a system more appropriate to changed social conditions and modern transport. The pareja is thus less common and is supplemented by the mobile patrols controlled by C.O.S. that consist of three or more men. Rapid and appropriate response to events is partly taking the place of a fragmented and often tediously bureaucratic system.

Turning from territorial to functional deployment, the same trend to specialisation is apparent. Specialisms, however, are fitted into the overall structure of the force in different ways, ranging from the considerable independence of the Agrupación de Tráfico to specialisms that are simply a matter of a training course.

The Agrupación de Tráfico was created in 1959 and reached its present size of 7,000 men in 1970. Its members are recruited from within the Guardia Civil and its duties are to police the roads and help in case of accident or breakdown. While it remains part of the Guardia Civil and is responsible through the colonel who commands it to the Director-General, it is also responsible for policy and technical matters and for materials to the Director-General de Tráfico, a subordinate of the Minister of the Interior, another dual control system that has often caused friction in the past. Nevertheless the Agrupación de Tráfico has become a well-respected unit, popularly considered strict but fair, and especially valued for the assistance given on the open road.

The Agrupación de Tráfico is grouped into 6 sectors, 50 sub-sectors (corresponding to provinces), and 258 destacamentos (detachments). The destacamentos are in most cases based on selected puestos, but a number are separately based, especially those built to cover the motorways. The Agrupación is independent enough to have its own specialised groups, including its own Intelligence Service. The basic specialisms are patrolling, carried out in pairs either in cars or on motorcycles, accident investigation (for which there are three-man teams, with specially adapted vans, called Equipos de Atestados e Informes), radar and photo-control with specially equipped vehicles, and roadside assistance, using two-man teams - driver and first-aider - in Land-Rovers that carry a stretcher and first-aid equipment as well as spare parts to deal with breakdowns. All of these men retain, of course, their full range of police duties, and are often involved in criminal and anti-contraband work. They are armed in the standard way and have the power to levy on-the-spot fines for road traffic offences.

Another important branch, though this time not constituted as a separate unit, is the Servicio Fiscal. Around 12,000 men are employed in this and the protection of coasts and frontiers. The latter task involves some 6,000 men, without special training, under regular local control. A further 5,000 (Especialistas) are qualified to work under the direction of Customs Officers in Customs Areas, assisted, if necessary, by 100 Matronas de la Guardia Civil, widows and unmarried orphans of civil guards, for female searches. Another 440 men belong to the Servicio Marítimo and control ports and bays, while special groups operating in plain clothes gather intelligence on excise and drugs offences. It is planned that the Guardia Civil's duties will shortly be expanded to cover territorial waters up to three miles out, with the provision of suitable patrol boats.

The service is co-ordinated by a section of the Director-General's Staff, co-ordination that involves contact with the Customs Department of the Ministry of Finance, with the Navy, with Policía anti-drug squads, with the Agrupación de Tráfico, and with the Servicio Especial de Vigilancia Fiscal, a body responsible to the Ministry of Finance that in part duplicates the Guardia Civil's work in the interior. Regionally there are fiscal and anti-drug groups at Zone and comandancia and sometimes compañía level. The major areas of concern to the Servicio Fiscal at present are large-scale smuggling of Virginia tobacco and drug traffic: some 12,000 kgs. of drugs were seized in 1981 compared with 4,800 kgs. in 1977. The major actions taken in response to this increase have been to treble the size of the plain-clothes groups, and to introduce drug-detecting dogs to most customs areas.

Under Franco the most feared and effective branch of the Guardia Civil was the Servicio de Información, the Intelligence Service, run by the Second Section of the Director-General's Staff. Starting from the files kept at the puestos, the S.I.G.C. built up a system of political,

240

social, and military intelligence that covered the whole rural population and was one of the essential bases of Franco's power. Since his death the emphasis has shifted to criminal and terrorist intelligence, but the structure, name, and much of the old information remain. However less mainstream political information is now recorded and the new data-processing system that has partly replaced the old _ficheros_ concentrates on criminal and terrorist intelligence and on making it accessible throughout the country. But it should also be remembered that the _Guardia Civil_ is part of the Armed Forces and therefore gathers military as well as police intelligence. Each Zone has a _Comandante de Información_, and there are specialist units at Zone, _comandancia_, and sometimes _compañía_ level. These units not only gather intelligence but are usually involved in the investigation of serious crime and terrorism.

Every civil guard is a member of the judicial police, but here too there is specialization, firstly, as we have seen, in that the S.I.G.C. investigates crime, but also through the system created in 1979 of _Equipos de Investigación y Atestados_ (Criminal Investigation Teams) supervised by the central _Servicio de Policía Judicial_. Like those of the _Agrupación de Tráfico_, with whom they have no connection, these are three-man teams, each with a specially-equipped van. There are at least two teams per province, each consisting of a warrant-officer or corporal in charge of the team and of interrogations, a photographer, and a fingerprint specialist. Their van has a rear compartment laid out for questioning and taking statements as well as carrying equipment - a mobile C.I.D. office, backed up by the province's laboratory and specialist staff. The team members receive two months' training. Official statistics record a total of 89,778 crimes dealt with by the Guardia Civil in 1981, with a clear-up rate of 44.6%.

Several other functions assigned to the Guardia Civil absorb further men. For instance, 3,000 are occupied in the external protection of civil prisons, and more in the regular guarding of public buildings of national importance. Transport of prisoners by road (31,000 in 1977), protection of communications, and the administration of weapons licences occupy others. The last of the functions assigned by the 1978 Police Law to the _Guardia Civil_, civil defence (_protección civil_) and its co-ordination, remains in its infancy, though the Ministry of the Interior now has a _Director-General de Protección Civil_ to advance matters here. In practice some of the special units of the Guardia Civil make an important technical contribution in the event of public disaster.

It is these special units, mostly recently created or strengthened, that now need to be examined. The Unidades de Montaña (Mountain Units) have their origin in the 1940's for defence of the Pyreneean frontier. Their rôle now is to guard this frontier against entry of terrorists and smuggling, general policing, and the provision of a rescue service. The units include 224 men deployed since 1981 in all the mountain areas of Spain in about 30 groups and teams. At Candanchú they are trained in skiing, climbing, and rescue work. Special units for underwater work are similarly attached to coastal provincial head-quarters.

Another recent development is the creation of the Grupo Antiterrorista Rural, three companies stationed in the Basque country. These are the Guardia Civil's specifically anti-terrorist forces, but they are supplemented not only by co-ordination with the Policía and army and the rest of the Guardia Civil, but also by other specialist units. Bomb disposal specialists were recognised as recently as 1975 and a Central Department for the Guardia Civil set up in 1979. Since then equipment and training has been extensively modernized. The Unidad de Helicópteros is another such back-up unit, often operating with the new Unidad Especial de Intervención (Special Intervention Unit), trained at the Centro de Adiestramientos Especiales (Special Training Centre) at El Escorial. Finally mention must be made of the mobile reserves held for public order purposes. These consist of one battalion per Zone.

Other police forces

Alongside the national police forces are a considerable number of other specialised or local forces. First one must mention the intelligence services since, though they are not strictly police forces, the demarcation lines are not very clearly drawn. Apart from the normal military intelligence services, the Minister of Defence has responsible to him the Centro Superior de Información de la Defensa (Higher Defence Intelligence Centre), formed in 1977 to replace the Francoist intelligence services. CESID has a staff of over 2,000, drawn from the military, the Guardia Civil, and the Policía, and includes two operational sections, one manned by 400 civil guards, the other by over 100 members of the Cuerpo Superior. It is responsible for foreign intelligence, counter-espionage, security of military installations, and 'internal defence'. The latter includes coverage of attempted coups, of extra-parliamentary political parties, and of terrorism. Since these are also covered by the <u>Guardia Civil,</u> the <u>Policía,</u> and the services' intelligence branches, there is wide scope for inter-organisational confusion, and for public suspicion of 'uncontrolled' operations.

Next come the <u>Policía Municipal.</u> Many municipalities, in particular the larger ones, have their own municipal police, responsible to the <u>Alcalde</u> (mayor). For much of the nineteenth and twentieth centuries Spanish town councils had very restricted powers, and together with the growth of the national police forces, this meant that the powers of local police were always equally restricted. Under Franco mayors were government appointees, local decision-making was at its lowest ebb, and the centralising tradition in Spanish administration reached its height. The 1978 Constitution reduces central domination and returns democracy to local affairs. Municipal police are now the affair of elected councils, but their powers remain restricted to dealing with traffic, parking, demonstrations, regulations on such matters as markets, begging, and street sales, and guarding municipal buildings. They also have a rôle in the maintenance of order, though in this they are subordinate to the national forces. They are armed with pistols.

In recent years reform of the Municipal Police Forces has been undertaken, though they remain separate bodies with separate regulations and more or less adequate reform programmes. The changes are very noticeable in a big city like Madrid where a new professionalism, a more modern style, and better equipment are obvious. Taken together these forces account for some 30,000 men and women.

Another group of some 5,000 is constituted by the <u>Cuerpo Especial de Guardería Forestal del Estado</u> (State Forest Guards), under the control of <u>ICONA</u> (The National Institute for Nature Conservation), who collaborate with the <u>Guardia Civil.</u> There are other small forces such as the agents of the <u>Servicio Especial de Vigilancia Fiscal,</u> chiefly concerned with the protection of the state tobacco monopoly. But the major remaining area is that of the <u>Vigilantes Jurados,</u> officially registered 'Agents of Authority' employed by private organisations. As in many countries private security forces have grown rapidly in recent years, taking many of their staff from public police forces. In Spain their status was regulated in 1978. Appointment as a <u>Vigilante Jurado,</u> which involves taking an oath of office, is made by a Civil Governor, but only on the proposal of the security company that is to employ him or her - no one can apply to become a <u>Vigilante Jurado.</u> Their function is to prevent offences, though they also have the power to 'identify, pursue, and arrest offenders', acting in this as subordinate to the public police forces. The Vigilantes Jurados must receive a fortnight's instruction from their company, and monthly target practice, as well as training in self-defence. They must always wear the company's approved uniform and carry a .38 revolver when on duty. They also carry a truncheon, hand-cuffs, and, when involved in transporting cash, a rifle. Their weapons and initial training with them are supervised by the Guardia Civil.

These registered private police are used extensively in the transport of cash and valuables and in guarding banks; indeed it is compulsory for most banks to have one and for security transport to employ them. But their use has spread into almost all areas of society, from railway police to guarding blocks of flats. Apart from banks and transport the Civil Governor's permission is required to use Vigilantes Jurados, but he has also powers to make their employment compulsory where he considers it necessary. He may even recommend their use for public buildings.

Spain, then, has basically three national police forces, municipal police forces, and registered but privately-employed security officers. But there is one further, very recent, and most interesting development to take into account, the creation of police forces by the autonomous communities. The powerful centralising tradition of most Spanish administrations since 1844 is intimately connected with the creation of the Guardia Civil in that year and the subsequent growth of national police systems. That centralising tradition came into more or less violent conflict with some regions of Spain, notably Catalonia and the Basque Country, creating the conditions for an armed struggle in the latter. Franco's repression of civil liberties and the methods used to deal with Basque Nationalism by his security forces meant that such movements had massive popular support. When the post-Franco governments tackled this regional problem by the system of Autonomous Communities, or regional devolution, offered in the 1978 Constitution, it was obvious that policing would be an important issue.

The Constitution itself lists areas that are specifically in the domain of the Autonomous Communities: these include the 'guarding and protection of its (the Community's) buildings and installations', and 'co-ordination in relation to local police forces in terms to be established by law'. The Constitution reserves to the state 'public security, without prejudice to the possibility of the creation of police forces by the Autonomous Communities in the forms to be established in the respective Statutes in the framework to be laid down by law'. The whole Spanish territory has now been divided into Autonomous Communities, to a total of fifteen on the mainland, plus the Canaries and the Balearics. They range from Andalusia with six-and-a-half million inhabitants and 34,000 square miles, to Rioja, a single province with a quarter of a million people in 2,000 square miles.

For political reasons the Statutes of Autonomy for Catalonia and the Basque Country were negotiated before the promised law on 'autonomous' police forces appeared, so that there is not necessarily any uniformity between the various Communities as to their police powers, nor is there any clear coherence between the various provisions. Political considerations are supreme here, since the critical objective is not police or local government reform, but the isolation of Basque terrorism from popular support by accepting the demands of moderate nationalists. So yet another kind of police force has been inserted into the system. It has been cogently argued that a logical system for modern Spain would be to create Community police forces everywhere, abolishing the national and municipal forces and getting rid of the urban/rural division, but such a radical reform seems politically out of the question at present. Instead a complex pattern will emerge with some communities having their own police, some not, and some opting for combinations of quasi-ceremonial forces and regional co-ordination of municipal police. Further careful demarcation and coordination will be essential.

To simplify matters and because it is the most interesting case we shall concentrate on the new situation in Euskadi, the Basque Country, that is, the three provinces of Guipúzcoa, Alava, and Vizcaya. The 1979 Statute of Autonomy for the Basque Country gives wide powers to the Basque Parliament that it set up. The Basque Government is empowered to set up and control its own police force 'for the protection of persons and goods, and the maintenance of public order'. To the State Security Forces are reserved powers that are extra- or supra-communitary, that is, the Policía's competence in immigration matters and identity documents, or the Guardia Civil's in arms control, protection of frontiers and points of entry, and in fiscal matters and contraband. Insofar as the Policía Autónoma, as these community police forces are known, are judicial police they are responsible to the courts.

Coordination with the national police forces is to be achieved through a Junta de Seguridad, a joint committee with equal representation of central and community government. This committee has the duty of deciding the regulations, numbers, structure, recruitment, and equipment of the <u>Policía Autónoma</u>, whose commanders are to be appointed from among officers of the Armed Forces and State Security Forces. The national police forces may still intervene in the maintenance of public order, either at the request of the Basque Government, or, where they consider the national interest is seriously threatened, on their own initiative but with the approval of the <u>Junta de Seguridad</u>. In especially urgent circumstances the national police forces may intervene on the sole responsibility of the central government. And in states of emergency all police forces come under central control.

Later legislation, in 1980, further defined the powers of the new Basque police. They are to look after Community officials, buildings, regulations, and ceremonial. They are to protect <u>seguridad ciudadana</u>, and to defend rights, persons, and goods. They should uphold national law, adopt crime prevention measures, and act for the judicial authorities. They will also participate in civil defence plans, help in disasters and private disputes, and guarantee essential public services. They are also given exclusive powers in traffic policing, though the national police forces may still take measures regarding all communication routes in connection with their own exclusive areas of competence.

The Basque government implemented this legislation by the creation of the <u>Ertzaina</u> (a Basque word meaning 'care for the people'). After some delays the first group of 278 appeared in public in October 1982 after six months' training. A further 800 were to follow shortly, while a later intake includes 100 women, to be treated with strict equality. At the same time 325 were in training as motorized traffic police and have now taken over these duties from the <u>Agrupación de Tráfico</u> of the <u>Guardia Civil</u>. As the name implies every effort is being made to project this new police force as having a quite new style, the emphasis being placed on service to the community. Above all this is the Basques' own police service, and for many Basque politicians only the beginning of a transfer of most police powers.

Achievements and problems

Basque and Catalan nationalism are movements of long standing, but the intractable nature of the situation in Euskadi is Franco's legacy to democratic Spain, and his police were at the heart of the creation of a situation where violent nationalists received mass support. The security forces acted as an alien army of occupation and were treated as such. They were literally alien (we have

246

seen how few Basques were in the Guardia Civil), finding the baffling Basque language a major obstacle to intelligence, and almost literally an army, officered by men trained as soldiers and steeped in the anti-democratic and centralist values of the Zaragoza Academia General Militar, home of Spanish military honour. After Franco's death in 1975 a purely repressive solution to the Basque situation was soon seen to have failed and the government embarked on the 'Spain of the Autonomies' as a political solution. Meanwhile the violence of ETA, the revolutionary Basque nationalist organization, continued, backed by massive popular demonstrations, and the government discovered that its security forces were counter-productive, since their harsh, massive methods of maintaining public order (they are said to have caused 27 deaths between 1975 and 1978 intervening against demonstrations)(4), and their frequent use of torture and ill-treatment, trained as they were to regard political opposition as the enemy, strengthened support for nationalism and made political solutions more difficult. Police reform was obviously urgent – the 1978 Police Law was one response.

But while political solutions in the late seventies were undermined by police actions, they were also inhibited by the threat of military reaction. Concessions to Basque nationalism were seen by opponents of democratization as weakening national unity and public order. Such opponents were principally in the armed forces, and the close links between army and police meant that a policy of devolution and police reform engaged the 'bunker', the old Francoist right, on a very broad front. Another complication was public suspicion that while the 'bunker' insisted on the importance of order and the crushing of separatism, there was nevertheless a sinister community of interest between extreme right and extreme left. The far right needed violence as a pretext for intervening against democratization, while ETA's hopes were that by precipitating an army coup by officers angry at the rising toll of deaths among the security forces, they could set off a revolutionary response. Under Franco police had associated with violent ultra-right groups both in and outside Spain. Why should they and army officers not still be manipulating terror for their own ends?

In this context of profound public mistrust and bitter Basque hostility, with the security forces, prisoners of their own past reputation, feeling isolated and, in some quarters, threatened by reform, the incidence of terrorist killings grew in the later 1970's: in 1978-80 235 deaths were caused by ETA, about three-fifths of them members of the security forces. The survival of the whole democratic experiment was at stake, as became dramatically clear in 1981 when Colonel Tejero, a Guardia Civil officer, stormed the Spanish Parliament with a group of civil guards, backed by a conspiracy of officers and civilians. A senior officer of a force on which the law laid the duty of upholding constitutional order was seen (and on television) trying to overthrow that order because of a supposed government softness on public order and national unity in the face of the Basque problem.

But only a minority of officers supported such views and the broad policy of devolution and police reform has continued, if warily and nervously at times. Terrorist killings have been reduced, ETA has become more isolated, and Basque opinion is slightly less bitterly hostile to the national police forces. More effective police work, a government policy of amnesty for repentant terrorists, and, at last, French co-operation, seem to be making headway, though by 1984 the situation still remained difficult. Assassination of ETA leaders in southern France by the mysterious GAL (Antiterrorist Liberation Group) led to renewed suspicions of police involvement in a 'dirty war', while growing polarisation of Basque society threatened to undermine the policy of devolution.

But there is another way in which the task of creating a police system for a parliamentary democracy was made more difficult by terrorism. The Constitution had in 1978 given citizens the civil rights expected in a democracy, but the growth of violence, both left and right, led the government to a series of laws in 1978, 1979, and 1980 to limit those rights in cases connected with terrorism. While in general anyone arrested must be either released or placed before the judicial authorities within 72 hours, those suspected of terrorist offences may be held for a further seven days with the approval of a magistrate. During this ten-day period the detainee may be held incommunicado (though in 1983 the presence of a lawyer was guaranteed). These provisions and their application are the subject of frequent criticism. The Spanish Asociación pro Derechos Humanos (Civil Rights Association), a highly-respected body, in its 1982 report, argues that magistrates do not always exercise proper supervision in such cases. It is from this ten-day period of incommunicado detention of terrorist suspects that most complaints of torture and ill-treatment currently arise. The Association concludes that torture and ill-treatment at the hands of the police forces do still occur, that there are more complaints against the Guardia Civil than against the Policía, but that matters have improved very substantially since 1978. Clearly reform has gone a long way towards eradicating the practices of the Franco era, hampered, however, by the struggle against political violence.

A different problem is that of relations between the various forces. It is difficult, for example, to co-ordinate fully two such distinct forces as the Policía and the Guardia Civil, with their different styles, functions, command structures, communications systems, and lines of responsibility to the cabinet. For instance, because postings in the Guardia Civil are a Ministry of Defence affair, the Ministry of the Interior were not officially informed when Tejero, a known anti-democrat, was given a Madrid posting. More broadly, difficulties arise from the fact that the Guardia Civil's major headquarters buildings are, for operational and functional reasons, usually in-side towns and cities that are the territory of the Policía. Their presence and availability there can and does lead to complaints of poaching.

At other times the Policía and the Guardia Civil are reported as both independently investigating the same crime, sometimes hindering each other's efforts. The creation of the Autonomous Police has also fostered new dif-ficulties over co-operation, since the national police forces and the autonomous authorities are often deeply suspicious of each other, while the modernization and de-velopment of the Municipal Police Forces has also revealed the urgent need for co-ordination.

More generally, a source of public criticism is that police practices and standing orders have not always been brought up-to-date. There are complaints of excessive force or numbers in preserving public order. Here the tradition of large urban comisarías that cover big areas, of the maintenance of sizeable reserves with a military-style training, and the lack of community or barrio polic-ing are inheritances from the past that play a part (and here again the threat of random political violence has in-hibited reform). Policemen themselves complain of inade-quate training in the use of weapons. Inappropriate and unmodernized standing instructions have also led to tragic incidents, the most recent being the death by shooting of a two-year-old child in a car that failed to stop at a Guardia Civil road-block, a case that has led to a review of rules for the use of firearms. Such incidents (there have been thirteen deaths at road-blocks in five years) also illustrate the need to complete the re-equipment of the police forces. The civil guards in this case did not have proper equipment for their road-block, other than their firearms.

The process of reform, apart from the proposed uni-fication of the Policía, has thus now become a matter of piecemeal changes of this sort. Neither full unification and demilitarization, nor regionalization are on the agenda. The socialist Ministers of Defence and of the Interior have, for instance, repeatedly emphasised their commitment to the Guardia Civil, and admired its reliability, to the point that now there are complaints of favouritism from the Policía. Indeed the new government has found itself tightly constrained in trying to implement its electoral programme. Inter-corps rivalry holds up structural reform and thereby a more efficient deployment of Spain's large number of police (if Municipal Police are included, about one per 250 of the population). The April 1984 announcement that the Municipal Police would be used as policía de barrio, community police, is a sign of the government's inability to go beyond makeshift measures. At the same time, though Spain still has crime rates among the lowest in Western Europe, the rise in crime has accelerated with the wave of heroin-addiction - three-quarters of all crime against property is now thought to be drug-related. Clear-up rates have fallen and new responses are needed. The courts have proved chronically incapable of coping with the volume of cases (it commonly takes two years for cases to come to trial) and when in 1983 the government introduced progressive reforms of the remand laws many of those awaiting trial were released because of the slowness of the courts. Public outcry at the crime-wave forced the government to modify the remand laws once more in 1984. Thus failure to complete the modernization of both the police and the judicial system have led to back-tracking on civil rights reform.

From the point of view of members of the police forces too, the process of reform and modernization remains uncompleted. They point out that, though now much better equipped and trained, many still operate from buildings that are antiquated and overcrowded, and with insufficient recognition in terms of pay. While labour rights have been broadly regulated - none of the forces have the right to strike, the Cuerpo Superior have several trade unions, while at present the Policía Nacional and the Guardia Civil are not permitted them - the legal framework has not been completed. The Law promised in the Constitution still does not exist, nor do the promised codes of practice to be based on resolutions of the Council of Europe. Policemen reasonably make the complaint that if they are to become part of a democratic society, their rights as well as their duties should be clear.

But most importantly policemen have to win and retain credibility as defenders of the rule of law. They have to convince the public of their complete commitment to the

Constitution and to the final eradication of Francoist practices and attitudes. An essential part of the latter is to be seen not to be shielding members of the forces who break the law. This is a problematic area in any police system, but it is doubly important in Spain where the public remember all too well police forces beyond the law.

It is notoriously difficult to judge, or even define consent but a poll in March 1983 showed 69% regarding as positive the performance of the Policía Nacional, and 67% that of the Guardia Civil, while 75% believed the security forces would develop for the better. Behind a broad satisfaction there were reminders of the past and of where improvement should be found: 75% felt the modern security forces were at the service of all, 56% felt protected by them, 73% said they had always been correctly treated, 56% agreed that the forces had adjusted to democratic practices, and only 44%, with 52% against, agreed that Spaniards worked with them.(5)

Clearly the system has changed, or at least evolved rapidly. In one sense there is a striking contrast between the recent history of the Spanish police and that of other West European forces, in that Spain has seen a remarkable liberalisation in terms of style and public acceptance. In other ways evolution has followed and will follow the patterns common to all modern Spanish institutions of bringing Spain closer to a general West European norm. If this is allowed simply to mean a technological catching-up operation it will remain a limping reform since the structure of the forces needs urgent attention. There are clearly too many sorts of police force for efficiency. But beyond efficiency it is to be hoped that technological modernity will not be the sole criterion, an easy temptation in a country that is still catching up economically. The failure so far to implement the stated ideal of a policía de barrio, community police, and the lack of local or real parliamentary accountability are eloquent. The Spanish police system has changed remarkably and surprisingly in the last eight years, but its mission as laid down in the Constitution remains a challenge: 'To protect the free exercise of rights and liberties and to guarantee the safety of citizens'.(6)

FOOTNOTES

1. See Policía Española, April 1983, p. 6, and May 1983, p. 5.
2. Temario de Seguridad Ciudadana, Madrid (Dirección General de la Policía), 1982, p. 57.
3. Francisco Murillo Ferrol, preface to Diego López Garrido, La Guardia Civil y los orígenes del Estado centralista, Barcelona (Grijalbo), 1982, p. 14.
4. Manuel Ballbé, Orden público y militarismo en la España constitucional (1812-1983), Madrid (Alianza), 1983, p. 470.
5. 'La Policía no está sola', Cambio 16, 7 March 1983, pp. 49-50.
6. I should like to thank Aberdeen University, the Carnegie Trust for the Universities of Scotland, and the British Academy for their support for the research for this chapter.

Further Reading

Ballbé, Manuel, Orden público y militarismo en la España constitucional (1812-1983), Madrid (Alianza), 1983.
Ballbé, M., and M. Giró, Las Fuerzas de orden público, Barcelona (Dopesa), 1978.
Bardavío, Joaquín, La estructura del poder en España, Madrid (Ibérico Europea), 1969.
Carr, Raymond, and Juan Pablo Fusi, Spain: Dictatorship to Democracy, London (Allen and Unwin), 1981.
Defensa: Revista Internacional de Ejércitos, Armamento y Tecnología, Extra No. 2, n.d. (special issue on Guardia Civil).
Guardia Civil, 1980-1982, Balance de realizaciones, Madrid (Ministerio del Interior), 1982.
López Garrido, Diego, La Guardia Civil y los orígenes del Estado centralista, Barcelona (Grijalbo), 1982.
Ministerio del Interior, Normativa básica, Servicios Centrales, Madrid (Ministerio del Interior), 1984.
Morales Villanueva, Antonio, Las Fuerzas de orden público, Madrid (San Martín), 1980.
Moya, Mauricio, La policía y sus sindicatos en España, Madrid (Fundamentos), 1982.
Policía, Realizaciones 1980-82, Madrid (Ministerio del Interior), 1982.
Tamames, Ramón, La República, La era de Franco, Madrid (Alianza), 1980.

Temario de Seguridad Ciudadana, Madrid (Dirección General de la Policía, Comisaría General de Seguridad Ciudadana), 1982.

Glossary

Academia General Militar - Army Officers' Academy, Zaragoza.

Agrupación de Tráfico - traffic police of the Guardia Civil.

Brigada Central - Central squad.

Brigada Regional - Regional squad.

Carabineros - Pre-1940 Anti-smuggling force.

COS (Centro operacional de servicio) - operational control system of the Guardia Civil.

Comandancia - Provincial HQ of the Guardia Civil.

Comandante - major.

Comisaría de Distrito - District Police Station (in a larger urban area).

Comisaría General - central operational division of the Policía.

Comisaría Local - Municipal Police Station.

Comisaría Provincial - Provincial HQ of the Policía.

Comisario - senior officer of the Cuerpo Superior (superintendent etc.).

Comisario Jefe Provincial - Provincial Chief of the Policía.

Compañía - company.

Cuerpo Administrativo de Seguridad - senior civilian staff of the Policía.

Cuerpo Auxiliar de Seguridad - auxiliary civilian staff of the Policía.

Cuerpo General de Policía - plain-clothes police, 1941-1978.

Cuerpo Superior de Policía - plain-clothes branch of the Policía.

Director de la Seguridad del Estado - Director of State Security, responsible for national police forces.

Documentación - documentation, branch of the Policía concerned with identification papers etc.

ETA (Euskadi Ta Askatasuna) - revolutionary Basque nationalist organisation.

fichero - file.

Grupo Antiterrorista Rural - anti-terrorist force of the Guardia Civil.

Guardia Civil - civil guard.

Información - intelligence.

Inspector de Guardia - station officer.

253

Jefatura Superior - Regional HQ of the Policía.

Policía - collective term for the Cuerpo Superior and the Policía Nacional. The English word 'police' is used to refer to police forces in general.

Policía Armada y de Tráfico - uniformed urban police, 1941-1978.

Policía Autónoma - police force of an Autonomous Community (region with devolved powers).

Policía Judicial - judicial police, C.I.D.

Policía Nacional - uniformed branch of the Policía.

Puesto - local station of the Guardia Civil.

Seguridad, Cuerpo de - uniformed urban police, pre-1941.

Seguridad Ciudadana - civil/citizens' security.

Servicio Fiscal - Fiscal Service of the Guardia Civil.

S.I.G.C. (Servicio de Información de la Guardia Civil) - Intelligence Department of the Guardia Civil.

Servicio Especial de Vigilancia Fiscal - Ministry of Finance excise guard.

Vigilancia, Cuerpo de - plain-clothes police, pre-1941.

Vigilante Jurado - registered private security guard.

Chapter 9

THE POLICE IN SWEDEN

Clive Archer

The role of the police in any society must inevitably reflect the traditions and present demands of law making and enforcing in that society. Sweden is perhaps one of the most law-abiding countries in Europe with the position of the Swedish police reflecting this basic quiescence. However, in the last twenty years the country has experienced some developments - political, social and economic in nature - which have increased disruption, particularly in the urban areas.

Background

Sweden is often seen as the archetype of post-industrial, social welfare societies. Although its economic advance in the early part of the century was based on a richness of raw materials -iron ore and wood in particular - Sweden's post-war wealth has been sustained by technological advance, specialist products, a highly-educated population and a well-ordered society. Being a neutral state in the 'quiet corner of Europe', Sweden has managed to avoid most of the disruption of war. The Swedes are a homogeneous people: apart from Lapps in the sparse north there are no geographic minorities, over 90% belong to the state Lutheran religion and until the 1960s there were few immigrants into the country. The domination of the reformist Social Democrat Party in government since the 1930s has provided Sweden with a long run of consensus politics and a degree of state social intervention not normally experienced in Western Europe. It also underlined the element of solidarity in Swedish society: the element that makes the Swede a very societal animal. The average Swedish citizen is more unionized, better educated and belongs to more interest groups than his or her West European counterpart.

The nature of Swedish society should mean that Sweden is easier to police than frontier America, religiously divided Ulster or locally atomized Italy. On the whole this has been true. As well as the unified nature of its society, Sweden has a small population (some eight and a half million) and thus it does not have many of the problems of the overcrowded areas of Europe - or at least only has them on a smaller, more manageable scale. The country is of interest because of the experimental nature of much of its legislation concerning justice and law-enforcement. However in the last decade some of the social problems felt by other European states - housing shortages, racial conflict, unemployed youth, terrorist incidents, political conflict - have been experienced by Sweden.

History

There is a long history of law-making and enforcement in the Scandinavian countries - Denmark, Norway and Sweden - and the Viking Atlantic outpost of Iceland. The process of law-making was most formalized in the Icelandic gatherings at the Althingi - held up until the eighteenth century - at which leaders met to hear the law recited and to agree on amendments. The dominance of farming families which typified the politics of Scandinavia until the sixteenth century could be seen in early Sweden. Slavery was abolished there in 1335 and localised law gathered together in the Code of Magnus Eriksson in 1350.(1)

From the sixteenth century the power of the nobility strengthened in Sweden leading to a battle with the royal court and an age of absolute government and war-like kings in the late seventeenth century followed by an Era of Liberty from 1719 to 1772 during which constitutional innovation was made and fundamental laws laid down. After another spell of absolutism (1772-1809), a new Instrument of Government (1809) introduced constitutional government and inaugurated progress towards democracy. In 1866 the old parliament of four estates - nobility, clergy, burghers and peasantry - was replaced by two chambers, one elected regionally and one by direct elections in the constituencies. 1909 saw male universal suffrage in the country and women obtained the vote in 1921.(2) By this time Sweden was already changing from an agricultural country into one with an important industrial sector. This process both caused and paralleled a move from the country to the town and from small towns to the larger towns and cities. By the end of the 1960s Sweden had become an urbanized industrial country with a growing tertiary, service sector.(3) For many Swedes this change from farm to factory to office had come in one generation and had been comparatively peaceful and painless. The country had seen a certain amount of industrial conflict at the turn of the century and during the 1920s, but the shock of unarmed strikers being cut down by armed militia in Adalen, 1931, helped to push labour, management and government towards compromise and cooperation.

This brief historical sketch serves to demonstrate four points about Swedish society important in the study of law-enforcement there. The first concerns the relationship of the individual and the state in Sweden. The Swedes have a long history of participation in the law-making process and there is little evidence of feelings of alienation by any sizeable group in the population against authority. The belief that the state should not distance itself from the populace is expressed in Chapter 1, Article 1 of the 1974 Instrument of Government:

'All public power in Sweden emanates from the people. The Swedish democracy is founded on freedom of opinion and on universal and equal suffrage and shall be realized through a representative and parliamentary polity and through local self-government.
Public powers shall be exercised under the laws.'

The second point is that the wide range of laws in Sweden are administered and enforced by a number of agencies and authorities. There are administrative agencies (separate from the ministries that make the law), local government authorities, semi-public boards and QUANGOs as well as the law courts and the police. As much legislation is social and economic in concern, it is considered necessary that it should be carried out by specialists in those areas. At its most negative this means that there is a wide range of authorities - social welfare agencies, tax inspectors, medical authorities, labour dispute arbitrators - who can take away from the individual his or her property, family, right to work, freedom of movement in a way that the ordinary policeman would find hard to do. However this must be done in accordance with the laws of Sweden and the individual has protection against maladministration or a miscarriage of justice by the Ombudsman system. This institution has been in existence in Sweden since 1809 and aims at protecting the citizen against injustice in the administraton of law.

The third point is that the nature of Swedish government over the last fifty years should have had consequences for justice in that country. A deeply democratic, reformist, socially aware government should be alive to the problems existing in society, should be willing to do something about them and able to execute change. A study of nineteen industrialized Western countries has shown a positive correlation between manifest political conflict and weak political influence of the working class on the one hand and repression in criminal policy on the other hand. Countries such as Sweden which have had a low level of industrial strikes and a regular involvement of the labour movement in the political process have shown a lower propensity towards repressive legislation and high rates of imprisonment.(4)

Finally, societal developments have affected the nature of crime in Sweden. Industrialization and urbanization have obviously brought a different pattern of crime than that which existed in rural Sweden of yesteryear. However, it should not be thought that the process has been one of larger cities bringing higher crime rates. As far as can be told, the rate of violent crime dealt with in the capital, Stockholm, varied greatly from the mid-nineteenth century until 1885. It then fell sharply until 1905, increased until 1910 and declined to a low point in the 1930s, a level maintained until the 1950s when it rose again. The Swedish criminologist, Sven Sperlings, holds that the rise of factory work with the industrialization of the 1890s led to more stable living conditions for Stockholm's working class – regular work, better housing conditions, the growth of the nuclear family and the decline of alcohol consumption.(5) It is quite possible that a disintegration of working-class consciousness after the achievement of a high material standard of living after the 1950s and the disruptions in settled family life brought by the post-industrial society has led to an increase in crime. However, one should heed the warnings of another criminologist, Nils Christie, about the problems of studying criminality over a period of time. Rates of crime change with the degree of interest taken by the authorities as well as the extent of reporting of crime.(6)

Development of the Modern Police Force

The police force in Sweden came about as a result of the process of industrialization and the growth of urban centres. By the mid-nineteenth century Stockholm had a force based on localities with most of the officers walking the beat. Since then the police force in the whole country has grown substantially and has undergone a process of specialization and centralization.

In 1864 a Detective Department was formed in Stockholm based on the few men who had been previously earmarked to look after people found guilty of serious crimes. The police authorities in the capital adjudicated over lesser cases with the city's governor-general acting as judge. The more important cases were dealt with by a magistrates' court. In 1869 a special police court was established to hear most minor cases.

According to Sperlings the Stockholm district police forces of the mid-nineteenth century had serious discipline problems with many of the constables taking on other jobs and drunkenness on duty being a problem. Further there did not seem to be enough policemen and those employed were badly trained and paid.(7)

In 1876 Stockholm established a central police department for training though its effectiveness was somewhat swamped by the influx of population into the city in the 1880s. In 1892 inspectors were appointed by the central department in an attempt to cut down the amount of misdemeanours committed by constables, and recruits were taken increasingly from the armed forces rather than from the working class. In 1884 a mounted police division and in 1887 a riot squad were added to the Stockholm central department. This specialization of police work in the big cities continued into the twentieth century.

In the rest of Sweden policing was the task of the local municipalities but even as early as the 1920s the difficulties of this localized effort had become clear. Many municipal forces were too small to be effective especially in times of emergency. However, suggestions of a more centralized police authority in the country were resisted until the early 1930s. A Swedish writer, Esbjörn Esbjörnson, pinpoints the incident in Adalen in 1931 (mentioned above) as a turning point.(8) Here an industrial dispute at sawmills in the north of the country led to a clash of workers and blacklegs. As the local police force was too small to control the situation, the police chief was obliged to call in troops from the local regiment. These were unable to respond to the intricacies of an industrial dispute with any subtlety: they shot five workers. After this, the Swedish parliament decided to create State Police units of some thousand officers. Grants allowed the larger municipalities to train extra officers who were then assigned to State Police units throughout the country with the intention that they should be able to deal with the sort of civil unrest experienced at Adalen.

As mentioned, the friction that sparked at Adalen was in fact dealt with by political compromise between employers and employees, encouraged by the new Social Democrat government of 1933. The State Police units continued dealing increasingly with traffic problems, criminal investigation into tougher cases and other cases with which the municipal police could not cope because of lack of manpower or expertise. The 1930s also saw the creation of a National Police College for training and the National Forensic Laboratory in Sweden.

From the 1930s until the mid-1960s the national system - State Police units, Police College and Forensic Laboratory - co-existed with the municipally-run police forces. There were increasing calls for the whole system to be reformed and a national police force to be established. These suggestions acted rather like 'planning blight': they discouraged the local authorities from investing large amounts of money in an organization which they suspected would be taken from them in the near future.

Other factors seemed to point towards reform. By the end of the 1950s both crime rates and the number of cars were increasing substantially in Sweden: figures for both doubled between 1954 and 1965.(9) The number of traffic accidents was increasing whilst the clear-up rate for crime was decreasing.

In the face of such developments, the organization of the Swedish police seemed somewhat outmoded. Except in the big cities, the local forces were often too small to provide a twenty-four hour watch and certainly could not support specialist policing. In 1964 Sweden had 554 police forces with over 70% of these having less than ten officers. One-third of the forces had fewer than five men.(10)

This fragmentation of police strength also caused problems of coordination and cooperation. 'Hot pursuit' into neighbouring districts was allowed, providing the police force there was notified. However, assistance to another force created financial complications: the municipality being helped had to pay those forces assisting them and this often led to 'an enormous amount of red tape'.(11)

The old system of local policing had grown up in a period before full urbanization so the distribution of police resources throughout Sweden did not, by the late 1950s, mirror that of population which had become concentrated in the centre and south of the country.

Finally, the old structure had little uniformity. The quality of policing differed from area to area, as well as the quantity. Small units could not easily take advantage of technological developments and became the poorer relations of the big city police. Police methods and working conditions varied widely.

As a result of these shortcomings, a government committee suggested reforms and in 1962 the Swedish parliament approved in principle the establishment of a national police force. This decision was unanimous, as was that taken in 1964 to adopt the detailed plan of action. On 1 January 1965 the 554 municipal police forces with their 18,000 employees were abolished and a national police force established.

Organization of the Swedish Police

In Sweden the Ministry of Justice has overall responsibility for the legal system and the Minister of Justice is answerable to parliament for that functional area. In the Swedish tradition government ministries do not normally administer their area of policy. This is done by boards or agencies which are controlled by legislation and are therefore rather indirectly answerable to government rather than to a particular minister. In the administration of justice in Sweden the police are now separated from the system of prosecution and the court organization.

The national police are themselves administered by the National Police Board (Rikspolisstyrelsen) which consists of a director general, his deputy and eight other members, six of whom are members of parliament and two of whom represent police personnel. The director general (or Commissioner) is appointed for a renewable six-year period by the government and during his term of office he is not subject to control by the Minister of Justice.

The headquarters of the National Police Board is divided into four functional departments (A, B, C and D) plus a division each for records and computers.

Division A (Operations) is divided into two divisions, one for the uniform police and one for criminal investigations. The first division plans patrol work, allocation of personnel and other resources, traffic supervision, air and sea supervision and also deals with emergencies. Resource allocation and coordination for criminal investigations is overseen by the second division which directs the National Criminal Investigation Unit (NCIU) consisting of over a hundred specialist detectives. The NCIU has five squads and a technical group. The work of the squads covers murder and other serious crimes of violence (squad A), narcotic offences (B), aggravated thefts and armed robberies (C), frauds (D) and criminal intelligence (E). These squads both co-ordinate national investigations and supply expertise for the investigation into serious crimes. B Department is concerned with technical aspects of national police work, including vehicles and telecommunications, as well as with training (see separate section below). The administration of the national police structure is undertaken by C Department.

D Department is perhaps the most controversial of the central organisation of the National Police Board - it deals with security questions. It is known as SÄPO - short for 'security policy' in Swedish and has three offices. Office A is concerned with counter-espionage and specialises in post interception, intercepting radio transmissions and with general defence security. Office B deals with bombs, terrorists, political extremists, cryptography, control of foreigners living in Sweden, foreign powers' activities and the exchange of information with other states' security networks. The third office is involved with the administration of the security service and the registration of those observed by the service. In the 1950s this office was staffed by people trusted by the Social Democrat government in order to exercise control over the 'secret services'. However, the 'watchdogs' eventually became socialised by the behaviour of their colleagues and once some of their indiscretions became known - including placing mildly left-wing public figures on their list of Marxists and revolutionaries - their wings were clipped and they were brought more closely into the SAPO structure.

From the start of the 1980s SÄPO's Budget has been increased (by some 15% in 1981-3) and the total number of people working for the department is now about 75. Over the past decade SAPO has been criticised for being ineffective and for placing too much emphasis on chasing left-wing groups. SAPO has replied by claiming that espionage has increased alarmingly since the end of the 1970s, especially in Sweden's important defence-related industries. It should perhaps be remembered that SÄPO's activities are by their nature dramatic compared with most police work but that their tasks are modest compared to equivalent agencies in Britain, France or West Germany.

All in all the operational tasks of the National Police Board are rather limited and involve investigation into crimes against the security of the state and those which have to be dealt with on a national level, security for state visits, supervision of the nation's traffic and air and sea patrol.

The regional level of police organization in Sweden is undertaken by twenty-four county administrations. The major task of the twenty-three regional County Police commissioners is that of supervision and co-ordination of police activities. This level is particularly suited to overseeing traffic activity which is done by the County Traffic Groups. At the local level Sweden is divided into 118 police districts – 115 divisions of the counties plus a district each for the three big cities of Stockholm, Malmö and Gothenburg. Every district has a Local Police Board made up of the Local Police Commissioner and six to eight other members appointed by the county council. This Board makes decisions concerning organization, finance and appointments. The Commissioner has operational command over the district's police. A normal police district consists of a secretariat, a uniformed branch (including both a public order and a traffic section) and a criminal investigation department usually with five squads – for general investigation, technical crime, theft, fraud and violence. Fourteen districts have crime prevention squads, three have an aliens squad, one an economic crime squad, whilst twenty-five have established special drugs squads.

Three points should be made about the organization of the police in Sweden. First, it has been truly national since the beginning of 1965 though its regional and local dimension should be noticed. Secondly there is an elected element at all levels of the control mechanism. The National Police Board, the county administrations and the district police boards are all dominated by those representing the public interest. Finally, despite the reform of 1965, the organization of the police is still somewhat over-bureaucratic. One Swedish commentator has estimated the ideal number of local districts to be approximately eighty and that six to eight regional authorities would be about right.(12)

Police Tasks

As in the rest of Western Europe, the general duty of the Swedish police is to maintain public order and safety. To do this, crime has to be prevented and detected, steps taken that the peace is not disturbed and the public provided with protection, information and other forms of assistance. The Police Instructions in the Swedish Code of Statutes require the police to cooperate with the Public Prosecutors and with the social welfare agencies. In order to assist the achievements of these general duties, there are a number of specialist police activities such as the National Police Board helicopters, marine units, and the mountain rescue service.

An important aspect of modern police work is traffic control. Sweden has some 3.5 million cars (1980 figures) and some five million valid driving licences. Every year

1,200 to 1,300 people are killed and 21,000 injured on the roads. The Swedish Central Bureau of Statistics issues data on traffic accidents every month and breaks down their incidence geographically. This information is used by the National Police Board and the regional and district boards to allocate their resources in the surveillance of the nation's roads. The county traffic surveillance groups carry out routine surveillance of the busier roads as well as specific operations. The Swedish police have adopted a new instrument called Traffipax for this surveillance. It is basically photographic equipment mounted in unmarked police cars and can record potentially dangerous traffic situations and superimpose on the pictures essential data such as exact time and date. The Traffipax can also be used at night as it has a dazzle-free flash attachment which takes good pictures up to forty-five metres. Traffic sections within the police districts cover those routes not under county supervision, undertake other duties concerning traffic regulations and help in road safety education in the schools. The National Police Board's helicopters also lend help in traffic control especially in the summer months. The Board also has an ambulance flight service to take people to hospital – quite often from the scene of a crash.

Since police reorganization in 1965 the National Police Board has governed the National Swedish Laboratory of Forensic Science, which is an independent institution. The Laboratory carries out technical investigations for the courts, prosecutors and police authorities and does paid work for other authorities and individuals, as time permits. The sort of work that the Laboratory undertakes includes handwriting investigation, forgery inspection, ballistics, causes of fires, chemical analysis, biological investigation, photographic services and other general work including that on clothing, locks, gambling machines etc. Forensic analyses in their chemical and serological form are carried out by the National Swedish Laboratory for Forensic Chemistry.

Use of both laboratories is made by the thirty or so technical detective squads in Sweden. Each regional county administration has at least one such squad which deals with the technical aspects of serious crimes – investigations of arson, reconstructions at the site of a murder or of a serious accident, identification of victims or suspects.

Training

The Swedish police has an extensive training programme

undertaken under the supervision of the Training and Technical Division of the National Police Board.

New policemen attend a basic course for forty-one weeks at the Police College at Ulriksdal before they go on for one year on uniformed duty and one year on plainclothes investigative assignment. At Ulriksdal the course consists of a study of the functions of the police and the legal basis of police operations followed by practical training with job-experience at local police stations. The subjects taught in the basic course include uniform police duty, traffic surveillance and legislation, use of service weapons, penal law, Swedish, English, psychology and psychiatry, physical training and civics. The College also provides a ten week course for sergeants.

Another police college, at Solna outside Stockholm, undertakes training for senior officers including inspectors, superintendents and chief constables. Both Solna and Ulriksdal give shorter training courses for detectives and instructors. The National Police Board's training division also has a traffic training section in Strängnäs and a course for dog handlers at Solleftea.

Regular physical training is carried out locally as is firearms training. Whilst the Swedish police are armed there is, on the whole, neither the opportunity nor the propensity to use firearms on a regular basis. Training makes sure that each man has about 150 shots, practice per annum and thus has a basic competence in the use of a gun should he be faced with a situation in which the strict regulations permit firearm use.

International Aspects

Sweden is a member of the International Criminal Police Organization - Interpol - which has its headquarters in Paris. Sweden's National Police Board acts as the country's national Interpol bureau and its Interpol section is manned round the clock with a staff of some twenty for this purpose. Two Swedish officers are seconded to the Interpol Secretariat in Paris and since 1977 Sweden has sent one officer each to Bangkok and The Hague, both capitals being of importance in the international drug trade, an area of particular interest for Interpol. Sweden may request through Interpol the arrest of a suspect with a view to extradition to Sweden, information on missing persons, statements from persons abroad to help in criminal investigation in Sweden, information from the criminal records of suspected persons, help for Swedish officers going abroad to investigate crimes, and may pass on to Interpol such assistance for other member states. The

Stockholm bureau is obliged to report to Paris drug offences and counterfeiting cases.

Formal relations between local police authorities in Sweden and authorities abroad are handled by the Interpol bureau in Stockholm. However a more direct method is used with the other Nordic countries. This is a result of the close co-operation and co-ordination between public authorities in the five Nordic states in matters of social and juridicial questions. For the last thirty years the interparliamentary and interministerial Nordic Council has overseen and encouraged such activities. The legal systems of the countries have a common background and in the post-war period governments have sought to make sure that new criminal laws do not create unnecessary differences. There also exists a close relationship between public offices and professional organizations in one Nordic country and their counterparts in the others. Civil servants often make direct contact with their opposite number in another Nordic state without going through the diplomatic service. This is true of the police services in these countries especially where practical circumstances demand such 'informality', as in the sparsely populated border regions of North Norway, Sweden and Finland.

Police and Society

During the last two decades the police in Sweden have had to face many of the difficulties confronted by other West European police forces. The force had to be built up after the reorganization of 1965. Yet this was a period of high standards of living in Sweden - one of the highest in the world, a growing teenage population showing signs of rebellion against the safe materialism of Swedish society, of unprecedented numbers of immigrants into Sweden and of a rising crime rate. More policemen were needed but in a highly trained society with full employment, it was hard to attract the right sort of person for the job. Incidents where demonstrators at an international tennis match and environmentalists trying to protect condemned trees in the centre of Stockholm were roughly handled by young policemen, as well as a number of running battles between policemen and youths in central Stockholm in the late 1960s and early 1970s gave Swedish citizens cause for thought about their police force.

A survey of Swedish police attitudes showed that in 1968 there was dissatisfaction amongst both recruits and senior policemen alike. They adjudged their level of security, pay, independence, training and social status to be below not only their level of expectation but also below what they considered acceptable. It is perhaps not surprising then that the 1969-70 wage negotiation round led to a series of wild-cat strikes affecting the police. With centralization and lack of employee participation in this period

> 'the development in police work in Sweden seems to have moved in a direction opposite to the value changes in society at large and to factual changes that have taken place in work towards increased democracy'.(13)

Since that time police pay and conditions of service have benefited to some extent by the militant approach taken in the mid-1970s by the TCO, the white-collared umbrella organization to which the policemen belong.

The Swedish police authorities have been aware of the need for the police force not being alienated from society. The instigation of their training programme demonstrates their wish to improve the quality and social responsibility of their recruits. The use of specially trained policemen to teach 'law and justice' classes in Swedish schools demonstrates the interest in ensuring that the citizens of tomorrow are aware of their responsibilities. One of the advantages of the new centralized system of control of the Swedish police has been that reforms can be made for the whole force - for example since a government commission on rising levels of crime made its recommendations in 1973 the Swedish police have switched their emphasis to the prevention of crime rather than its detection. With built-in democratic controls, the Swedish police have been anxious to avoid the disadvantages of a centralized force, aiming in the words of an American commentator at 'State Police not Police State'.(14)

These moves have met with limited success: the Swedish police is not immune from the type of criticism aimed at colleagues in other West European forces. Much of the comment is about forces in the larger cities. Recent adverse remarks have been about the narcotics police acting as <u>agents provocateurs</u> by offering to buy or sell drugs and then arresting the dealers.(15)

Reports of police violence have also appeared in the press though substantiation seems difficult.(16) More often the press, especially the more popular papers, seem uncritical of the police. One commentator, Jan Guillou, has complained about the hand-in-glove relationship between police and press. In particular he gave as evidence the case in which a Yugoslav restaurant-owner was condemned in the popular press as the 'spider in the web' of drug-trafficking and international terrorism. After the man was found to be innocent, it became clear that the newspaper reports had been based on police information. Guillou wrote: 'It is no longer crystal clear who is police and who is journalist.'(17) Another accusation is that the police have become too 'gun-happy' and have been trying to copy detective series.(18)

Are the Swedes well policed? 1982 saw a rise in reported crimes of some 45000 or 6% on the previous year's total. For the first time the number of crimes reported broke the 800,000 mark - some five times the number reported to the police in 1950. Between 1950 and 1964 the average annual increase in crime statistics was 13,000 whilst the equivalent figure for the period 1969-1982 was 25,000. Robberies, narcotic crimes and violence have been noticeably on the increase. Violence against women within the home was reported to be 29% higher in 1982 than in 1981. This figure provides a clue to some of these statistics. All of them concern crimes reported and dealt with by the police. Some - for example, drug offences - represent a definite change in criminal behaviour: more drug dealing. Others, such as 'wife-beating' may represent more a recognition by society of existing anti-social behaviour and a need to remedy it. The statistics also had their brighter side for the police - the 'clear-up' rate in 1982 was 40% compared with the 35% average for the previous five years. Again the figures may not tell all the story as narcotics dealing - strongly on the increase in reported crime - had a high clear-up rate.(19)

Another area where the Swedish police are meeting an upsurge of activity is in that of terrorism. This should be placed in perspective: Sweden has not experienced the widespread violence of the IRA, the Baader-Meinhof Gang, of the Basque ETA or the Italian Red Brigade. However, these movements have sometimes spilt over into Scandinavia - back in 1975 the West German embassy in Stockholm was set alight by a terrorist bomb, and a member of the staff there shot. Even before this incident the Swedish authorities had been made aware that their country was not immune to terrorist acts. In February 1971 Croat exiles occupied the Yugoslav consulate in Gothenburg and later assassinated the Yugoslav ambassador to Sweden. In 1972 Croats highjacked an SAS airliner, demanding the release of members of their group from Swedish jails,. an order to which the Swedish authorities capitulated. Three years later the Swedish Embassy in Kuala Lumpur was attacked by the Japanese Red Army and the chargé d'affaires taken hostage.(20)

There has been some debate in Sweden as to what extent the security police should go to protect the state and its citizens against potential terrorist acts. After the Wennerström spy scandal of 1963, in which a Swedish colonel was imprisoned for spying, internal security was tightened up. The Police Register Act of 1965 led to a registration of those suspected of being a security threat. However, complaints from political activists and civil liberties groups led to a Personnel Control Ordinance being issued in 1969 that prevented registration of people just because they held certain political opinions or belonged to a particular organisation, even an extremist one advocating violent activity. Existing information was destroyed. After the SAS hijacking in 1972 (mentioned above) these regulations were slightly amended to allow registration of certain organisations that may engage in subversion including violent acts or the threat of such. The list drawn up in 1973 after the passing of an 'Anti-Terrorist' Act included the Croat Ustasja movement, the Palestinian Black September, the Japanese Red Army and, two years later, the Baader-Meinhof group.(21) However this sort of proscription and the subsequent enquiries made by SAPO have not gone unchallenged: there have been cases in which SAPO have been accused of hounding left-wingers, in particular a TV-editor who had shown some sympathy for the case of the Baader-Meinhof group.(22)

The response of the Swedish police to the threat of terrorism has been fairly restrained. The Stockholm Police District has established a 'mobile picket' to intervene in dangerous situations whether they be armed robberies or terrorist acts. This group, established in 1979, consists of 108 policemen drawn from a list of volunteers and trained in the use of guns, tear gas etc. It is noticeable that press reports of the group tried to balance the more sensational aspects of their activities, such as dealing with hostage-taking, with assurances about the care taken to choose members of the group and their reserve about using arms – they have only had to fire their guns twice since 1979.(23) In discussions about the role of the police in counteracting spying and terrorism, it would seem that Swedish opinion is as yet uncertain about the balance between civil rights and internal security.

FOOTNOTES

1. Sigurdur Lindal 'Early Democratic Traditions in the Nordic Countries', in F. Wisti (ed) Nordic Democracy, Copenhagen: Det Danske Selskab, 1981, chapter 1.
2. Constitutional Documents of Sweden, Stockholm: the Swedish Riksdag, 1975, pp 7-9.
3. See S. Koblik Sweden's Development from Poverty to Affluence 1750-1970, Minneapolis: University of Minneapolis, 1975.
4. Leif Lenke 'Criminal Policy and Repression in Capitalist Societies - the Scandinavian case', Scandinavian Studies in Criminology, volume 7, pp 5-30.
5. Sven Sperlings 'Violent Criminality and Social Control during Stockholm's Industrialization', Scandinavian Studies in Criminology, volume 7, pp 125-134.
6. Nils Christie 'Changes in penal values', Scandinavian Studies in Criminology, volume 2, pp 161-172.
7. Sperlings op.cit. pp 134-7.
8. Esbjörn Esbjörnson The Re-organization of the Swedish Police, Stockholm: mimeo, May 1976.
9. Ibid. p 7.
10. Ibid. p 3.
11. Ibid.
12. Ibid. pp 9 and 11.
13. Jan Forslin 'Work Adjustment of Swedish Policemen', Scandinavian Studies in Criminology, volume 7, p 172.
14. John R. Kleberg 'Sweden: State Police Not Police State' Some Facts about the organization, resources and operation of the Swedish Police, G7, Stockholm: National Swedish Police Board, August 1980, p 1.
15. Thomas Nordegren, 'Bekämpa brott med brott?' (Fighting crime with crime?) Dagens Nyheter 2 September 1982.
16. For example: 'RA vägrar ta upp misshandel' (Public Prosecutor declines to take up maltreatment [case]) Dagens Nyheter 30 July 1983, and 'Sverige som kriminalroman' (Sweden as a crime-novel) Dagens Nyheter 15 November 1982.
17. Jan Guillou, 'Den tredge statsmaktens vanmakt' (The Third Estate's impotence), Dagens Nyheter, 20 November 1982. Guillou himself was sentenced to ten months in jail in 1974 for disclosing the activities of a Swedish intelligence agency.
18. Ibid. and 'Sverige som kriminalroman' cited in note 16.

19. 'Storsta ökningen nagonsin' (The largest increase ever), Dagens Nyheter 25 August 1983.

20. The connections that the Baader-Meinhof group had in Sweden have been detailed in Bertil Haggman, Terrorism - var tids krigföring (Terrorism - the warfare of our time), Stockholm: Berghs, 1978, pp. 140-4.

21. Jacob Sundberg, 'The Antiterrorist Legislation in Sweden' in R.D. Crelinsten, D. Laberge-Altmegd and D. Szabo, Terrorism and Criminal Justice, Lexington: D.C. Heath, 1978, pp. 75-83

22. Ibid. pp.76-86.

23. 'SÄpo har jobbat i utmarken' (SÄPO has dabbled in the outer region) Dagens Nyheter, 22 January 1983. Svante Stockselius, 'Sa arbetar attackpolisen' (This is how the Attack-police work) Expressen 31 March 1984.

Further Reading

1. Leif Lenke 'Criminal Policy and Repression in Capitalist Societies - the Scandinavian case', Scandinavian Studies in Criminology, volume 7, pp. 5-30.

2. Sven Sperlings 'Violent Criminality and Social Control during Stockholm's Industrialization', Scandinavian Studies in Criminology, volume 7, pp. 125-134.

3. Esbjörn Esbjörnson The Re-organization of the Swedish Police, Stockholm: mimeo, May 1976.

4. Jan Forslin 'Work Adjustment of the Swedish Policemen', Scandinavian Studies in Criminology, volume 7, p. 172.

5. John R. Kleberg 'Sweden: State Police Not Police State' Some Facts about the organization, resources and operation of the Swedish Police, G7, Stockholm: National Swedish Police Board, August 1980, p.1.

Chapter 10

EUROPEAN POLICE COOPERATION

Paul Wilkinson

There are three basic reasons why West European governments and police forces should be persuaded that increased
European police cooperation is both a logical and desirable development: (a) the increasing internationalization
of serious crimes, including fraud, robbery, narcotics and
arms smuggling, and terrorism; (b) the shared experience
of common crime and policing problems, affording rich opportunities for mutual assistance and learning from each
other; and (c) the general historical movement towards
European integration at both economic and political
levels, which has far-reaching implications for legal
systems and law enforcement agencies in the European
Community member states.
    Western Europe's multiplicity of frontiers, and free-
dom of movement within and across national borders, combined with the presence of skilled and sophisticated international criminals, make the whole region a particularly attractive target, not only for indigenous criminals, but also for international gangs. It should be obvious enough that the prevention and punishment of specifically international crimes such as drug smuggling and
international terrorism can only be accomplished if the
police forces of all the countries involved work closely
together. The general public may be less aware that much
of what is regarded as conventional domestic crime in
Western states has international ramifications. Fugitive
criminals move to foreign countries where they believe
they will be safe from extradition and where they can
spend their ill-gotten gains. The proceeds of domestic
crime will end in secret bank accounts abroad. Stolen
goods are often more easily disposed of in an overseas
market where no awkward questions will be asked.
    It could be argued that in addition to these funda-
mental common interests in police cooperation, the Western
European states present a more conducive setting for such

developments than most other regions of the world. These states have the advantage that their political and legal systems share common underlying values and norms. One comparative justice researcher has characterised what he terms the Western Democratic Centralized Model as including:

> "multiparty political systems, no clear obligations of the citizen to the state, centrally organized court systems, centralized police functions, and an integrated correctional system".(1)

In addition Western Europe has over 35 years of experience in cooperation in the most integrated alliance system it has achieved in its history. If NATO can provide such a successful system of collective defence against external threats, it might be argued, surely an equally developed system of coordinating internal security and law order should be within their capacity? And if one is looking for a potential mechanism for integration in this field there are the institutions of the European Community, now augmented by a directly elected European Parliament. Even when the present acute internal differences between member states are taken into account, these arrangements constitute far and away the most advanced regional cooperation system in contemporary international relations.

In view of this favourable context it is perhaps not altogether surprising to find that the international police cooperation achieved by the European states is _relatively_ more advanced than that prevailing in any other world region. However, when we examine it more closely it becomes clear that police cooperation has proved one of the most difficult and intractable endeavours even among the West European allies. Let us briefly survey the major developments involved, and then proceed to examine some of the major reasons why progress in police cooperation is so difficult. The essay concludes with a discussion of some of the fundamental moral and political issues raised by the development of international police cooperation, and the prospects for the future.

The Development of International Police Cooperation

The first attempt to establish an international organization for police cooperation(2) was made in Europe in 1914. At the invitation of Prince Albert I of Monaco, jurists, magistrates, and police officials from 14 countries met in Monaco between 14th and 18th April. The conference showed considerable interest in pursuing progress towards agreeing extradition procedures and the development of an international criminal record office, but these projects had to be shelved when the First World War broke out.

The next major development came in 1923. Perhaps rather appropriately the initiative was taken by Johann Schober, an Austrian policeman, born in 1874, who had become President of the Austrian police by 1918. As head of the police, Schober made a useful contribution during the political tumult in Austria at the end of the war by ensuring the loyalty of the police to the new republican regime. A natural conservative in politics, he became chancellor of Austria June 1921 to 1922 and again in 1929 to 1930. With the support of the Christian Socialist Party and the Pan-Germans, he took the major step of re-establishing friendly relations with the new states that had been created out of the old Hapsburg Empire. His government made the Treaty of Lanty with Czechoslovakia in December 1921. But Schober failed to secure a union between Austria and Germany, and found himself in bitter dispute with the Pan-Germans in the Austrian parliament. Following his resignation from the chancellorship in 1922, he returned to his post in the Vienna police. Schober was interested in reviving the idea of international police cooperation that had veen voiced at Monaco. There was widespread support for the idea of making Vienna the venue for a second criminal police congress. Vienna was geographically central and the Austrians had a reputation for expertise in maintaining international criminal files, and in dealing with international criminals. 130 delegates from 20 countries and territories attended, and they approved a scheme which led to the formation of the International Criminal Police Commission (ICPC). This was essentially a European organisation, though some leading European countries did not join until later: for example the United Kingdom declined the invitation to participate in the 1923 congress. In 1927 Britain was again invited to attend an international conference. The Commissioner of Police for the Metropolis could not be persuaded to attend. However, Sir Leonard Dunning, one of His Majesty's Inspectors of Constabulary, did participate.

Dunning reported favourably on the conference and recommended that the United Kingdom should be represented at future conferences by a senior member of the Criminal Investigation Department. Following this it became standard practice for the Assistant Commissioner (Crime) of the Metropolitan Police to lead the UK delegation. The first Secretary-General of the ICPC was Dr. D. Dressler, editor of the publication Internationale Öffentliche Sicherheit.

This organization became the basis of the renamed International Congress of Criminal Police (1930), which performed many of the key functions later taken over by Interpol: maintaining a Central International Bureau, the suppression of counterfeiting, publishing a journal (International Public Security), maintaining an International Criminal Records Office and fingerprint and photographic records of international criminals, and a department for countering passport forgery. By the mid 1930s they had added an international radio network.

These developments were interrupted by the Second World War, and it was not until 1946 that the original member states of the ICPC were able to revive the machinery of international police cooperation. A leading spirit behind this move was Monsieur F.E. Louwage, Inspector-General of the Belgian police, and the international conference was held in Brussels. It was decided to revise the constitution, to establish an Executive Committee and a President, both independent of the HQ, and an elected Secretary-General. The HQ of the organisation was moved to Paris. The telegraphic address was to be INTERPOL. Only nineteen countries were members of the new body at the initial post-war launching. But by 1963 INTERPOL covered 78 countries and held records of over 200,000 international criminals. There are three main types of international criminals included in Interpol's extensive files: those who operate in more than one country; those whose crimes affect other countries (e.g. criminals who counterfeit foreign banknotes), and those who commit crime in one country, but flee to another. Interpol's records contain details of identities, any known 'aliases', associates, and known habits and methods. Information gathered is sent by confidential circular to member states.

Interpol's constitution was drawn up at Vienna in 1956. It is important to note that it is not designed to be an international police force. It has no teams of agents operating internationally, but relies entirely on the police forces of the member states to carry out requests for assistance. In essence it is a specialized inter-governmental organization with the following general objectives, as laid down in Article 2 of its constitution:

1. To ensure and promote the widest possible mutual assistance between all criminal police authorities within the limits of the laws existing in the different countries and in the spirit of the Universal Declaration of Human Rights;

2. to establish and develop all institutions
likely to contribute effectively to the prevention and suppression of ordinary law
crimes.

Interpol's constitution also states that any intervention or activity of a political, military, religious or
racial character is strictly forbidden. In the view of
many member states this precludes the organization from
recording or exchanging information on politically motivated terrorists. In practice, however, the Interpol Secretariat has often taken a more pragmatic view, and has
sometimes helped substantially in the effort to bring terrorist offenders to justice.

From the size and range of its membership Interpol is
clearly no longer a purely European organization. Any
country may join provided its membership is approved by
two thirds of the member states, and provided it designat-
es an official police body with criminal police functions
to act as the Interpol National Central Bureau for the
country. Nevertheless, the organization is the longest-
established and most significant international organization for police cooperation. All Western European police
forces are represented within it. It is therefore
necessary to examine its structure and modus operandi.(3)

Interpol is governed by a General Assembly and an Executive Committee. The former meets once a year and makes
all key decisions on general policy, financing, working
methods, instruments of cooperation, programmes of activities, and elected officers. Each member state has one
vote in the Assembly. There are 13 members elected by the
General Assembly to serve on the Executive Committee.
Their task is to ensure that all Assembly policies and
decisions are enacted, to prepare the Assembly agenda, to
approve the programme of activities and draft budget for
submission to the Assembly, and to supervise the Secretary
General's management of Interpol.

Day-to-day administration and technical matters are
the responsibility of the General Secretariat and the
National Central Bureaux. The former centralises records
and maintains links with national and international authorities. The Secretary General is elected by the Assembly
for a 5 year term, and he is responsible for three major
sections' activities; General Administration, Police Cooperation, Research and Studies. The staff is made up of
police officers seconded by their own countries, together
with administrative and technical personnel recruited directly by Interpol under contract. The General Secretariat
staff is now over 200 strong and is drawn from over 30

countries. Official languages of the organization are English, French, Spanish and Arabic. Information and materials in other languages are translated into an Interpol language.

The National Central Bureaux centred in each member country have a vital role in working with the General Secretariat in three major activities: the exchange of police information, for example concerning persons arrested, under surveillance or under suspicion; the identification of wanted persons or persons wanted for questioning; the arrest of those who are wanted, on a warrant issued by the appropriate judicial authorities, usually in conjunction with a formal request for extradition. The General Secretariat therefore can only act as a coordinating and regulatory body. It is up to the National Bureaux to undertake the necessary police operations requested by other countries and to make requests for similar operations by other countries' Bureaux. Even in the key role of information gathering and the collection of international crime statistics the General Secretariat is completely dependent on the material provided from the National Bureaux. The quality and quantity of this data is limited in three major ways: (i) there is an enormous discrepancy in resources and professional expertise available to national police forces, and in many cases the information required is simply not available to the domestic authorities; (ii) there are still crucial gaps in Interpol membership: for example the Soviet Union and most of its Warsaw Pact allies do not belong. Romania, however, joined in 1974.

The United States participates through a National Central Bureau in Washington, DC. Interpol's world-wide radio communications system is divided into five zones: the Far East, centred in Tokyo; South America (Buenos Aires); Africa (Nairobi) Europe (Paris); and North America (Washington and Ottawa).(4) The Americans have also used the State Department Telex link to Paris for Interpol messages.

Interpol has become increasingly involved in cooperation with a wide range of other international organizations. For example they have worked with UNESCO on problems of Narcotic Drugs and Social Defence, with the International Civil Aviation Organization (ICAO) on problems of aviation security, and with other international professional bodies, such as the International Association of Airport and Seaport Police, on such matters as marine fraud, which has cost companies hundreds of millions of pounds in lost cargoes and claims. This is an example of the type of rapidly growing international crime which an international organization for police cooperation should be particularly well placed to combat. One particularly brazen recent case of fraud involved a consignment of cement which was supposed to have been shipped from the Pacific to the Middle East loaded in two ships. A simple check of one of the ships would have revealed that her tonnage was too small for her to carry the consignment claimed.(5) Rapid communications, data gathering, and exchange of information are clearly crucial for combating this type of crime. The same is true of international computer fraud, described at an Interpol conference as "a new international crime world of mind-boggling proportions".(6) One report describes how one man succeeded in programming a bank computer in the US to transfer a million dollars into his own Swiss bank account. He immediately caught a plane to Zurich, drew out the money and bought diamonds. His plan was to import them into the US and sell them at °10,000 profit. He then intended to repay the million dollars and order the computer to erase all record of the transaction. Unfortunately for him customs officers found a diamond on him.(7) But this case vividly illustrates the potential complexity of modern international crime.

However it has been correctly observed that "one finds no great enthusiams"(8) for Interpol's performance as a means to prevent international crime. This is a widely shared view. Some would argue that this judgement does not make sufficient allowance for the difficulties under which the organization operates. Interpol has to contend with differing legal and police systems, political differences between members, and severe limitations of funding and technical resources. For example, its records are badly in need of computerization. In addition there is little doubt that Interpol is suffering from the growing habit of direct bilateral inter-force contacts. For all these reasons the organization is severely limited in its capacity to develop international police cooperation. It is recognized that it is making a valuable contribution in certain fields, such as combating drug trafficking. But in many important aspects of crime it is being increasingly bypassed by bilateral cooperation between national police forces. As Lewis has pointed out,(9) this process gains momentum through the development of closer personal relationships between the officers of the various police forces. Many officers simply find it easier to telephone a colleague in another European force direct than to go through the slow moving bureaucracy and communications of Interpol. On the other hand police forces in many countries know that cooperation with Interpol is fully supported by their government. They are aware that it has a well established mechanism for international police cooperation. In some states it is even illegal for a police officer to provide assistance to a foreign police force which is not processed through Interpol.

However, Interpol is not alone in the international police cooperation field. One important step in Europe was the establishment of the permanent Cross Channel Conference. This comprises those French, British, Dutch, Belgian and German police operating on Channel coastlines. They have been largely concerned with preventing drug smuggling, catching smugglers, illegal immigrants, and maritime and port crime. It has been extremely successful, but again it provides an alternative mechanism to Interpol. Another international organization interested in similar problems, though wider in membership and purely advisory in nature, is the International Association of Airport and Seaport Police. This body has taken an active part in the campaign to crack down on marine fraud, and has had discussions with Interpol on the problem. But this is another illustration of the extent to which important areas of international crime are now being combated by means of cooperation arrangements and organizations outside Interpol. It must be borne in mind that there is some limited machinery for international cooperation in the field of penal law, despite the absence of an agreed international criminal code and court system. In addition to the limited avenues for international criminal police cooperation we have already examined, there are five main methods of judicial cooperation: (i) extradition agreements; (ii) mutual agreements for assistance in criminal matters; (iii) transfer of proceedings in criminal matters; (iv) transfer of the enforcement of judgements; and (v) transfer of supervision.

Extradition means, in essence, that a person is surrendered on the basis of a judicial order, and with the agreement of the interested states, to the authorities of the requesting state. The extradition may be requested for the purpose of prosecution for some specific and preestablished offence or offences, or in order to ensure the enforcement of a sentence of imprisonment. The European Convention on Extradition (1957) is a significant mechanism for cooperation in this field. Parties to this agreement include Austria, Denmark, the Federal Republic of Germany, Greece, Ireland, Italy, the Netherlands, Norway, Sweden, and Switzerland. There are some notable West European states missing from this list, including Great Britain and France. Difficulties in securing extradition treaties may be due to differences of legal system and tradition or to deep political differences or a combination of these. Even where the agreement exists it tends to be a very laborious and difficult method of bringing individuals to justice.(10) In many instances extradition proceedings fail not as a result of positive proof of the innocence of the individual for whom extradition is sought, but because of technical legal complications. Partly for this reason many states have increasingly sought to circumvent the stiff judicial requirements of extradition processes by resorting to refusal of entry and administrative deportation. This is a very swift but inevitably somewhat arbitrary procedure handled executively by the immigration authorities of the state concerned.

Many states are parties to formal agreements to afford mutual assistance in criminal matters. This takes the form of help provided by the judiciary and police of one state to further and support criminal proceedings in another state. This may involve supplying documents or information or engaging in extensive criminal investigations. Among European states the crucial agreement on this aspect of cooperation is the 1959 European Convention on Mutual Assistance in Criminal Matters. This treaty is in force between Austria, Belgium, Denmark, France, the Federal Republic of Germany, Greece, Israel, Italy, Liechtenstein, Luxembourg, the Netherlands, Norway, Sweden and Switzerland. (Note again the absence of the United Kingdom from this list.)

Transfer of proceedings covers all measures through which a state competent to perform criminal proceedings, by virtue of international agreement or domestic law, takes over responsibility for commencing criminal proceedings for a criminal offence committed in another state. This task can only be lawfully performed if the state where the offence was committed agrees to the transfer of proceedings. The transferred proceedings will of course be carried out according to the laws of the state in which they are conducted. This is clearly a relatively advanced form of international judicial cooperation. It is therefore hardly surprising to find that the key European instrument, the European Convention on the Transfer of Proceedings in Criminal Matters (1972) is of very recent date, and so far there are very few contracting parties. The main West European states have not yet acceded to the Convention.

Transfer of the enforcement of judgements is the agreement by one state to enforce the sentences imposed by another state. Once again this can only be done with the agreement of the state that originally imposed the sentence, and it must, of course, be in full accordance with the provisions of its own law. The European Convention on

the International Validity of Criminal Judgements (1970)
only had six contracting parties ten years after its introduction. There appears little likelihood of any of the
major West European countries acceding to the Convention.

When a state is, by formal international agreement,
empowered to supervise a person convicted in another
state, this constitutes transfer of supervision. This applies when a person is placed on probation without sentence being pronounced, or if a person is conditionally
sentenced or conditionally released from custody. This
right of supervision applies for the entire period of probation. The relevant international agreement here is the
European Convention on the Supervision of Conditionally
Sentenced or Conditionally Released Offenders (1964). Six-
teen years after its introduction only 6 European states
had decided to adhere to this agreement.

Practically the only specialised crime field which
has brought major developments in international police cooperation in Europe is terrorism. The main network of
police cooperation in this field simply could not be Interpol. (As we noted earlier, its constitution forbids it
intervening in political, religious and military spheres,
and it has been naturally reluctant to deal with cases of
politically motivated terrorism.) In view of this the EEC
Ministers of the Interior have been compelled to develop
their own network for police cooperation in this sensitive
field. Since 1977 they have developed the TREVI (Terrorism, Radicalism, and International Violence) network to
exchange information and coordinate international police
cooperation against the increasingly internationalized
terrorist campaigns. Each EEC country has a police co-
ordination with the TREVI network. The police and security service chiefs meet at six-monthly intervals to review
progress, and there have been frequent meetings between
Ministers of the Interior on the subject of terrorism.
Other international fora, such as the meetings of the
western leaders for their annual economic summits, have
also considered the subject and issued general declarations of policy.(11) Yet even in this particularly dangerous and growing field of terrorist crime, national governments and police forces have been jealous of their
national sovereignty. Even governments with serious terrorist border problems in common, such as Britain and
Ireland and France and Spain, have failed to develop the
full trust, cooperation and physical assistance necessary
to defeat the problem.(12) National differences, public
prejudices and suspicions have quite evidently prevented
wholehearted cooperation from the Irish government against
the IRA or from the French against ETA. Recently, more

282

top-level efforts have been made to improve border cooperation in both these cases, but the level is still far
short of what is required.(13) The French government continued to insist on giving ETA terrorists refugee status
long after Franco's regime had been replaced by a democratic government in Madrid. And the Dublin government
continues to oppose the extradition of terrorist offenders
from the Republic, despite the fact that the IRA wish to
overthrow democracy throughout Ireland, on the grounds
that it is against their constitution! If West European
governments cannot even cooperate effectively on the life
and death matter of terrorism, what prospects are there
for improving European police cooperation generally?

Main Obstacles to International Police Cooperation

The major obstacle to international cooperation by the
police, as in other spheres, is the fact of national sovereignty. Despite their occasional taste for the rhetoric
of European integration, all West European governments remain stubbornly attached to the principle of autonomous
national decision making in the light of perceived national interests. Nor is this simply an expression of the
vested interest of national political leaders and bureau-
crats. There is overwhelming evidence that national public opinion also regards the defence of national and sec-
toral interest as the supreme priority. Hence the violent
demonstrations of French farmers and the bitter recrimina-
tions of many groups of British workers against EEC policies, and the lack of any genuine mass movement for European integration.

Policing is _par excellence_ regarded by governments
and public opinion alike as a domestic matter, strictly
the concern of national and local governments. Police
work, particularly in the field of public order, during
this period of recession and increasing social tension, is
difficult enough when carried out by indigenous and locally controlled police. An integrated 'Europolice' would be
totally unacceptable to the vast majority of Europe's citizens. They much prefer to live with their own national
police traditions and organizations, each naturally reflecting their own politics, history and culture.

Of course this allegiance to the concept of national
and local police does not preclude improvements in inter-
governmental and inter-force cooperation, but it does act
as a very considerable constraint. But there are other
key obstacles which have been implicit in the earlier
brief survey of international police cooperation. Differences between the legal systems of European states, in-

cluding differences of jurisdiction and procedure, are bound to handicap cooperation. For example, no British national can be proceeded against in a British court for crimes he is alleged to have committed outside British jurisdiction. Yet other European countries have the right to try their own nationals for crimes committed abroad, including those carried out in the United Kingdom.

There is a major difference between the extradition process customary in common law Britain and that used in the continental civil law states. Under the European Convention which most continental countries adhere to, an unsupported allegation, provided it is supported by an examining magistrate's request to investigate, is accepted as a basis for arresting a suspect and returning them to another state to face a preliminary investigation. British courts, used to different procedures and with different extradition treaties, are not willing to operate in this manner: they are slower and have more complex procedures, and many of the treaties are very outdated. Indeed extraditing a suspect from Britain is considered so difficult that many countries have practically given up the attempt. Inevitably Britain is seen to be something of a sanctuary for criminals wanted by continental countries. It is very difficult for Britain to get the cooperation it needs on other matters when these anomalies cause such ill-feeling between national judicial authorities and police forces.

Thus it must be admitted that a key obstacle to improved European police cooperation is the absence of an agreed European criminal code and judicial and police procedure.(14) When the community is apparently finding it impossible to agree to quite modest and sensible reforms of its comparatively well-established Common Agricultural Policy and budgetary system, one can have little confidence in their ability to develop common policies on the traditionally sensitive and emotive issues of law and order.

Another key barrier to European police cooperation, clearly demonstrated in our survey of the present machinery, is the incomplete ratification of the various treaties and conventions for legal and police cooperation. How can they have much impact when only a handful of small states adhere to them? Even when there is more widespread support for an international convention, as with the European Convention on the Suppression of Terrorism (1977) a major weakness stems from the absence of any mechanism for ensuring enforcement. It is also evident that national authorities can take advantage of the vague and ambiguous nature of international convention texts in order to evade obligations.

284

Conclusions

It could also be argued that any serious attempt to create a more integrated and centralized 'Europolice' system, even if politically feasible, would be highly undesirable on grounds of democratic theory. The vast centralization and bureaucratic complexity that would inevitably be involved in any attempt at police integration would undermine democratic control and sensitivity to local needs. One of the serious dangers of overemphasis on European police coordination and centralized command, control and communication, is that the climate of public consent and cooperation, so vital for democratic policing, could be put at risk.

However, in the light of the severe limitations of current European police cooperation and the serious obstacles to its further development which have been described above, it would be foolish to exaggerate these dangers. As shown by the national case studies in this volume, sophisticated police organisations tend to develop well _after_ their parent centralized governmental systems become fully developed. Judging by experience any significant breakthrough in European police cooperation will be entirely dependent on major progress in European political integration. There is nothing inevitable about such a process. It must be said that the notion of Europe acquiring genuinely supranational legal and police systems is entirely theoretical. On the other hand the processes of ad hoc and bilateral international cooperation among police forces are now so well established that they repay closer examination and research.

FOOTNOTES

1. Jefferson S. Duffey, "An Embryonic Model for Comparative Justice" in William Jones (ed.) Criminal Justice Administration, New York: Dekker, 1983 pp. 88-9.

2. For an overview of the development and role of Interpol see A.J. Forrest, Interpol, London: Wingate, 1955, and International Criminal Police Organization Review 50th anniversary edition, June-July, 1973.

3. For differing views on the functioning and effectiveness of Interpol see Tom Tullett, Inside Interpol, London: F. Muller, 1963; Ben Whitaker, The Police in Society London: Methuen, 1979; Roy Lewis, A Force For the Future London: Temple Smith, 1976 Chapter 8; and Police Review, 17 January 1975.

4. Iris Noble, _Interpol: International Crime Fighter_, New York, Harcourt Brace, 1975.

5. _The Times_, 29 November 1978.

6. _The Sunday Times_, 23 December 1979.

7. Ibid.

8. Roy Lewis, _op.cit._, p. 232.

9. Ibid., p. 235.

10. For a discussion of the difficulties of using extradition to deal with international terrorism see Paul Wilkinson, "Proposals for a liberal-Democratic Government Response to Terrorism" in _Terrorism and Beyond_, Santa Monica: Rand, 1982 pp. 203-232.

11. For a discussion of these responses see Paul Wilkinson, "Terrorism: the Internatinal Response", _The World Today_, January 1978, pp. 5-13, and "State-sponsored international terrorism: the problems of response", _The World Today_, July 1984, pp. 292-8.

12. For details, see "Irish to arm more police in drive against terrorists", _Daily Telegraph_, 9 January 1984, and "Face to the ETA Gun", _The Economist_, 4 February 1984.

13. As evidence for this, assassinations and bombings actually escalated in both border areas in the first quarter of 1984.

14. This point is brought out very well by the former Secretary-General of Interpol, Jean Nepote, in his contribution to _The Proceedings of the 1978 Cranfield Conference on the Prevention of Crime in Europe_, London: Peel Press, 1980, pp. 216-9.

Further Reading

A.J. Forrest, _Interpol_, London, Wingate, 1955.

B. Whitaker, _The Police in Society_, London, Methuen, 1979.

I. Noble, _Interpol: International Crime Fighter_, New York, Harcourt Brace, 1975.

T. Tullett, _Inside Interpol_, London, F. Muller, 1963.

INDEX

BRIXTON AND AFTER

Complaints against the
  police 4
Ethnically diverse society
  1-4
Police accountability 6
Police Act 1

Police and Society 1-2
Police discipline 4
Police recruitment 2-3
Police training 3
Policing methods 5-6
PSI Study 6-7

POLICE AND SOCIAL ORDER

Brixton riots 25-27
Butler, R.A. (Lord) 20
Cromwell, O. 21
Edward III 21
France 17-18
Germany 17
High police 17-18, 21
History of police 15-16,
  20-21
Justice of the Peace Act 21
Local government 27, 30-31
police 17-19
MI5 19, 22
MI6 22

Northern Ireland 23
Peel, Sir Robert 21
Police accountability 25,
  30-31
Police authorities 21-22
Police Bill 21
Police Federation 24
Police functions 17, 31
Police power 19-20, 25-27
Police state 16-17
Police Superintendents' Law
  Association 24
Toynbee, Arnold 22-24
USA 19, 22

THE BRITISH POLICE

Alderson, John 38, 54
Anderton, James 38
Association of Chief Police
  Officers 41, 44, 65
Bereitschaftspolizei 46

Newman, Sir Kenneth, 34,
  50, 53, 56
NGA dispute 65
Northern Ireland Emergency
  Provisions Act 44

Brixton 33, 46, 53, 54, 56, 61
Bundesgrenzschutz 44f
Burgh Police (Scotland) Act 62
Centralisation 39
Citizen in uniform 36
Civic Government (Scotland) Act 62
Civil liberties 35f
CND 51
Common Law 33f, 35f, 40f
Commons Home Affairs Committee Report on 'The Law Relating to Public Order' 39f, 54, 64
Criminal Investigation Departments (CID) 37
Demonstrations 40, 41, 42, 43, 51-54, 61f
Diplomatic Protection Group 53
Director of Public Prosecutions 36
Edinburgh 37
Emergency 36, 46
Ethnically diverse society 48f
French CRS 44, 46, 50
French Gendarmerie 37
French Gendarmerie Mobile 45, 46
Gibson, Wilford 43
Glasgow 37
Greenham Common 61f
Grunwick 65
Hargadon, James 51
History of British Police 35f
Home Office Memorandum 1980 42
IRA 53
Ireland 35f
Irish Police Act 36
Local Improvement Act 37
McNee, Sir David 43, 48, 56
Manchester Tactical Aid Group 50
Mark, Sir Robert 38, 51

Notting Hill 53
Oxford, Kenneth 58
Parish Constables 36
Peach, Blair 56
Peel, Sir Robert 36
Police accountability 34, 38, 58ff, 68
Police Act 1964 38, 59, 65
Police and Criminal Evidence Bill 36
Police authorities 34f, 37ff, 42f, 58ff, 68
Police duties 36
Police equipment 34, 45
Police organisation 44-47
Police powers 36, 41-44, 64
Police staff associations 39
Police strength 39, 46, 47
Police training 34, 66
Police weapons, 58, 66
Prevention of Terrorism Acts 41, 42
Procurator Fiscal 36
Public Order Act 39, 40, 41, 42, 43, 51, 61, 62, 63, 64
Race Relations Act 63
Red Lion Square 47, 50, 53, 54
Rees, Merlyn 41
Roman Law 33f, 35f, 40
Royal Commission on the Police 1960/1962 38, 59
Royal Irish Constabulary 36
Royal Ulster Constabulary 36, 44, 53
Scarman, Lord 40, 48f, 50, 54, 55, 56, 57, 58, 61, 62
Scotland 35f, 62, 63
Shackleton, Lord 42
Southall 53, 54, 56
Special Branch 37, 41
Special Patrol Group 45, 46, 50, 53, 56
St Paul's Bristol 46f
Terrorism 49, 61
Toxteth 46, 54, 57, 58

Metropolitan Police Act 37
Moss side 55
Municipal Corporation Act 37
National police force 38, 46
NCCL 57

Trade Union legislation 65f
Unemployment 55
Wales 35f
Whitelaw, W. 60, 66

IRELAND

Army 80, 82, 83, 97
Black and Tans 75
Bloody Sunday 82
Blueshirts 77
Border, passim
Civil War 75-77
Complaint procedure 98
Community policing 99
Conroy Commission 90f, 94
Crime statistics 85, 88f, 90, 92
Criminal Justice Bill 98f
Criminal Law Act 78
Criminal Law Jurisdiction Act 86
Dublin Metropolitan Police 76
Emergency Powers Act 78, 79, 82
European Convention on the Suppression of Terrorism 87
Ewart-Biggs, murder of 78-80
Garda Siochana, passim
Development and Structure of the Garda 89-96
Garda - RUC Coordinating Committee 84
The Historical Perspective 73-77
Internment 78, 96f
IRA 74, 77, 78, 79, 80, 87 96

Irish Extradition Act 87
Irredentism 73
Law, respect for 73, 75
Legitimacy 73-76, 89
Liberation Struggle 73-76
Offences against the State Act 78, 80, 82
Oriel House CID 93
Permanent Defence Force 82f, 85
Police authority 76f, 90f
Police overtime 91
Police powers 80, 98f
Police recruitment 76, 91
Police training 90ff
Political interference 90ff, 97ff
RIC 75, 77, 90
Riots 90ff
RUC 76, 84-86
Ryan Report 91
SAS 84
Security costs 81, 87f
Special Branch (Intelligence and Security) 93
Special Criminal Court 78, 79, 80, 87
Special Garda Task Force 84
State of emergency 78ff
Sunningdale 84f
Terrorism, passim
War of Independence 73-75

FRANCE

Bureau de Sûreté 108
Centralism 107, 109, 126, 132
Civil Liberties 112

Mitterrand 112f, 116, 125
Napoleon 109f'
National Guard 109
Police accountability 129

Community policing 113
Compagnies de District 126
Compagnies Républicaines de
  Securité, CRS 111, 117,
  119, 121, 126, 131f
Declaration of Rights 109
Direction de la Surveillance
  du Territoire, DST 114,
  118f
Ethnic minorities 111
Forces d'Intervention des
  Corps Urbains, FICU 116,
  126
Fouché 109, 133
Gardes Mobiles de Réserve
  111
Gardiens de la paix 110,
  113, 131
Gendarmerie Mobile 117,
  120, 121, 126, 132
Gendarmerie Nationale 109,
  111, 114, 116, 119-128,
  124
Groupe d'Intervention de
  la Gendarmerie Nationale,
  GIGN 121f
La Haute Police 109
History of Police 107-113
Legislation 122-126, 128
Lieutenant-General of
  Police 107, 109
Louis XIV 107
Louis Napoleon 110
May 1968 113, 121, 126, 127
Minister of Police 107, 109,
  110, 118

Police authority 108, 110,
  111, 112, 114, 115, 117,
  121, 122f
Police discontent 112, 130f
Police equipment 113, 129
Police functions 109f,
  113-121
Police Judiciaire 111, 117,
  122
Police Nationale 111, 113,
  115, 116, 117, 124, 126,
  128, 130, 131, 132
Police powers 122-126, 128
Police reforms 113-121, 128,
  131, 132
Police Spéciales des chemins
  de fer 110
Police strength 113-121
Police training 113, 114,
  129
Police Urbaine 116
Police weapons, 113f, 129
Renseignements Généraux 110,
  114, 118-119
Sécurité publique 111
Sergents de ville 110
Sûreté Nationale 110, 115
Surveillance 107, 108, 109,
  110, 114, 117-121, 123,
  128
Surveillance du Territoire
  111
Terrorism 109, 112, 113,
  121
Vichy Government 111, 119

WEST GERMANY

Absolutism 147
ALR 148
Civil liberties 148, 169,
  180
Community policing 159,
  177f
Crime statistics 153, 178
Danger 147f, 164, 166
Data storage 160f
Democracy crisis 144f

Police laws 146-148, 156f,
  163-172
Police organisation
  154-158
Police pay 157
Police powers 147ff, 159-163,
  164
Police state 147f
Police strength 154f, 157f,
  160

De-policing 150, 154f, 171, 177

Ecological movement 144f, 153, 167

Federalism 143, 150f, 154ff, 172

Federal Special Branch 161-163

Foreign workers 143, 163

Gestapo 149f

History of police 146-154

Intellectuals 180

Kohl government 170-172

Legitimacy of the state 143f, 146, 153f

Media 153f, 165, 169, 178-180

Militarisation 159, 178

Overtime 157

Police authorities 143, 154f, 159-163

Police crisis 145, 150, 154, 178

Police forces 148ff

Police functions 146-150, 151, 159-163, 164

Police weapons 151, 159, 171, 172-176

Political conflict management 169f

Political police 150

Potsdam agreement 150

Pre-emptive policing 147f, 166, 171

Public prosecutor 164

Putter, J.S. 147

Restoration 148

Special police forces 159-163

SS 149f

Student rebellion 144f, 153f, 167, 168, 169, 173

Surveillance 170f

Terrorism 144f, 153, 164, 171

Third Reich 144, 145f

Trade Union Organisation 158-159

Wolff, Christian 147

ITALY

Carabinieri 185, 186-188, 189, 191-193, 194, 195, 196-198, 200, 201, 202, 204, 205, 206, 207

Capitanneria del Porto 188

Celere 196

Chiesa, Carlo Dalla, General 185, 199, 200,

Civil rights 201

Commissario 186

Corpo Forestale 188

Crime statistics 189f, 203

Gendarmerie Nazionale 188

Guardia di Finanza 187f, 206

Independent police forces 187f

Interior Ministry Police 186, 189, 193, 194, 195, 196-197, 204, 206

Police authorities 185-188, 206

Police crisis 189f, 198

Police from Giolitti to Mussolini 190-193

Police functions 186-188, 189

Police image 198, 199, 206

Police in the Nineteenth Century 188-190

Police in the Post-War World 195-198

Police laws 194

Police powers 200

Police recruitment 187

Police training 196, 206

Police under Fascism 193-195

Pre-emptive policing 189

Prefects 186, 193, 195

291

Mafia 184, 202-205
March on Rome 200, 193
Media 207
Milizia Volontaria
   Sicurezza Nazionale 193
Moro, Aldo 197, 200
Neo-fascism 198
Police and Society 205-207
Police and the Mafia
   202-205
Police arms 205

Public Security Guards 186
Questor 186, 195
Red Brigades 185, 199-200
Resistance 194, 195
Security Services 200, 205
Structural duality of the
   Italian police 185-188
Student unrest 198
Surveillance 187, 189
Terrorism 185, 187, 189,
   198-202, 205, 206, 207

SPAIN

Civil War 215, 219
Constitution 216-217, 220,
   243, 244, 248
Courts 223-224
Crime statistics 227-228,
   241
Effectiveness of police
   220, 223
Franco 215, 216, 247
Garcia Lorca 215
Guardia Civil 215, 217,
   218-222, 232, 233-242,
   243, 244, 248-249
Judicial system 218
Militarization 219
Nationalism 217, 246
Police authorities 221-222,
   223, 225, 227, 228,
   229-230, 233, 242, 244,
   245
Police equipment 236-237
Police function 218-220,
   221, 222-232, 241, 243-244

Police law 221-222, 228,
   233, 234, 241, 244-245,
   246, 247
Police organisation, cf.
   Guardia Civil, Policia
Police recruitment 224, 226,
   234-236
Police strength 223-232,
   234-242, 243, 246
Police training 223, 224,
   226, 234-236, 249, 250
Police weapons 215, 224, 225,
   237, 249, 250
Policia 219, 221, 222-232,
   243, 249
Regionalism 215-216, 217,
   234, 244-250
Second Republic 215, 219
Tejero, Colonel 215
Terrorism 227, 229, 241,
   242, 247-248
Torture 217

SWEDEN

Adalen 257, 259
Background 255f
Crime statistics 258, 260,
   266, 268
Detective Department 259
Development of modern police
   force 258-261
History 256-258
Housing shortage 256

Nordic Council 266
Ombudsman system 257
Police and Society 266-269
Police arms 265, 269
Police dissatisfaction 266f
Police organisation
   261-263
Police pay 259, 266f
Police Register Act 269

International aspects 265f
Judicial system 256-258
Local police forces 259f
Local Police Boards 261ff
National Criminal Investi-
  gation Unit 261
National Police Board
  261-264
National police force 261ff
National Swedish Laboratory
  of Forensic Science 264

Police tasks 261f, 263f
Police training 259f, 264f,
  266f
Police union 267
Press 267f
Racial conflict 256
Security Police (SAPO) 262,
  269
State Police units 260
Terrorism 262, 269
Unemployment 256

EUROPEAN POLICE COOPERATION

Cross Channel Conference
  282
Dunning, Sir Leonard 277
ETA 284f
European Convention on
  Mutual Assistance in
  Matters 283
European Convention on the
  International Validity of
  Criminal Judgements 284
European Convention on the
  Supervision of
  Conditionally Sentenced or
  Conditionally Released
  Offenders 284
European Convention on the
  Suppression of Terrorism
  284, 286
European Convention on the
  Transfer of Proceedings
  in Criminal Matters 283

International Association
  of Airport and Seaport
  Police 280, 282
International Congress of
  Criminal Police 278
International Criminal
  Police Commission (ICPC)
  277f
Interpol structure 278ff
        function 279ff
        problems 279ff
IRA 284ff
Judicial cooperation 282ff
Legal systems 286
Louwage, F.E. 278
Monaco police congress 277
Schober, Johan 277
Terrorism 275, 279, 284f
TREVI 284
Vienna police congress 277

For Product Safety Concerns and Information please contact our EU
representative GPSR@taylorandfrancis.com
Taylor & Francis Verlag GmbH, Kaufingerstraße 24, 80331 München, Germany

* 9 7 8 1 0 3 2 4 2 7 0 9 6 *